PRAISE FOR ALTERNATIVE RESUMES//

" Michael Howard's resume books have been a highly effective resource in the YWCA Vancouver employment resource centres that work with job seekers 15-30 years of age. In fact, the books are so successful that they keep getting stolen! "

Melanie Hardy, Program Manager
YWCA Vancouver, Career Zone

" Alternative Resumes provides samples of highly visual, innovative resumes, providing alternatives to conventional methods. This book is ideal for youth engaged in their quest to land a first job, or youth unsure of how to present their skills & experience. This book is like a breath of fresh air!"

Denise Young, Manager, Youth Employability Project
Centre for Entrepreneurship Education & Development

" Readers will be inspired by the practical advice, case studies & samples that demonstrate how to display assets to best advantage. Alternative Resumes is truly a valuable contribution to the resume writing industry. "

Sandra Lim, CHRP, CPRW, CECC
Career Management Specialist
A Better Impression Resume & Career Counselling Services

" A treasure for both youths & adults with minimal experience & skills wishing to enter or re-enter the current labour force. I recommend it to employment counsellors who aspire to highlight their clients' resumes with strong, truthful & well-thought anecdotes."

Gabrielle Musick, Employment Service Advisor
Community Employment & Resource Centre

WRITING
ON STONE
PRESS
www.writingonstone.ca

ALTERNATIVE RESUMES
DEFINITELY NOT YOUR PARENTS RESUME BOOK

BY MICHAEL HOWARD

WRITING
ON STONE
PRESS

The techniques in this book have helped job seekers land interviews,
land jobs and supported their job search. We have been careful
to provide accurate information, but it is possible that errors and
omissions crept in. Your results will vary depending on your
qualifications, personal situation, job search strategies, job market
fluctuations, economic conditions and other factors.

All the names of individuals and organizations in this book are
fictional creations for the purpose of supplying resume samples.
There is no intended relation or allusion to actual individuals or
organizations, either contemporary or historical.

Howard, Michael G. (Michael Gordon), 1967-
Alternative resumes : definitely NOT your parents' resume book!
/ by Michael Howard.

ISBN 978-0-9811529-1-2

1. Résumés (Employment). 2. Young adults--Employment. I. Title.

HF5383.H74 2010   650.14'2   C2010-900791-3

WRITING
ON STONE
PRESS

Cover Design: Joanne Howard, Small Dog Design
Editor: Marilyn Inglis
Interior Design: Talia Cohen

Dedicated to Ashley and Kimberly.

One who walks in another's tracks leaves no footprints.

ACKNOWLEDGMENTS//

Many friends, family members, and colleagues provided personal and valuable contributions to this book.

Because they have been around since the very beginning, I extend my first appreciation to Fred and Maryelle Howard. Although my unconventional career path was likely a source of concern for many years, they never lost faith and no one has been more thrilled with my achievements. Thank you for trusting my vision.

Several past co-workers played a role in my professional development and ultimately this book, notably Rachel Young and Heidi Gerhart. However, no colleague had a greater impact than Jo-Anne Nadort, a gifted and compassionate mentor who was instrumental in helping me identify my talents and find a new, fulfilling direction for my career.

My thanks to Becky Zeeman, an early patron and supporter, who instilled me with confidence at a critical time by showing me that my work had value to people. My appreciation and respect also go to Deborah Envik Howard and Christine Boudreau, pivotal figures in the shaping of my ideals.

Finally, this book would not be possible if it wasn't for the love, enthusiasm, trust, and cooperation of my wife and partner, Marina Dawson. From day one she has been my proudest supporter and loudest advocate, accompanying me every step of the way on this unpredictable journey.

Thank you for all that you do.

TABLE OF CONTENTS//

FAQ LISTINGS//

Alternative Resumes provides one-page answers to the most frequently asked questions about resumes and resume design. Here's a quick reference list for all the FAQ's in the book.

INTRODUCTION//

This is definitely NOT your parents' resume book. Good thing too. Their book uses only a few conventional resume formats such as chronological, functional, and hybrid. It recommends using only standard resume sections such as objective, summary of qualifications, employment history, education, and interests and hobbies. Your parents' book would show you how to make a resume focused mainly on work experience, and offer limited options for your resume's appearance. Their book would help you make a resume that looks like everyone else's.

But you are not your parents.

As a teenager or young adult, your job search is very different from theirs. With less training and experience, fewer skills and achievements, more competition, and different job targets, your job search faces unique obstacles and requires a unique approach. Using your parents' resume book will result in frustration. You are different from your parents, and you deserve a resume book that understands your needs and circumstances.

Alternative Resumes is your resume book. This book ignores conventional resume formats and encourages you to design your own. It proves that you don't have to use the standard sections found on everyone else's resume. This book helps you uncover and highlight many

qualifications besides work experience such as your availability, personal projects, or travel history. It provides you with countless ideas for your resume's appearance to help you stand out from the crowd. Most importantly, this book will help you get job interviews.

Whether you're a middle or high school student learning how to create your first resume, or a twenty-something with a few years of career experience, Alternative Resumes has something for you. Each chapter contains sample resumes from a job sector that hires youth, such as retail, hospitality, trades/labour, office/technical, and community service. The final chapter has miscellaneous jobs that don't fit into the other categories. Each chapter begins with "Designing My Alternative Resume," a case study for a resume in that job sector. Each chapter includes resume writing tips in "Frequently Asked Questions" style. There is also an eleven-page worksheet to help you design your alternative resume.

Using your parents' resume book might be easier – all you have to do is follow a standard format and slot your qualifications into predetermined sections. But you will end up with a resume that looks similar in content and appearance to everyone else's. And seriously, do you want to look like your parents?

RETAIL

Chapter 1

One of the largest employers of teens and young adults, the retail industry provides jobs in several areas working with countless products.

Common entry-level positions include Greeter, Stock Clerk, Cashier, Sales Associate, and Visual Merchandiser. Advanced positions can be found as Key Holder, Department Supervisor, Assistant Manager, and Store Manager. This chapter begins with an analysis of a Visual Merchandiser resume, and continues with 30 more resumes and four FAQ tips.

DESIGNING MY ALTERNATIVE RESUME//
MELANIE LANE : VISUAL MERCHANDISER

Melanie Lane is a college student in a fashion marketing and merchandising program. She is seeking a visual merchandiser position with a ladies' fashion chain.

She has over a year of retail employment as a cashier and sales associate, but no actual experience in visual presentation. Since both her training and experience are in retail, she can prioritize her qualifications in a few different ways. Melanie's resume can be viewed on the following page.

Most applicants with her background would list either education or experience at the top of their resume. Those opting for education would argue it's directly related to the job she is targeting, while those preferring experience would say her employment is in retail, she hasn't yet earned her diploma, and actual experience is generally regarded more highly than training by employers. Rather than choosing a normal Employment History or Education and Training section as the focal point of her resume, Melanie chooses to showcase one particular element of her diploma program.

1. Visual Merchandising Project

Melanie's greatest achievement to date at Bradshaw Community College is earning the top grade on a two-month project where she compared the visual presentation methods and standards of a group of ladies' fashion retailers. This project thrust Melanie into the world of ladies' apparel merchandising, much more than her coursework or previous experience had done. She gained significant knowledge of her chosen field while meeting with store managers and visual merchandisers and analyzing their methods and achievements. Although other aspects of her background will also interest employers, Melanie feels her success on this project is the best way to distinguish herself from her competitors. She highlights it prominently on her resume and makes the report available for employers to view.

2. Retail Training

Melanie separates her project from the rest of her diploma program so she can use the eye-catching title of Visual Merchandising Project, which is sure to attract the reader's attention. She then lists the supplementary details of her college program under the heading Retail Training, a title that will pique more interest than one simply labelled Education. Here she outlines the overall program and includes her course listing and academic success.

3. Retail Employment

Melanie lists both her retail jobs but doesn't go into great detail because they were not related to visual presentation and, since she is staying in the same industry, employers will know what she did in those positions. She includes the fact that she sold ladies' fashions because that is the commodity she wants to work with as a merchandiser and some employers may not be familiar with the small specialty boutique where she worked.

MELANIE LANE
Visual Merchandiser, Ladies Fashion Retail

MAILING ADDRESS • HOME PHONE • CELL PHONE • EMAIL ADDRESS

❶ VISUAL MERCHANDISING PROJECT
Fashion Marketing Program, Bradshaw Community College

- Conducted a comprehensive comparative analysis of the visual presentation techniques and standards and in-store marketing systems for 5 competing ladies' apparel retailers. Met with all contributors in advance to obtain authorization and discuss the project with store managers and visual presentation specialists.

- Visited the same 5 locations every Saturday for 6 weeks. Photographed in-store visual displays and window presentations, including mannequins and promotional signage. Noted current themes, the visual impact of each display, the overall cleanliness and organization, the location of clearance items, and changes from the previous week.

- Studied the effective and efficient use of a variety of merchandising fixtures including circle racks, 4-way racks, 2-way racks, tables, showcases, benches, waterfalls, faceouts, slat wall panels, shelving, pegboards, mannequins, and bust forms.

- Evaluated all elements of a successful merchandise presentation including story-telling, product selection, price points, signage, fabric coordination, colour blocking and linking, folding, hanging, balance, symmetry, sizing, tag placement, adjacencies, cleanliness, lighting, and overall attention to detail.

- Received 93% on the final project submission, earning the highest mark in the class. Full report available for viewing upon request.

❷ RETAIL TRAINING

- BRADSHAW COMMUNITY COLLEGE, City   20XX – Present
Recently finished the first year of a 2-year program leading to a Diploma in Fashion Marketing and Merchandising. Averaged 90% in courses such as Introduction to the Retail Industry, History of Art Design, Colour Management, Business Communications, Advertising, Fundamentals of In-Store Marketing, Design and Fabrication, Promotional Marketing, Design Illustration, and Digital Imaging.

❸ RETAIL EMPLOYMENT

- SHOPCO FOODS, Cashier, City   Feb 20XX – Present
Process customer transactions for a high-volume discount retailer. Maintain a high level of accuracy with no variances greater than $1. Earned "Employee of the Month" twice.

- MELISSA, Seasonal Sales Associate, City   Nov 20XX – Jan 20XX
Sold women's junior apparel and accessories in a specialty boutique during a very busy Christmas season. Declined manager's request to stay on afterwards due to relocation.

MALIK YUEN
Retail Sales and Service Associate • Fluent in English and Mandarin

Mailing Address • Email Address • Home Telephone • Cell Telephone

RETAIL SALES SKILLS

- **Greeting** customers to make them feel welcome and to aid in loss prevention.
- **Approaching** customers in a friendly manner, avoiding pressure or intimidation.
- **Identifying wants or needs** by asking relevant and open-ended questions.
- **Showing and demonstrating products** that meet the needs or wants of the customer.
- **Overcoming objections** with strong product knowledge and problem-solving skills.
- **Adding on additional products** that are on promotion or complement their purchase.
- **Closing the sale** and thanking them for their business.

EMPLOYMENT HISTORY

Sales Associate – The Sophisticated Man, City
February 20XX – Present
Promoted from shipper/receiver after 1 month. Earned "Top Monthly Sales" award twice and "Top Units per Transaction" award once, on a team of over 20 associates. Trained 2 new employees on the cash desk and the retail sales cycle. Complimented by the district manager for creative visual merchandising skills.

Server – Antonio's Pasta Experience, City
June 20XX – October 20XX
Promoted from bus person to server after 2 months. Awarded "Employee of the Month" twice. Scored "exceeds" or "meets" expectations on all categories on September 20XX performance evaluation. Received letter of appreciation from a customer for delivering outstanding guest service. Trained 2 new servers.

EDUCATION

Atlantic Business and Technical Institute, City
20XX – Present
Enrolled in general business courses including Marketing, Business Communications, Accounting, Economics, Business Applications, and Information Technology.

COMPUTER SKILLS

Proficient with Windows systems; limited knowledge of Mac. Trained in MS Word, Excel, PowerPoint, and Outlook. Skilled in online research and Web 2.0 technologies.

DONNA LEE

MAILING ADDRESS ~ TELEPHONE ~ EMAIL ADDRESS

extensive knowledge of:

Classic / Progressive Rock	R&B / Soul	Alternative / Garage
Latin Pop / Latin Jazz	Pop / Disco	Punk / Hardcore
Rap / Hip Hop	Jazz / Blues	Heavy Metal

moderate knowledge of:

Christian Rap / Hip Hop	Country	Musicals
Christian Rock / Pop	Bluegrass	Reggae
Christian Country	New Age	Gospel / Devotional

limited knowledge of:

Classical / Opera	Children's	Lounge / Oldies

EXPERIENCE

Musical Coordinator for 3 school plays, 2 in junior high and 1 in senior high. Consulted with teachers on song selections, setup and operated stereo and speaker equipment, and played music according to scripted cues. Also assisted with lighting and stage setup and design.

EDUCATION

Sabre Senior Secondary School, City   20XX – Present
Currently enrolled in Grade 12. Maintaining a B+ average with such electives as Information Technology, Marketing, Accounting, and History. Volunteered 30 hours in the computer lab.

AVAILABILITY

Monday / Wednesday	4:00 – Close	Friday	3:00 – Close
Tuesday / Thursday	1:00 – Close	Weekends	Open – Close

RELIABILITY

Proven to be very reliable and punctual; copies of high school report cards, showing zero absences throughout senior high school, available upon request. Hold a valid driver's licence with access to a reliable vehicle; willing and able to work on short notice when required.

~ references available from high school drama teacher and career advisor ~

ATTENTION HIRING MANAGER:

With a combination of retail experience, excellent computer skills, and a positive attitude, I would like to apply for a Stock Assistant position in your department store. I am often described as enthusiastic, mature, and motivated, and I am confident I will prove beneficial to your team. Please review the following skills and qualifications I offer:

- **Customer Service Certificate.** Completed a 2-day course on the importance of delivering a high level of customer service and the skills and techniques required to do so.

- **Communication Skills.** Fluent in English and conversant in spoken French. Capable of following verbal and written directions quickly and easily.

- **Teamwork Skills.** Worked effectively as part of a team during a 4-week work experience placement at Fashion World. Completed several group projects in school.

- **Technical Skills.** Experienced with Word, Excel, Outlook, Publisher, and Photoshop on both Windows and Mac operating systems. Keyboard 40-50 wpm.

Although I am just starting my career, I have gained some important work experience that is sure to help me excel in future jobs:

- **Stock Clerk - Fashion World**, March 20XX
  Completed a 4-week, full-time work experience placement. Worked with 3 other stock clerks to receive and verify up to 6 pallets of new merchandise a day. Transferred stock to the sales floor and maintained an organized warehouse. Prepared boxes and pallets for shipment to other locations. Performance report available upon request.

I understand the importance of availability and flexibility when working in any business that is open long hours. Although I am currently in high school, I do get early dismissal every Friday and have no other commitments that would interfere with a job. Therefore, my availability is as follows: Mon-Thurs, 4pm-close; Fri, 2pm-close; weekends/holidays, open-close. I also live within walking distance and would be happy to come in on short notice when needed.

- South Robson Junior Secondary School, 20XX-Present
  Currently enrolled in Grade 10 and taking French, Computer Systems, Algebra, and Foods. Worked in the school cafeteria during lunch hour for one semester, preparing entrées, salads, desserts, and beverages. Maintaining a B average.

I am confident my resume shows that I possess not only the technical skills you may need in a Stock Assistant, but also the right attitude and personality for retail employment. May we meet and discuss any opportunities you may have? I will contact you early next week, but in the meantime I can be reached at 555-555-5555. Thank you for your time and consideration, and I look forward to talking with you soon!

Wayne Crawford

3 Years' Retail Sales Management Experience • Bachelor of Arts Degree with a Marketing Major

COUNTER MANAGER, COSMETICS/FRAGRANCES
Barnsworth Department Stores, City • 20XX–20XX

Promoted from cosmetician after just 4 months.

Sales Management. Directed a team of 6 full-time and part-time cosmeticians in pursuit of head office and vendor sales objectives. Monitored and analyzed key performance indicators such as units-per-transaction, dollars-per-transaction, and productivity-per-hour. Created business plans, set and assigned sales targets, and provided ongoing coaching and staff motivation.

- Led counter from 12% below sales target to 5% above target after just 3 months.
- Increased sales from $1M in 20XX to $1.3M in 20XX, averaging 9% growth per year.
- Surpassed annual sales goals by an average of 4% per year.
- Improved counter ranking from 43rd in the company to 22nd after just 18 months.
- Ranked 3rd in sales out of 39 counters in the region during the 20XX Christmas season.

Marketing, Promotions and Event Planning. Partnered with the assistant store manager and the account executive on the conception, planning, and execution of in-store events and marketing promotions. Recruited demonstrators, estimated stock needs, procured door prizes and testers, ordered refreshments, and liaised with other store departments for cross-promotions.

- Conceived, organized, and facilitated monthly facial events that doubled the customer contact list after 4 months and generated significant exposure in the community.
- Created and executed a 20XX Valentine's Day promotion that was selected by the marketing department for use in their advertising plan.
- Planned and conducted a marketing event during the 20XX Christmas season that generated the 4th highest sales in the company.
- Contributed to the planning and execution of a major "grand opening" event at a new store in conjunction with the counter manager and account executive.

Human Resources. Oversaw all recruiting, hiring, orientation, training, team development, and performance management, in addition to continuous product knowledge and skill development. Prepared and conducted semi-annual performance evaluations. Administered bi-weekly payroll.

- Created a sales training program that was commended by the assistant store manager and account executive, and adopted by every other cosmetics counter in the store.
- Recruited, interviewed, and hired 1 full-time and 4 part-time cosmeticians, and 30+ contract demonstrators and photographers for special events.
- Developed and led one cosmetician to a counter manager promotion at another location.

Inventory Management. Controlled the inventory flow and merchandise presentation including receiving shipments, authorizing invoices, ordering replenishments, creating product displays, coordinating allocations among stores, processing vendor returns, and tracking inventory shrink.

- Conducted annual inventory counts and maintained inventory shrink below 1.5%.
- Lowered stock-on-hand 14% by planning and implementing quarterly clearance events.

BUSINESS SERVICES ASSOCIATE
Office Supplies Warehouse, City

SKILLS

General Services
Copying / Printing
Fax Services
Courier Shipping

Custom Printing
Business Cards
Brochures
Flyers
Manuals
Presentations
Letterhead
Envelopes
Signs
Banners
Labels
Forms
Stamps
Embossers
Posters

Finishing Services
Machine Folding
Cutting
Machine Stapling
Booklet Assembly
Bundling
Laminating
Mounting
Wireless Binding
Cerlox Binding
Coil Binding

Digital Services
CD Burning
Photo Scanning
Document Scanning
Desktop Publishing

EMPLOYMENT

COPY CENTRE CLERK, Full-time   20XX–20XX
AJ's Print and Copy Centre, City

Provided a wide variety of custom printing and document management services to personal and corporate clients in a high-volume, 10,000 sf. print and copy centre. Worked directly with customers, creating tailored document solutions designed to exceed their expectations while meeting their budgets. Assisted self-serve customers with basic needs. Operated and maintained all related equipment. Worked as part of a team of 15.

CASHIER, Part-time   20XX
Supply Depot, City

Processed customer purchases, returns and exchanges in a large-format office supplies and equipment store. Worked evenings and weekends while in school. Operated and maintained computerized cash registers and debit/credit machines. Balanced cash and receipts at shift-end. Awarded "Employee of the Month" in October 20XX.

BUS PERSON, Part-time   20XX–20XX
Antoine's Bar and Grill, City

Worked evenings and weekends in a fine dining restaurant while still in high school. Cleared and prepared tables and supported serving staff in providing optimum service to all guests.

EDUCATION

POTTER COMMUNITY COLLEGE, City   20XX–20XX

Completed the first year of a business administration program, earning all As and Bs in such courses as Economics, Business Communications, Marketing, Financial Accounting, Managerial Accounting, Business Math, Organizational Behaviour, and Professional Sales.

SAMPSON HIGH SCHOOL, City   20XX–20XX

Graduated with an Honours Diploma and several workplace certificates including First Aid Level 1, Workplace Safety, and Conflict Resolution.

CONTACT

SVEND PAHLSSON
Mailing Address - Home Phone - Cell Phone - Email Address

GILLIAN MASTERSON
Financial Services Representative

HOME PHONE • CELL PHONE • FAX NUMBER • EMAIL ADDRESS • MAILING ADDRESS

FINANCIAL EDUCATION • Financial Management Certificate, 20XX

- Earned a Financial Management Certificate from Morris Pendleton Community College after completing a full-time, 9-month program.
- Courses included Accounting I/II, Financial Accounting I/II, Managerial Accounting, Taxation, Auditing, Business Applications, Business Mathematics, and Economics.
- Graduated high school in 20XX, completing such courses as Accounting 11/12, Advanced Accounting 12, Information Technology 11, Keyboarding 11, and French 11/12.

CASH MANAGEMENT EXPERIENCE • Organic Wonders, 20XX-20XX

- 2 years' cash handling and reconciliation experience as a cashier and relief cash office clerk in an organic grocery store generating $22M per year in sales revenue.
- Processed all tender types on a computerized register and scanning system including cash, bank, and credit cards, traveller's cheques, coupons, and foreign currency.
- Reconciled cash and receipts to computer and terminal totals at the end of each shift, either balancing all totals or researching and accounting for any overages or shortages.
- Covered for the cash office clerk as needed. Calculated, prepared, and delivered daily bank deposits, placed change orders, and calculated and reported on safe contents.
- Received the following recognition on August 20XX performance review: "Congratulations and thanks for stepping in and performing so well in the cash office while Marianne was ill. You learned the job remarkably fast!" MARK PAVELICH, GENERAL STORE MANAGER

ADDITIONAL CUSTOMER SERVICE EXPERIENCE • Arts & Crafts Superstore, 20XX-20XX

- 2 years' experience in retail sales and customer service in a high volume arts and crafts store. Promoted from merchandiser to service associate after just 2 months.
- Earned a score of "exceeding expectations" on 80% of the customer service component on a June 20XX performance evaluation. Received "meeting expectations" on the rest.
- "You have made a great contribution to the success of our store through your dedication to providing our customers with the very best service. Your problem-solving and communication skills have been a lesson to other staff members." PERFORMANCE EVALUATION, JUNE 20XX
- "Gillian's compassion and empathy for our predicament was exemplary. We ran into trouble with our wedding scrapbook but she consistently provided us a friendly smile, a patient ear, and superior product knowledge." CUSTOMER APPRECIATION LETTER, MARCH 20XX

PERSONAL CHARACTER • References and 3 Letters of Recommendation Available

- Strong work ethic. Attended Morris Pendleton Community College 35 hours per week while also working 20-30 hours per week at Organic Wonders.
- Quick learner. Graduated in the top 5% of the Financial Management program.
- Reliable. Missed only 1 day of work due to illness in 4 years with Organic Wonders and Arts & Crafts Superstore. Performance evaluations and attendance records available for viewing.
- Trustworthy. Trusted with cash office duties and safe combination at Organic Wonders.

ALTERNATIVE RESUMES FAQ//
WHAT IS THE PURPOSE OF A RESUME?

Why do companies put flyers in your mailbox? To advertise their products and services. In other words, to persuade you to contact them with potential business.

They design convincing brochures and e-newsletters that show how they can solve your problem, why they can be trusted with your hard-earned money, and where they can be contacted for more information.

Is this any different from a resume? Why do you send it to places you want to work? To persuade the hiring manager to contact you for an interview. That's why, just like in advertising, your resume needs to show how you can solve their problem, why you should be trusted with their hard-earned money, and how you can be contacted for an interview.

As a job-seeker, you are a product that can fill a need for a company, whether it's to pump gas, sell electronics, or serve food. To advertise that product, you use marketing materials such as resumes, cover letters, reference letters, and portfolios.

Your resume is an advertising tool and its purpose is to convince the employer, through these steps, to contact you for an interview:

1. Get Their Attention

When managers have a large list or stack of resumes to go through, they typically skim each one for a few seconds before deciding whether it will go in an A folder to examine in more detail, a B folder as a backup, or a C folder for rejections. Your resume has to get their attention to make the A folder. How will it stand out from the hundreds of others they receive? Appearance plays a big part.

2. Generate Interest

Once your resume has caught their attention, something about it needs to convince them to read through to the end because most hiring managers don't have time to read every resume they receive. While the appearance may grab their attention, the structure and content will determine their level of interest. Is it targeted to their industry? Does it have applicable section headings? A relevant job title? Are your key qualifications near the top?

3. Elevate Their Interest To Desire

As they read your resume, you want their casual interest to escalate to desire so that they feel a strong need to meet you. To do this, your resume has to give the reader some reason to think you can benefit their business. They won't call you just because they get the impression you're a nice person, but they will if they think you could be a valuable addition to their team.

4. Promote Action

Once they have an enthusiastic desire to meet you, they will take action by contacting you for an interview. At that point, your resume has worked.

In almost all cases, your resume alone will not get you a job. Contrary to popular opinion, that's not its intent. The intent is to get an interview. Whether it's a twenty-second screening or a lengthy series of in-depth panel interviews, most employers will want to get more information from you and possibly check references before making a hiring decision. Rather than designing your resume with the goal of answering every question they may have for you in an eventual interview, concentrate on getting their attention, generating interest, elevating desire, and promoting action. Then WOW them in the actual interview!

GWEN ARNOLD
Bookseller

4 Years' Retail Experience
English Literature Major
Customer Service Certificate
Excellent Scheduling Availability

PHONE • EMAIL • MAILING ADDRESS

Chapter 1: Knowledge of Books and Literature

- Favourite genres include classics, drama, historical fiction and poetry. Personal collection includes over 150 books, mostly in these categories.
- Favourite authors include Jane Austen, the Brontë sisters, Margaret Mitchell, Tennessee Williams, T.S. Eliot, Diana Gabaldon, and William Wordsworth.
- Advanced knowledge of classic literature. Intermediate knowledge of travel, mythology, art, history, geography, theatre, film, TV, computers, and cooking.
- Completed such university courses as Shakespeare, Women in Literature, English Literature and Composition, Creative Writing in Prose, Poetic History, and Drama and the Novel.
- Earned a literature award for a 3rd year university essay.
- Attended the 20XX and 20XX Downtown Writers' Conference.

Chapter 2: Retail Skills and Experience

- 4 years' experience in retail customer service. Employed as a cashier with Super Save Foods since 20XX. Worked as a Sales Associate with Henry & Sons from 20XX to 20XX.
- Highly skilled in face-to-face customer service and sales.
- Strong cash handling abilities, including the use of computer systems and bank terminals. Experienced with reconciling cash trays and bank receipts.
- Earned a rating of "exceeding expectations" on almost all categories on September 20XX performance evaluation with Super Save Foods. Copy available upon request.

Chapter 3: Education and Training

- Currently enrolled in 3rd year university courses at Chadwick University. Majoring in English Literature with a minor in European History.
- Graduated with a high school diploma from Culver Senior Secondary School in 20XX.
- Earned a Customer Service Skills Certificate in high school.

Chapter 4: Additional Qualifications

- Fluent in English; conversant in verbal and written French.
- Excellent availability for scheduling: Monday to Wednesday, 1:00pm to close; Thursday and Friday, 3:00 to close; weekends and holidays, anytime.
- Live within a 5 minute drive from your location. Able to work on short notice when needed.

"The best of a book is not the thought which it contains, but the thought which it suggests; just as the charm of music dwells not in the tones but in the echoes of our hearts." - JOHN GREENLEAF WHITTIER

Demetri Ronin

Mailing Address • Home Phone • Cell Phone • Email Address

Leading sales associate with Camera World relocating from back east. 2 years' experience in the retail camera industry, coupled with an additional 2 years' experience in men's fashion. Exceptional record of sales success and customer satisfaction in both fields. Demonstrated a high level of professionalism and competency, resulting in a promotion to Staff Trainer after just 6 months.

ACHIEVEMENTS

✓ Surpassed 20XX sales target by 13%, second highest on a team of 12 sales associates. Exceeded 20XX goal by 7%.

✓ Received the top customer satisfaction score on a 3-month promotion focused on generating customer feedback.

✓ Awarded the "Top Dog" prize for a nation-wide Christmas contest in 20XX.

✓ Earned numerous bonuses and awards for excellent performance in monthly contests and promotions.

✓ Trained 5 new associates on sales techniques, product knowledge, cash register operation, and company policies and procedures.

✓ Selected by the General Manager to cover for the Assistant Manager in her absence; authorized to hold store keys and retain safe combination.

EDUCATION & TRAINING

SALES WORKSHOPS   20XX – 20XX
Participated in and facilitated numerous company training courses such as Building the Sale: How to Add On Additional Merchandise; Identifying Wants and Needs; The 7 Steps of Selling; Closing With Confidence; and Don't Aim to Satisfy.

CAMERA COURSES   20XX – 20XX
Completed numerous camera and photography courses through high school and Regional Continuing Education including The Digital Camera Industry, Advanced SLR Photography, Lenses in Focus, Digital Video Magic, Outdoor Photography, Memory Formats, Advanced Photoshop, and Introduction to Photo Imaging.

EMPLOYMENT HISTORY

Camera World, City	*Sales Associate / Trainer*	20XX – 20XX
Mills Fashions, City	*Sales Clerk*	20XX – 20XX
Justine's Diner, City	*Server / Host*	20XX – 20XX

HOME PHONE • CELL PHONE • **VALERIE RINNA** • EMAIL • MAILING ADDRESS

Part-time cashier at House & Home World seeks a full-time cashier position at the brand new Home Renovators store opening soon. Two years' part-time experience, averaging 20 hours per week while attending high school. Graduated with a diploma in May 20XX from Porter Senior Secondary. Achieved excellent ratings on performance evaluation last month:

EMPLOYEE NAME	Valerie Rinna	EVALUATION DATE	June 19, 20XX
JOB TITLE	Part-time Cashier	EMPLOYMENT PERIOD	Nov 20XX – Present
COMPANY	House & Home World	NUMBER OF LATES	Zero
LOCATION	Darlington Plaza	NUMBER OF ABSENCES	One (excused)

	EXCELLENT	ABOVE AVERAGE	AVERAGE	BELOW AVERAGE	NEEDS TO IMPROVE
EFFORT TO MEET STORE GOALS	✓				
SKILL WITH TOOLS & EQUIPMENT		✓			
RESPONSE TO CRITICISM/ADVICE			✓		
TIME MANAGEMENT SKILLS	✓				
PRODUCT KNOWLEDGE		✓			
CO-WORKER COMMUNICATION		✓			
CUSTOMER COMMUNICATION		✓			
PROBLEM-SOLVING SKILLS	✓				
WORKS INDEPENDENTLY		✓			
WORKS AS PART OF A TEAM			✓		
WORK ETHIC & ENERGY LEVEL	✓				
LEADERSHIP SKILLS		✓			
WORKS WELL UNDER PRESSURE	✓				
INITIATIVE & SELF-MOTIVATION	✓				
FLEXIBLE; ADAPTS TO CHANGE		✓			
DRESS & GROOMING			✓		
COURTESY & CONSIDERATION		✓			

Great job Valerie! We are very happy with your work, especially your energy and determination.

You do a great job of keeping your co-workers on their toes. Thanks for the great effort. You are

a pleasure to have on our team!   ANN MAH, STORE MANAGER, HOUSE & HOME WORLD

MICHEL SAVARD
Home Phone • Cell Phone • Email Address • Mailing Address

Art Store Sales Associate, Art Gallery Host

Over two years' retail customer service and cash handling experience.
Training in fine arts from the Madison Art Institute.
Skilled in drawing, sculpting, and oil, acrylic, and water colour painting.
Extensive knowledge of Renaissance, Impressionist, and Modern art.
Fluent in English and French.

EDUCATION

Currently enrolled in second year of Fine Arts Diploma program at Madison Art Institute.

EXHIBITIONS

Earned "Honourable Mention" in the amateur youth category for a painting shown at the County Art Festival in November 20XX.
Received "Artist of the Future" award for a painting submitted to the Brower Valley Art Exhibit contest in March 20XX.
Displayed paintings at Garden City and Metro Mall exhibitions in 20XX.

WORK HISTORY

SUBURBAN FOODS, City • 20XX–Present
Cashier / Stock Person

Operate a computerized scanning register system and bank terminal. Process cash, debit, credit, and cheque payments. Memorize numerous product codes for produce and bakery items. Assist customers with carrying purchases to their vehicles. Stock shelves with products from the warehouse. Help customers locate items.

CASUAL CORNER, City • 20XX–Present
Sales Associate / Cashier

Greet and approach customers. Ask open-ended questions to determine needs. Show suitable merchandise and demonstrate product knowledge. Suggest additional and/or alternative items. Process sale, refund, and exchange transactions. Reconcile cash and receipts to computer and bank terminal totals. Merchandise wall and floor displays. Maintain a clean and organized store.

LOTTERY CLERK

EXPERIENCE

Lottery Terminal: 18 months
Cash Handling: 4 years
Customer Service: 4 years

CERTIFICATIONS

Lottery Terminal Operator
Conflict Resolution
Occupational Health & Safety

AVAILABILITY

Any Day or Shift Needed
Weekdays and Weekends
Full-Time or Part-Time
Able to Start Immediately

HIGH SCHOOL GRADUATE

KELLY CARMINE

Mailing Address Line 1
Mailing Address Line 2

Home Phone: 555.555.5555
Cell Phone: 555.555.5555
Email Address: Email Address

EMPLOYMENT HISTORY

ROSEMARY SHOPPING MALL   Location
20XX–20XX

Lottery Booth Attendant

- Sold and redeemed all authorized lottery tickets including lotto, dailies, scratch-and-win, and sport betting.

- Operated and maintained a government authorized lottery ticket terminal.

- Explained and interpreted gaming rules and regulations as needed.

- Processed cash transactions; balanced cash and receipts to terminal totals at the end of each shift.

- Counted all lottery tickets at the beginning and end of each shift and reconciled totals with terminal reports.

- Rated as "exceeding expectations" on performance reviews in January 20XX and July 20XX.

THE GROCERY BARN   Location
20XX–20XX

Cashier

- Operated a scanning system, cash register, and bank terminal.

- Processed cash, debit, credit, cheque, and coupon transactions and reconciled all totals at the end of each shift.

- Awarded "Employee of the Month" on 3 separate occasions.

ALTERNATIVE RESUMES FAQ//
WHAT ARE THE DESIRED QUALIFICATIONS FOR RETAIL AND HOSPITALITY?

Retail and hospitality employ more teens and young adults than any other industries.

There are jobs in department stores, boutiques, big-box retailers, grocery stores, video stores, convenience stores, drug stores, fast food and full service restaurants, catering companies, movie theatres, gas stations, hotels, amusement parks, and many more. Here are some common qualifications and character traits that hiring managers look for:

Customer Service Experience

Almost all entry-level jobs in retail and hospitality involve serving customers. If you have this kind of employment or volunteer experience, make it clear on your resume. Emphasize the type of on-premises, face-to-face customer service most often found in retail and hospitality, but also include other service experience such as door-to-door sales, help desk, or telemarketing.

Cash Handling Experience

Many entry-level jobs in retail and hospitality involve cash handling. In smaller boutique stores, most employees handle cash in addition to their other duties, while in larger establishments, such as grocery stores, many positions don't involve cash. If you have operated a register and processed cash, credit card or bank card transactions, highlight this experience on your resume.

Availability

Retail and hospitality companies are open long hours, usually seven days a week, and they need employees who can work weekdays, weekends, holidays, and sometimes even overnight. If you believe you have better scheduling availability than most other job-seekers who may apply for the same positions, feature it on your resume.

Reliability

Punctuality and dependability are extremely important in retail and hospitality because if employees are late or don't show up, customers are left waiting. However, it's not convincing enough to simply state on your resume that you are dependable. Be sure to prove it using excerpts from letters of recommendation, performance evaluations, and school attendance records and report cards.

Flexibility

Scheduling changes are common in these industries and managers want employees who are flexible. This may include staying late or coming in early when it's busy or when a co-worker doesn't show up, working on a day off when someone calls in sick, or working at other locations when needed. Demonstrating your positive attitude using examples such as these from school or past jobs will show your willingness to go the extra mile.

WOODY GREEN

June 12, 20XX

Attention: Paulette Wong, Hiring Manager, ShopVille Superstore

Could you use a new Customer Greeter with the following qualifications?

CERTIFICATES
- Service Skills Plus, 20XX
- First Aid Level 1, 20XX

CHARACTER
- Customer-focused. Earned the highest mark in the class on the Service Skills exam. Oversaw sales and marketing functions for a hypothetical company during a 3-month group project in school.

- Punctual/Reliable. Received an Outstanding Attendance Award in Grade 11. Never late or absent for school cafeteria shifts; copy of performance evaluation available for viewing.

- Team Player. Worked as part of a 6-person team in the school cafeteria for 2 semesters. Member of basketball team in high school for 2 years. Member of track & field team for 1 year.

- Quick Learner. Achieved honour roll standing in both Grade 11 semesters. Self-taught Windows computer programs including Word, Excel, Publisher, WordPerfect and Photoshop.

AVAILABILITY
- Monday / Thursday / Friday
- 4:00 to Close
- Tuesday / Wednesday
- 1:00 to Close
- Weekends / Holidays
- Open to Close

EXPERIENCE
- Juniper Secondary School Cafeteria, Fall Semester 20XX

  Worked in all areas of the school cafeteria during morning and lunch hours, including food preparation, counter service, cash handling, dishwashing, and general clean-up. Prepared and served lunch meals including wraps, sandwiches, hamburgers, pitas, macaroni and cheese, lasagne, salads, and pastries.

Ms. Wong, I welcome the opportunity to meet with you and discuss how your company can benefit from my work. I will contact you early next week. In the meantime, I can be reached at 555.555.5555. Thank you in advance for your time and consideration!

Respectfully,

Woody Green

Sophia Cammalleri
RETAIL EVENT PLANNING / VISUAL PRESENTATION

Creative young woman seeking a position in event planning and/or visual presentation. Skilled in fashion coordination, event organization and production, marketing, promotions, and visual design. Able to start immediately and work any day or shift needed. Fluent in English and Italian.

FASHION EXPERIENCE

Visual Merchandiser, Danni Designs. Performed visual merchandising for this high-end ladies fashion store over a busy Christmas season. Created wall and table displays, followed head office planograms for the merchandising of fashion accessories, designed attractive window displays, managed all markdowns and clearance movement, and coached staff on visual presentation. Christmas 20XX

Volunteer Event Planner, Cheshire Fashion Show.
Assisted with the planning and production of the annual fundraising fashion show. Marketed the event to retailers to solicit donations, oversaw the pickup and return of all apparel and accessories, directed the models via headsets, chose the order of the presentation, selected suitable music, and used creative problem-solving skills to ensure the show ran smoothly. Position lasted for one month each year. 20XX–20XX

EDUCATION

High School Diploma, River High School. Completed business courses such as Marketing, Accounting, Entrepreneurship, and Leadership. Earned an award for Outstanding Leadership for planning school events. Member of the basketball team for 2 seasons, and the field hockey team for 1 season. 20XX

ADDITIONAL EXPERIENCE

Volunteer Event Planner, Children's Community Festival.
Supported the planning and organization of the annual children's festival. Designed and distributed advertising posters, called local businesses and organizations to solicit sponsorship and participation, recruited and coordinated volunteers, and provided input into other marketing and event ideas. Position lasted for approximately one month each year. 20XX–20XX

Gymnastics Instructor, Kid's Club. Instructed beginner and intermediate children aged 5–10 in a variety of gymnastics programs. Provided regular updates to parents on each child's progress. Prepared lesson plans in advance. Developed and implemented a student recognition and reward system. 20XX–20XX

Volunteer Event Set-Up, River High School Graduation.
Assisted with planning and organizing the graduation dinner and dance, including fundraising and venue setup, as a member of the school graduation committee. 20XX

Volunteer Event Set-Up, Annual City Marathon.
Assisted with setting up the starting gate and registration tables, distributing water, and registering participants. 20XX

Office Assistant, Cammalleri Design. Assisted with office administration, client service, planning and setting-up mall displays, coordinating deliveries with clients, monitoring product shipments, communicating with suppliers, and answering phone and email inquiries. 20XX–20XX

Home Phone • Cell Phone • Email • Mailing Address

PAOLO CHAVEZ
Men's Fashion Sales Associate

Motivated, mature, and customer-focused young man seeking a part-time position in a men's clothing and accessory store. Willing and able to work in any position, whether it is front-line sales and service, or back-end receiving and merchandising. Highly professional with a cheerful and enthusiastic attitude!

RETAIL SKILLS & EXPERIENCE

ROBSON CLIQUE, City, December 20XX – January 20XX
- Completed a 4-week work experience placement during the busy Christmas season, receiving training and experience in all areas of the store.
- Utilized the "6 steps of selling" on the sales floor: greeting and approaching customers, asking open-ended questions, showing the product, overcoming objections, suggesting related merchandise, and closing the sale.
- After 2 training days, regularly surpassed daily sales goals by 15-25%.
- Operated a computerized register system, accepting cash, credit, and bank card payments; operated a bank terminal; processed refunds and exchanges.
- Reconciled cash and banking receipts to computer totals at shift-end; balanced perfectly every shift except for one 50¢ overage on Christmas Eve.
- Merchandised products on the sales floor; created attractive floor and wall displays incorporating balance, colour, fabric, lighting, and story-telling; dressed window mannequins; replenished stock from the backroom.
- Received new shipments; verified and authorized packing slips; processed new merchandise including unwrapping, pricing, hanging, folding, and steaming; maintained accurate inventory receipts and records.
- Participated in the January physical inventory count of the entire sales floor and backroom using hand-held scanning units.

EDUCATION

EASTSIDE SENIOR SECONDARY SCHOOL, City
- Currently enrolled in Grade 11 with expected graduation in 20XX. Received a Certificate of Merit for improved grades last semester. Earned an Outstanding Attendance Award in Grade 10. Past member of basketball team.

AVAILABILITY

Monday, Tuesday, Thursday	4:00 pm – Close
Wednesday, Friday	1:00 pm – Close
Saturday, Sunday, Holidays	Open – Close

LORI NAKAMURA
Convenience Store Clerk

Mailing Address • Home Phone • Cell Phone • Email Address

2 YEARS' CONVENIENCE STORE EXPERIENCE

Store Associate   **24 Plus! Convenience Store**   **20XX–Present**

- Worked part-time through high school and full-time since graduation in this A-volume, 24-hour store. Work all shifts including weekdays, weekends, and overnights.
- Serve customers a selection of food, beverages, and other products with the goal of ensuring a pleasant experience. Used problem-solving skills to resolve disputes.
- Operate a cash register, bank terminal, and lottery machine. Process cash, credit, debit, and coupon transactions. Balance cash/receipts to register totals at shift-end.
- Monitor stock to reduce inventory loss. Perform daily, weekly, and monthly inventory counts. Verify shipments and authorize packing slips. Coordinate vendor returns.
- Maintain a clean and visually appealing store. Display point-of-purchase signs and promotional posters. Follow cleaning schedule. Clean parking lot and stock room.
- Described as "extremely courteous" and praised for "demonstrating a high level of professionalism while dealing with a difficult customer" on a May 20XX mystery shop.
- Selected as "Employee of the Month" out of 18 staff on 3 separate occasions.
- Earned 3 wage increases in less than 2 years.

20XX Performance Review	Poor	Satisfactory	Good	Excellent
Quality of Work				✓
Quantity of Work			✓	
Teamwork				✓
Customer Service				✓
Communication Skills				✓
Work Habits				✓
Product Knowledge			✓	
Time Management Skills			✓	
Technical Skills			✓	
Problem Solving Skills				✓
Reliability				✓
Personal Grooming				✓
Enthusiasm / Initiative				✓
Adapting to Change			✓	

HIGH SCHOOL DIPLOMA, 20XX

ROSS HORRIGAN, Retail Manager		Mailing Address • Email Address • Home Phone • Cell Phone
Diploma of Technology, Marketing Management Burnside Technical Institute, 20XX		Associates Degree in Business Administration West Coast University College, 20XX
EMPLOYER	**ACCOUNTABILITIES**	**ACCOMPLISHMENTS**
Assistant Store Manager Book and Media Emporium Location 20XX–Present	• Managing a free-standing, 18,000 square foot book, music, and DVD store as part of a 4-person management team. • Generating annual sales exceeding $8M. • Supervising a staff of 20-30 full-time and part-time employees. • Controlling over $2M in inventory turnover per year. Maintaining an inventory shrink level below 1.5%. • Averaging a minimum of 85% on monthly mystery shops.	• Increased annual sales 8% in 20XX over the previous year while keeping labour costs below budget levels. • Recruited and hired 9 new sales and stock associates. Created an improved orientation and training program. • Recorded 1.4% and 1.3% shrink on manual inventory counts conducted in January and July of 20XX. • Averaged 88% on monthly mystery shops in 20XX, and 92% so far in 20XX.
Store Manager Accessory Bonanza Location 20XX	• Managing a 1,200 square foot fashion accessory store targeting teens. • Generating at least $1M in annual sales. • Supervising a staff of 6-9 part-time sales associates. • Maintaining less than 2.5% shrink.	• Surpassed sales objective 12 out of 14 months by an average of 6%. • Generated $1.1M in sales for 20XX. • Recruited and hired 3 new associates. Promoted 1 to Assistant Manager. • Recorded 1.9% shrink in January 20XX.
Assistant Store Manager Movie World Location 20XX–20XX	• Managing a 1,500 square foot video store as part of a 3-person management team. • Generating $1.5M in annual revenues. • Leading a team of 10-15 part-time sales associates. • Reducing inventory loss below 2%.	• Exceeded 20XX revenue target by 11%. • Broke monthly sales records during the 20XX Christmas quarter. • Covered for the store manager during a 5-week absence. • Recorded 1.8% inventory shrink in 20XX.

SEASONAL CASHIER and SALES ASSOCIATE
Essence Card and Gift Shop

Available to work any days/shifts needed, including weekdays, evenings, weekends, and holidays, from November 1, 20XX to January 4, 20XX. Moving out of town on January 5.

QUALIFICATION SUMMARY

- 6 years' retail experience in specialty, big-box, and department stores. Gained strong customer service experience with Home Plus, Mansfield's, and Fashion City.
- Exceptional cash handling skills during peak periods. Chosen by management of Home Plus to serve as lead cashier during last 2 Christmas seasons.
- Strong loss prevention awareness. Contributed to the apprehension and conviction of 2 shoplifters while working in the cosmetics department at Mansfield's.
- Willing to work overtime as needed. Comfortable standing for long shifts and working in excess of 8 hours per day when necessary during high volume periods.

EMPLOYMENT HISTORY

•	Home Plus	Cashier, Home Improvement	20XX–20XX
•	Mansfield's Department Store	Sales Associate, Cosmetics/Fragrances	20XX–20XX
•	Mansfield's Department Store	Sales Associate, Fashion Accessories	20XX–20XX
•	Fashion City	Sales Associate, Unisex Apparel	20XX–20XX

PERFORMANCE RECORD

- Earned 82%, 87%, and 93% on semi-annual performance reviews with Home Plus.
- Recorded no shortages greater than $1 as a high-volume cashier with Home Plus.
- Selected by the Cosmetics Sales Manager at Mansfield's Department Store to serve as the Assistant Sales Manager for a 3-week vacation period.
- Formally recognized by the General Manager at Mansfield's Department Store for generating the highest sales in the department during the Christmas 20XX season.
- Received grades of B+ and A- on 2 performance evaluations with Fashion City.
- Missed only 1 day of work due to illness in the last 6 years.

RETAIL TRAINING

•	Front-Line Loss Prevention Awareness, Home Plus	20XX
•	Workplace Safety and Security, Home Plus	20XX
•	Sales and Service Excellence, Mansfield's Department Store	20XX
•	Workplace Harassment Awareness, Mansfield's Department Store	20XX
•	7 Steps of Retail Selling, Fashion City	20XX

JACKIE MOORE • MAILING ADDRESS • CELL PHONE • EMAIL ADDRESS

ROGER KING

personal profile	Mechanically inclined Grade 11 student with labour and service experience seeks an entry-level position in a gas station. Developed skills in minor auto mechanics and maintenance through personal study and high school shop courses. Excellent references and scheduling availability. Able to start immediately and work full-time or part-time!

mechanical skills

Check engine **oil** level
Confirm **transmission fluid** level
Fill windshield **wiper fluid**
Ensure sufficient **battery** water

Verify proper level of **brake fluid**
Check coolant level in **radiator**
Ensure proper **tire** pressure
Visually check wear & tear on **belts**

education & training

ServicePlus – received a customer service skills certificate in April 20XX
First Aid – earned certificate in Standard First Aid and CPR in May 20XX
High School – currently completing Grade 11 courses on a part-time basis

work availability

Currently attending Westside Learning Academy, with much better work availability than a typical high school student. Westside is an alternate school that encourages students to have a job while they complete high school part-time. Classes can either be completed in the mornings (8:30 to 11:30), afternoons (1:00 to 4:00) or evenings (6:00 to 9:00) to work around a job schedule. No other commitments that would interfere with availability.

work experience

Lawn Care. Landscaped lawns and gardens during summer/fall of 20XX, including mowing, weeding, planting, and pruning. Also helped design and install a backyard pond and bridge, and assisted with paving a driveway.

Flyer Delivery. During the summer of 20XX, placed brochures and other advertising flyers on car windows for restaurants, dry cleaners, grocery stores, fitness studios, and carpet cleaners. Worked independently and met strict deadlines and quotas for delivery.

contact

Roger King • Mailing Address • Home Phone • Cell Phone • Email Address

ALTERNATIVE RESUMES FAQ//
WHAT DO I PUT FOR AN OBJECTIVE?

While it is very important to target every resume you design for a particular job, company or industry, typical objective statements such as the following are outdated and should NOT be on your resume:

OBJECTIVE: To obtain a full-time position as a Replenishment Supervisor with a big-box retailer.

What's wrong with objective statements like this? They usually express what the job-seeker wants, not what the companies care about. Hiring managers want to know what they will gain by employing you, not what you will gain from your employment. These statements also don't project a qualified or confident image. If you want to be something in the future, that implies you aren't one now. Employers would rather hire an out-of-work replenishment supervisor than someone who wants to become a replenishment supervisor.

Emphasizing a job title in a prominent spot on your resume is a more assertive and concise way of stating who you are. A job title serves as an objective, while using as few words as possible. Make it a focal point using bold, caps or underlining so it will be easily noticed. Consider the following two examples comparing a typical objective to a job title:

1.   **LISA BUTLER**
Mailing Address | Home Phone | Email Address
Objective: To obtain a full-time position as a
Replenishment Supervisor with a big-box retailer

2.   **LISA BUTLER**
Retail Replenishment Supervisor
Mailing Address . Home Phone . Email Address

In the first example, Lisa projects the image of someone who wants to be a Retail Replenishment Supervisor. From this top portion of her resume, the reader has no reason to believe she is qualified for that position. She may or may not be, but her objective doesn't portray a confident candidate.

In the second example, Lisa emphasizes a job title and projects the image of a qualified Replenishment Supervisor. She may not have any experience in that position but it's a more confident approach and there's a better chance her entire resume will be read.

Additional options for your objective include job function (the type of work you want), job level (the level of position you want), or industry (the field you want). Here are other possible objectives that Lisa could use:

- Retail Operations and Distribution Supervisor
  (open to different job functions)

- Retail Replenishment Specialist
  (open to different job levels)

- Warehouse Replenishment Supervisor
  (open to different industries)

- Retail Replenishment: Supervisor, Team Leader,
  Department Manager (options for job level)

Targeted resumes with clear objectives in the form of job titles are most successful. Employers don't have the time or desire to determine the best use of your talents, so you have to tell them.

LISA BUTLER
Retail Replenishment Supervisor
Home Phone • Cell Phone • Email Address
Mailing Address

REPLENISHMENT COORDINATOR   20XX–Present
Heartland Home & Garden, City

- Promoted from an entry-level position on the merchandising team to Replenishment Coordinator after 2 months. Lead the overnight stock team in the transfer of merchandise from the warehouse to 12 departments on a 75,000 square foot sales floor. Supervise up to 15 employees at a time, including all training, coaching, and progressive discipline. Accountable for inventory integrity and visual presentation at store opening.

- Selected by management to receive specialized training on a new operating system. Created and facilitated a 2-hour training workshop with a PowerPoint presentation for all employees. Selected by the Regional Manager of Operations to supervise the 6-week setup of the entire warehouse racking system for a new 90,000 square foot store in Fairfield.

- Co-chair of the Occupational Health & Safety Committee; lead and participate in risk assessments, accident investigations, and monthly safety inspections throughout the store. Member of the Equal Partners Action Team, a new committee that aims to bring staff concerns and ideas to upper management to help promote a better work environment.

MERCHANDISE ASSOCIATE   20XX–20XX
Shop-Easy Superstore, City

- Moved from an entry-level position on the maintenance team to a challenging role on the overnight stock crew after 2 months. Worked with a team of 20+ associates on the accurate and timely placement of a wide variety of soft and hard goods on a 120,000 square foot sales floor. Consistently met strict morning deadlines while complying with very detail-oriented planograms for visual presentation.

- Trained 12 new merchandise associates in 4 departments. One trainee was quickly promoted to Merchandise Coordinator at an out-of-town store.

PITA SHACK   20XX–20XX
Cashier / Prep Cook, City

High School Graduate ~ MW Lancaster Senior Secondary ~ 20XX

CERTIFICATES

Level 2 First Aid
Forklift Driver
Workplace Safety
Hazardous Materials

COMMODITIES

Bath & Beauty
Bed & Bath Linens
Children's Apparel
Cosmetics/Fragrances
Electronics
Fabric & Sewing
Fashion Accessories
Fast Food
Footwear
Furniture
Garden Supplies
Giftware
Greeting Cards
Grocery/Confectionary
Hardware
Home Décor
Housewares
Jewellery
Junior Apparel
Kitchen
Ladies Apparel
Men's Apparel
Music & Video
Office Supplies
Pet Products
Photo/Camera
Sporting Goods
Toys & Games

Geoffrey Watson
COMPUTER SALES & SERVICE

Email Address • Home Phone • Cell Phone
Mailing Address

COMPUTER SKILLS & ACHIEVEMENTS

- Windows, Mac and Linux operating systems; MS Word, Excel, PowerPoint, and Outlook; Lotus SmartSuite; Photoshop; Corel Draw.
- Troubleshooting, removing and installing hard-drives, disk-drives, sound/video cards, burners, RAM, processors, and motherboards.
- Preparing recovery/backup disks for hard drives and operating systems.
- Installing virus and spy protection software, and setting up firewalls, email spam controls, and parental controls.
- Created a home wireless network with 4 computer systems and a mini-server.

WORK CHARACTERISTICS

- Business and sales training. Managed the marketing and sales departments of a hypothetical company during a 4-month group project in Entrepreneurship 11 class. Delivered a formal business presentation to fellow students.
- Very reliable and punctual. Earned the Outstanding Attendance Award in Grade 11 for not missing any days the entire school year. Received the Certificate of Merit for volunteering at the school.
- Excellent leadership potential. Elected to student council in Grades 10 and 11. Liaised with school administrators on a variety of issues important to students. Organized and led a protest campaign supporting teacher pay equity.
- Strong communication skills. Fluent in English. Conversant in French, having finished up to Grade 11. Follow written and verbal directions quickly and easily.

VOLUNTEER EXPERIENCE

- Volunteered in the school computer lab 5 hours per week throughout Grade 11. Monitored student activity, and investigated and repaired hardware and software problems. Reference available from the Information Technology teacher.

EDUCATION

- Williams Harris Senior Secondary, City   20XX – Present

  Currently enrolled in Grade 12, taking several business and computer courses such as Marketing, Communications, Accounting, and Information Technology.

GINA TAYLOR

Supermarket Cashier

Attention: Laura Shepherd, Earth Foods General Manager

Often described as a motivated, determined, and outgoing young woman, I am excited about applying for the part-time cashier position advertised in the *Central City Courier*. I am confident in my abilities and would like to take this opportunity to demonstrate how I can benefit your business.

Although I balance work with school, I take my job seriously. As an example of that, I memorized your store directory, as shown on the right, to prepare myself for working with your company. I feel it's important to take this initiative with my training because it will allow me to progress quickly. This excerpt from a reference letter from my principal will further demonstrate my dedication and maturity:

"She has proven dedicated to not only her own studies, but also the school in general. Her organization and direction of the Global Conscience Committee is testament to her desire to see things done right, and her maturity in recognizing and valuing the world outside her own – something many teens struggle with."
- JACK KOPP, STORYBOOK HIGH PRINCIPAL

I have also proven to be a reliable employee. While managing an *Urban Fare* paper route for the past 18 months, I consistently met all delivery deadlines and provided excellent service to subscribers. This paragraph from a customer's letter will confirm:

"Gina has always been an excellent paper carrier. I need the paper delivered by 6:30am every morning as I leave for work at that time. Gina has never disappointed me, even though I know she has a large route. She is also a warm, friendly young lady who would be an asset to any company that employs her. I wish her all the best!"
- SANDRA CUTLER, *URBAN FARE* SUBSCRIBER

Ms. Shepherd, may we meet to discuss my qualifications in person? I look forward to describing in more detail how I would make a great cashier for your store. Thanks for your time and consideration!

Sincerely,

Gina Taylor
Mailing Address
Home Phone • Cell Phone • Email Address

**EARTH FOODS
STORE DIRECTORY**

Aisle #1
Bakery

Aisle #2
Floral

Aisle #3
Produce

Aisle #4
Prepared Foods

Aisle #5
Frozen Foods

Aisle #6
Packaged Foods

Aisle #7
Bulk Foods

Aisle #8
Snacks

Aisle #9
Beverages

Aisle #10
Household

Aisle #11
Health/Body Care

LIAM TANG   **Mystery Shopper / Retail Merchandiser**

Experienced retail professional seeking a part-time, flexible position in mystery shopping and/or merchandising. Currently employed part-time as a library assistant with the Northwest School District. Available afternoons, evenings, and weekends in addition to summers and holidays. Three years' prior experience in retail; skilled in all aspects of retail merchandising and inventory control. Professional communicator and extremely detail-oriented. Clean driver's licence with a reliable, late model vehicle. Own newer home computer and have advanced software skills.

MERCHANDISING

- Two years of progressive experience in retail management with a focus on merchandising and stock turnover. This included one year as Merchandise Supervisor with Shop-Mart and one year as Assistant Store Manager with Sam's.
- Initially hired as part of the renovation team at Shop-Mart, travelling to many locations over a four-month period to re-merchandise all departments according to detailed planograms. Later organized and supervised a Store Planogram Team at the Scottsville store.
- Experienced with merchandising tools and equipment for both hard-lines and soft-lines, such as shelving, pegboards, vendor display racks, store display racks, and mannequins.
- Created effective merchandise displays incorporating product themes, signage, marketing POP, symmetry, balance, price-points, color coordination, lighting, and attention to detail.
- Utilized creative problem-solving skills to resolve merchandising or planogram conflicts.

INVENTORY CONTROL

- Planned and conducted physical inventory counts at Style Time, Shop-Mart, and Sam's.
- Utilized portable scanning equipment to accurately record product data and inventory totals.
- Maintained organized stockrooms to ease merchandise replenishment and deter internal theft.
- Received and counted/verified new product shipments and authorized invoices.
- Prepared merchandise for the sales floor, including unwrapping, pricing and ticketing, barcode scanning, folding, hanging, assembling, and steaming.
- Followed-up with vendors on shortages/overages, missing shipments, and late deliveries.
- Placed product re-orders with vendors according to stock levels and sales projections.
- Supervised markdown teams at Shop-Mart and Sam's. Monitored all price-changes, entered data into the computer system, and maintained detailed records to assist with loss prevention.
- Accurately processed and recorded store transfers, refunds/exchanges, and vendor returns.

SALES / CUSTOMER SERVICE

- Enthusiastic service provider, consistently striving to exceed the customer's expectations.
- Accustomed to interacting with store management and staff and respecting service priorities.
- Effective communicator and sales representative; able to explain and market sales promotions.
- Knowledge and understanding of the role of the vendor representative on the sales floor.

Retail	SAM'S, City, 20XX – 20XX	Assistant Store Manager
Employment	SHOP-MART, City, 20XX – 20XX	Merchandise Supervisor
History	STYLE TIME, City, 20XX – 20XX	Store Manager

Mailing Address   ·   **Email Address**   ·   **Home Phone**   ·   **Cell Phone**

CHARLOTTE TOWNSEND
Home Phone • Cell Phone • Email Address
Mailing Address

EXPERIENCE	EDUCATION

EXPERIENCE

Sales Associate, Wireless Products
Electronic Outlet, City • 20XX–Present

- Sell cellular phones and accessories to consumers and corporate clients.

- Work alongside a sales manager, a department supervisor, and 11 other associates in a $1.8M department.

- Utilize the "7 steps of selling" with each customer that enters the department:
  - Greet and approach
  - Initiate communication
  - Identify needs
  - Show suitable products
  - Overcome objections
  - Add-on complementary products
  - Close the sale

- Participate in vendor-facilitated product knowledge seminars on a regular basis.

- Contribute to the visual presentation of the department by displaying and maintaining promotional signage.

- Assist management with ordering new stock as needed.

- Conduct monthly inventory counts of all merchandise in the department.

Achievements

- Earned "Star of the Month" for the entire store in February, May, July, and December of 20XX.

- Awarded "Star of the Month" for the department on 9 different occasions, the highest in the store.

- Placed 2nd for "Employee of the Year" in 20XX out of 115 staff.

- Won the back-to-school wireless sales contest in 20XX.

EDUCATION

High School Diploma with Honours
Glenwood High School, City • 20XX–20XX

- Graduated with an A average.

- Completed a variety of business and technical courses including:
  - Accounting 11 / 12
  - Advanced Accounting 12
  - Marketing 11 / 12
  - Business Communications 12
  - Information Technology 11 / 12
  - Business Applications 11
  - Graphic Design 12
  - Entrepreneurship 12

- Prepared a comprehensive business plan for Entrepreneurship 12 class that earned a grade of 98%, the highest ever awarded by that teacher.

- Earned several workplace certificates:
  - Occupational First Aid Level 1
  - Customer Service Excellence
  - Workplace Health and Safety
  - Conflict Resolution
  - Workplace Hazardous Materials

- Completed a 2-week work experience placement in the accounting office at Whole Foods. Reference available.

- Received a "Certificate of Merit for Outstanding Attendance" in Grades 10, 11, and 12.

- Member of the debate team in Grades 11 and 12. Elected captain in Grade 12. Won provincial award in 20XX.

- Served as treasurer for the graduation committee in Grade 12.

- Member of the track and field team in Grade 11. Specialized in the javelin throw, winning gold at the 20XX finals.

ALTERNATIVE RESUMES FAQ//
WHAT SECTIONS SHOULD I INCLUDE?

Many resume writers and job-seekers design resumes backwards.

They find samples or templates and see common sections such as Objective, Summary of Qualifications, Employment History, Education, Volunteer Experience, and Interests and Hobbies. They believe all these sections are required, so they slot each of their qualifications into these pre-determined categories.

The problem with this method is every job-seeker is unique, and their range of qualifications is also unique. What works for some may not work for all. The sections listed above are the most common, and can be used if they will show your qualifications in the best light, but they aren't mandatory.

Rather than starting with those sections, begin by listing all your qualifications that may be relevant or appealing to your job target. These could come from work, school, or your personal life, and may include experience, education, training, skills, achievements, or character traits. Then separate them into groups based on common themes to determine your sections.

For example, say you want to include the following qualifications:

- Assisted teachers with chaperoning Grade 8 students on a weekend ski trip.

- Excellent report-writing skills and use of business English, having achieved A in both Business Communication 12 and English 12.

- Placed 2nd in the election of class valedictorian in Grade 12.

- Strong computer skills including proficiency with Windows and Mac operating systems, extensive experience with MS Word, and 65 wpm keyboard speed.

- Fluent in verbal and written English; conversant in verbal French.

- Requested by management of Harris Corp. to assemble and lead a social committee.

Rather than slotting these into whatever common section seems like the closest fit, present them in the following way to differentiate yourself from your competitors and leave a stronger impression with the reader:

Communication Skills

- Excellent report-writing skills and use of business English, having achieved A in both Business Communication 12 and English 12.

- Strong computer skills including proficiency with Windows and Mac operating systems, extensive experience with MS Word, and 65 wpm keyboard speed.

- Fluent in verbal and written English; conversant in verbal French.

Leadership Experience

- Requested by management of Harris Corp. to assemble and lead a social committee.

- Assisted teachers with chaperoning Grade 8 students on a weekend ski trip.

- Placed 2nd in the election of class valedictorian in Grade 12.

RETAIL SALES, MERCHANDISING, and OPERATIONS
Mailing Address • Email • **Omar Puri** • Home Phone • Cell Phone

RETAIL SKILLS and EXPERIENCE

Sales and Customer Service
- Greeting and approaching customers soon after they enter the store.
- Asking open-ended questions to identify customer needs and wants.
- Showing products that meet their needs and wants.
- Overcoming objections using creative problem-solving skills.
- Suggesting and showing additional related merchandise.
- Closing the sale and thanking the customer.

Merchandising and Inventory Control
- Receiving shipment deliveries, counting inventory, and authorizing invoices.
- Preparing merchandise for the sales floor including pricing, folding, and hanging.
- Merchandising wall displays and 4-way, circle, and H-racks. Incorporating price points, colour and fabric coordination, lighting, story-telling, and attention-to-detail.
- Organizing and conducting annual physical inventory counts.
- Processing vendor returns, store transfers, markdowns, and price changes.

Cash Management
- Operating computerized cash register systems with optical scanners.
- Processing cash, credit cards, bank cards, traveller's cheques, and foreign currency.
- Reconciling cash and receipts to computer and bank terminal totals.
- Calculating, preparing and delivering bank deposits.
- Maintaining accurate sales reports and accounting records.

ACHIEVEMENTS

Retail
- Awarded "Sales Associate of the Month" 5 times at Teez Pleez.
- Recorded the highest personal sales in the company in December 20XX.
- Received a cash bonus and letter from the president for Christmas success.
- Trained 4 new employees in product knowledge and the sales cycle.
- Rated as "excellent" or "above average" in all areas on last performance review.

Academic
- Graduated with a high school diploma in May 20XX.
- Served as campaign manager for the winning Student Council President.
- Volunteered in the library before and after school throughout Grade 11.
- Earned a Certificate of Merit for business success in Entrepreneurship 12 class.

EMPLOYMENT HISTORY

3rd Key Holder • Teez Pleez, Laughlin Shopping Centre   September 20XX – Present
Sales Associate • Teez Pleez, Delta Hills Mall   January 20XX – September 20XX
Sales Associate • Casual Corner, Delta Hills Mall   October 20XX – January 20XX

Dorothy Winslet
Home Phone | Cell Phone | Email Address | Mailing Address

FLORIST ASSISTANT

I am a mature, professional young woman with a life-long love of flowers and gardening. Having been taught how to plant, nourish, and care for large flower gardens since childhood, I am confident I have the skills necessary to contribute to the success of your flower shop. My range of knowledge includes roses, tulips, carnations, lilies, freesia, anthuriums, sunflowers, irises, and asters.
In addition to my floral experience, I have often been described as a "people person" with a warm, outgoing personality and a positive attitude. I will consistently strive to deliver the best possible service to your customers!

EDUCATION

Serenity School of the Arts, City | 20XX–Present
I am currently enrolled in Grade 11 at this alternative school that focuses on performing and fine arts. In addition to academic classes, I completed artistic courses such as sculpting, painting, and drawing. In Grade 10, I earned an Outstanding Attendance Award and a Certificate of Merit for school participation. I have volunteered with the school library for the past 5 months and served on a student committee researching fundraising opportunities.

AVAILABILITY

Monday	4:00–Close	Friday	1:00–Close
Tuesday	4:00–Close	Saturday	Open–Close
Wednesday	1:00–Close	Sunday	Open–Close
Thursday	4:00–Close	Holidays	Open–Close

I can start immediately and work up to 20 hours a week while in school. I live within walking distance of your store and am happy to work on short notice when needed. With email and two phone numbers, I am easy to contact for schedule changes.

REFERENCES

"Dorothy has volunteered in the Serenity School Library for five months and has been a pleasure to work with. She performs many valuable tasks including book shelving and assisting students with locating and accessing materials. She is highly dependable and always comes in when needed. Her work ethic is superb – she always asks for more to do when she is finished a task, and constantly seeks new responsibility. I'm confident Dorothy will succeed at any job she undertakes." KAREN NEELY – LIBRARIAN

"Dorothy Winslet has been a highly valued babysitter for my family over the past three years. We have three children, including one seven-year-old son diagnosed with ADHD. Dorothy has always exercised the necessary patience and tolerance when dealing with my children, and has consistently shown her maturity. Dorothy will surely be a benefit to all her future employers and I highly recommend her." NAOMI POLLACK – CHILD CARE EMPLOYER

PAUL KENNEDY
Mailing Address
Email / Cell

JOB OBJECTIVE

To provide a pleasant shopping experience for Media World customers as a sales associate!

Extensive Musical Knowledge
Rap, Hip Hop, Pop, Alternative Garage, Punk, R & B, Soul, Gospel

Moderate Musical Knowledge
Classic Rock, Disco, Latin Pop Jazz, Blues, Reggae

Limited Musical Knowledge
Country, Classical, Opera, Heavy Metal Hardcore, Oldies, Children's

Extensive Movie Knowledge
Drama, Crime, Thriller, Cult Gangster, Science Fiction

Moderate Movie Knowledge
Comedy, Action, Adventure Horror, Romance, Art

Limited Movie Knowledge
Epic, Fantasy, Children's Family, Documentaries

CAPABILITIES

◊ Greeting customers as they enter the store
◊ Directing them to appropriate sections of the store
◊ Answering questions regarding music and movies
◊ Processing sales transactions through the register
◊ Receiving new product shipments in the stock room
◊ Merchandising new stock on the sales floor
◊ Making sure the sales floor and stockroom are clean
◊ Completing all other duties as needed

QUALIFICATIONS

◊ Extensive knowledge of music and movies
◊ Certificate in Customer Service Excellence
◊ Bilingual – fluent in English and French
◊ Completely open availability for the summer
◊ One year volunteer experience in school library
◊ Reference available from school librarian
◊ Friendly and outgoing personality
◊ Well-groomed; very presentable appearance

Volunteering in my school library in Grade 11 has prepared me for a job at Media World in these ways:

◊ SYSTEMS – Both jobs require stock to be merchandised in specific systems. I am skilled at understanding and following category systems and product flows.

◊ MEMORY SKILLS – I have become accustomed to learning and memorizing departments and sections of large floor layouts, and directing visitors to desired areas.

◊ ALPHABETICAL SKILLS – My library experience has developed my ability to organize or quickly locate items according to alphabetical or numerical systems.

◊ PRIORITIZING – I have learned the importance of giving great service to visitors and prioritizing that service over other duties.

JANYA PREET
SALES ASSOCIATE, LADIES FASHIONS

FEATURE	BENEFIT
Earned 2nd highest grade while completing Service Excellence: Fundamentals of Customer Service.	Previous training and certification in customer service will enable me to learn quicker and serve your customers better.
Held lead and co-lead acting parts in two theatre productions in Grades 8 and 9 at Carson Junior High School.	Acting in theatre demonstrates my ability to perform a role, to express my personality, to be vibrant and outgoing, and to memorize.
Strong computer skills; proficient in MS Word and Excel with a keyboard speed of 50 wpm.	Computer literacy will help me to learn your register system quickly and easily.
Participated in a school-wide, team-building "ropes course" training program that lasted a full day in 20XX.	Having learned to trust teammates and work together for a common goal, I will make a smooth transition to your team.
Received a Certificate of Merit for exceptional improvement in Math 10, after progressing from C– to B+.	I will also put in the extra effort necessary to overcome any weaknesses that my manager or I discover on the job.
Fluent in verbal and written English and Hindi with limited knowledge of French.	I'm able to follow instructions easily and communicate with co-workers and customers.
Attend classes weekday mornings until 12:30. Available to be scheduled anytime after 1:00 on weekdays; anytime weekends & holidays.	Better availability than most students means more options for the scheduling manager with regards to weekday afternoon coverage.
Only missed one day of school in the past two years at Bronson Alternate School, where I am currently completing Grade 11.	I will be a dependable and punctual staff member for your store, ensuring all customers will be attended to when needed.
Live within close walking distance of both your store and my school.	Not relying on public transit or access to rides means less chance of arriving late to work.
I can be reached at two phone numbers, at home and on my cell, in addition to email.	Being easy to reach means I'm more accessible if needed to work on short notice.
Students at my school are allowed to miss class in the event of a job interview.	I am able to come in for an interview any time that is convenient for you.

HOME PHONE • CELL PHONE • EMAIL ADDRESS • MAILING ADDRESS

ANDREI KOZLOV • MAILING ADDRESS • EMAIL ADDRESS • HOME PHONE • CELL PHONE

May 27, 20XX

ATTENTION: CHERYL MOFFATT, SPORT CITY MANAGER

Although Sport City is quite new to the sporting goods/apparel market in our city, it has been very successful across the country for the past five years. This is why I am applying for an entry-level position with your company. I am a motivated and determined Grade 10 student, and I am very confident my energy and enthusiasm will benefit your store and customers.

To prepare myself to work in this industry, I researched both your store and your competitors. I visited each one last Saturday afternoon, the busiest period of the week. While observing the staff, I noticed the successful ones used certain techniques when talking with customers. For example, most customers said they were just looking and walked away when asked IF they need any help, but the good salespeople would ask different questions such as, "Are you looking for a gift or something for yourself?" That always seemed to get the customers talking more, and allowed the salesperson to show them items they may like. These are skills I will learn quickly so that I can make a positive contribution to your team. I made notes during and after my store visits, and I thought you may like to see the results:

	Sport City	**In The Paint**	**Sport Market**	**The Net**	**Jim's Jerseys**
Location	Crescent Mall	Parkway Drive	Diamond Street	Diamond Street	Crescent Mall
Product mix	Apparel, shoes, equipment	Apparel, shoes, collectibles	Apparel, shoes, equipment	Apparel, shoes, collectibles	Apparel, collectibles
Current sale	½ off second pair of shoes	Nothing	Markdowns clearance sale	Additional 25% off clearance	15% off hockey jerseys
Clearance items	Mixed	None	Front of store	Front of store	Back of store
Was I greeted?	Yes	Yes	No	No	Yes
# staff on floor	8	3	11	4	2
Cleanliness	Very clean	Very clean	Very messy	Average	Very clean
Window display	Posters	None	Boring	Eye-catching	Eye-catching

If you wish, I can provide a picture comparison of the main window displays. After comparing the five stores, I quickly realized how an effective window display can draw customers in. I am very interested in learning more about sales, store operations, and merchandising with your company.

I would like to meet with you to discuss any part-time jobs you have available. I can be reached, or a message can be left, anytime at 555.555.5555. However, I will come back within the week to talk to you in person as well. Ms. Moffatt, thank you for your time and consideration!

Regards,

Andrei Kozlov

Jennie Lynn
RETAIL SALES MANAGER
Home Phone • Email Address
Mailing Address

Sales Manager • Benton Department Store • Location • 20XX–20XX

Scope

- Oversaw multiple departments generating $8M in annual revenue including fashion accessories, jewellery, footwear, hosiery, luggage, and handbags/wallets. Managed over 25,000 square feet of selling space on 2 floors.

- Accountable for department P&L, sales, payroll and expense budgets, recruiting and hiring, training and development, inventory control, loss prevention, merchandise management, strategic planning, visual presentation, and in-store marketing.

- Provided leadership, guidance, and support to a team of 35 including 4 supervisors, 3 visual merchandisers, and 28 sales associates. Reported to the General Manager.

Accomplishments

- Surpassed annual sales budget by 19% in 20XX and 11% in 20XX. Exceeded targets 11 out of the past 12 months. Averaged 21% sales increases year-over-year.

- Improved divisional sales ranking from 56th out of 110 stores to 21st in just 2 years.

- Increased dollars-per-transaction from $34.91 to $39.63 and units-per-transaction from 1.32 to 1.88. Improved dollars-per-transaction ranking from 44th to 23rd.

- Reduced labour costs by 8% in 2 years, improving efficiency by 14%.

- Lowered inventory shrink from 1.5% to 1.1%. Sourced a more efficient and reliable contractor to provide inventory count services for the entire store.

- Recorded an average of 92% on 10 quarterly operational audits conducted by head office, highest among all departments in the store.

- Scored an average of 86% on 12 mystery shops in the past year, 2nd highest in the store. Improved from an average of 73% in 20XX.

- Hired, trained, developed, and led 2 sales associates to sales manager promotions in other stores. Awarded 8 promotions in total.

- Virtually eliminated cash and receipt variances greater than $1.00 by creating a cash desk system that was implemented throughout the company.

- Oversaw the $1.5M renovation of the footwear and luggage departments in 20XX.

- Awarded "Sales Manager of the Year" for the store in 20XX. 3rd runner-up for "Sales Manager of the Year" company-wide the same year.

Bachelor's Degree in Marketing ~ University of the Southern Region

DEREK LAWSON
VIDEO STORE CLERK

A LAWSON FAMILY PRODUCTION

Hard-working, motivated, and mature young man seeking a part-time position in a video store. Extensive movie knowledge and excellent people skills. Currently enrolled in Grade 10 at Jefferson High School. Able to start work immediately and comfortable working up to 24 hours/week.

20XX

DEREK LAWSON ✦ Video Store Clerk

★★★★ FOUR-STAR REVIEWS ★★★★

Full letters of recommendation available from:

- Scout Leader – known and worked with for four years.
- Soccer Coach – known and played with for two years.
- Guidance Counsellor – known for two years.
- Math Teacher – known for one year.

SPECIAL FEATURES

- Movie buff: excellent movie knowledge with over 200 films in personal DVD collection.
- Team player: six years soccer experience in an organized league, and seven years with Scout Pack.
- Great availability: 4:00 to close M-W, 1:00 to close on TH and F, and anytime on weekends and holidays.

DEREK M. LAWSON

MAILING ADDRESS 1234 MAIN STREET, CITY

HOME PHONE 555.555.5555   CELL PHONE 555.555.5555

EMAIL ADDRESS EMAIL ADDRESS

HOSPITALITY

Chapter 2

The hospitality industry includes businesses such as hotels and motels, fast food and full service restaurants, coffee shops, bars & nightclubs, catering companies, theatres, airlines, and amusement parks.

Because most positions are entry-level, hospitality is a major employer of teens and young adults. This chapter opens with a case study examining the resume of a Hotel Concierge, before continuing with 25 additional sample resumes and three FAQ tips.

DESIGNING MY ALTERNATIVE RESUME//

IRENE CHAN : HOTEL CONCIERGE

Irene Chan has three years' experience in the hotel industry, including her most recent position as a concierge at the Waterfront Palace Hotel and Convention Centre.

She is seeking the same position with a new five-diamond resort property that will be opening soon. Her goal is to demonstrate her expertise and success as a hotel concierge through her resume. Irene's resume can be viewed on the following page.

1. Guest Appreciation Letter

Irene works in a job where the only true measure of success is customer satisfaction, and because her intent is to prove her success as a concierge, she headlines her resume with an excerpt from a letter of appreciation her supervisor received from a guest. Although the hotel received several such letters, Irene chooses this one because it clearly describes the steps she took that impressed these guests. It doesn't just say they're happy, it states what Irene did to make them happy.

2. Accomplishments In Guest Service

There is no "above and beyond"…there is only "the call of duty". Irene uses this unique heading for a section highlighting her achievements in guest service to express to readers that because the whole purpose of her job is to go above and beyond, doing so is the norm. She provides four examples of her stellar guest service to illustrate her problem-solving expertise and commitment to exceeding guest expectations. Rather than just proclaiming she has the ingenuity to solve any problem or meet any request, she clearly illustrates it through factual examples.

3. Employment

Irene lists every position she has held in her hospitality career but she doesn't provide further details because her targeted employers will recognize the hotels she worked for and understand what she did as a concierge and front desk clerk. Instead of wasting space with duties and responsibilities, it's much more important to show how well she did her job, as she has done in the previous section.

4. Education

Irene includes her post-secondary education on her resume, as is customary. She doesn't expand on her experience in university and college because she now has a few years of career employment behind her. She does, however, indicate that she graduated from the advertising option of her marketing management program. It may seem irrelevant since she is not working in that field, but her training in advertising has contributed to her overall creativity and success as a concierge, and employers may find that aspect of her education appealing.

irene chan ✦ concierge

"Irene was an amazing resource to us on our recent visit. Not only did she secure cruise tickets for us with a day's notice, she also ensured our hotel room would still be available on our return four days later. Also, she was able to get us theatre tickets to a sold-out event with only a few hours notice! Irene must have a vast network of contacts to complement her total dedication to providing guests with the ultimate in service. Your hotel is very lucky to have her on staff!"

❶ GUEST APPRECIATION LETTER, SEPTEMBER 20XX

---

❷ there is no "above and beyond"... there is only "the call of duty"

A family visiting from Sweden was in a terrible car accident that left the son in stable condition in the hospital. I arranged for three members of the local hockey team to visit the young fan, including his favourite player. They brought sticks, posed for pictures, and signed autographs.

A guest wanted to surprise her husband and family with tickets to the Sun Bowl two days prior to the event. She wanted 14 tickets together. After discovering the game was a sell-out, I made several phone calls and arranged for the party to rent a skybox from an owner who was travelling.

An elderly guest wanted to locate her brother whom she had not seen in over ten years. He was no longer residing at the last address she had for him. After a few days of phone calls to social service agencies, I tracked him down at a senior's home in the suburbs. The next day, the guest was provided with full use of a driver and limousine to visit her brother and tour the city.

Two guests came to town to attend a major concert but unfortunately left their tickets at home. They had no family in that city to help them out. I contacted the concierge at our hotel in that city and arranged for the landlord to provide him access to their suite. He retrieved the concert tickets and couriered them to me so that my guests would make the concert on time.

---

employment ❸

Hotel Concierge • Waterfront Palace Hotel and Convention Centre	20XX to 20XX
Front Desk Clerk • Waterfront Palace Hotel and Convention Centre	20XX to 20XX
Front Desk Clerk • Pacific Western Inn and Suites	20XX

education ❹

Marketing Management Diploma, Advertising Option, Concord Business College	20XX
Bachelor of Arts Degree, Economics Major, Templeton University	20XX

contact

Mailing Address • Home Phone • Cell Phone • Fax Number • Email Address

---

~ fluent in English and Mandarin, conversant in French ~

AUSTIN CAMPBELL

Professional Bartending Diploma
Columbia Bartending College, City, September 20XX – January 20XX

Completed this 3-month diploma program that included courses on local alcohol regulations, liquor inventory, bar etiquette, cost control, customer service, equipment and glassware, intervention procedures, and POS training, as well as the proper preparation of numerous alcoholic and non-alcoholic drinks.

Serving It Right Certificate / Food Safe Certificate
Columbia Bartending College, City, January 20XX

Customer Service Excellence Certificate
Thompson Senior Secondary School, City, October 20XX

First Aid with CPR Certificate
Care Training Institute, City, March 20XX

Prep Cook / Cashier
Vegopolis, City, October 20XX – Present

Record customer orders and process payments on a computerized register. Prepare a variety of lunch and dinner entrées, as well as appetizers, salads, and desserts. Resolve customer concerns and ensure satisfaction. Maintain a clean and organized kitchen. Count and order inventory.

Available 7 days a week...24 hours a day.

Fluent in English and conversant in German. Travelled much of the world, including Europe, Southeast Asia, North America, and South America.

Valid driver's licence. Always punctual and reliable.

Mailing Address / Home Phone / Cell Phone / Email Address

BARTENDER

Mabell Young
Mailing Address
Home Phone / Cell Phone
Email Address

May 27, 20XX

Randy Tyler, General Manager
BUTLER'S GARDEN RESTAURANT
Mailing Address Line 1
Mailing Address Line 2

Dear Mr. Tyler:

When you hire a new hostess or bus person, what qualifications do you look for in applicants? Do you require excellent teamwork skills? A mature attitude? Strong work ethic? Dependability? Leadership potential? I would like to take this opportunity to demonstrate why I would make an excellent hostess or bus person for your restaurant:

- **Teamwork Skills.** I understand the importance of every member of a team working together for the betterment of the business. I have worked on teams ranging in size from 4 to 10 on various school projects, including a group marketing project that lasted 4 months. You will find I will make a strong addition to your team.

- **Maturity.** My background includes 2 years' babysitting experience, caring for newborns as well as children up to the age of 8. In addition, I have demonstrated my maturity more than once by travelling alone to Europe to visit family members. I have confirmed that 2 of my teachers will act as references and verify that I am regarded as mature for my age.

- **Strong Work Ethic.** I am accustomed to juggling many priorities in my life. For the past 2 years, I have balanced 30 hours per week of school with 10 hours of babysitting and 5 hours skating practice, with homework on top of that. I am now retired from competitive skating and would like to replace babysitting with an entry-level position in your restaurant.

- **Dependability.** My references will also confirm that I am reliable and punctual. I have only missed 2 days of school in the past 2 years, due to a death in the family, and I am never late for class or work. I also live very close to you and don't have to rely on public transit.

- **Leadership Potential.** I am currently taking a leadership course at Jacksonville Secondary, where I am enrolled in Grade 10. I feel I have natural leadership ability and will learn the job quickly and grow into more responsible positions when the opportunities arise.

Mr. Tyler, may we meet and discuss my qualifications in greater detail? I will call you on Tuesday to inquire about a date and time. Thanks in advance for your consideration.

Sincerely,

Mabell Young

Mabell Young

PETER SCHLOSSER
Amusement Park Games Attendant

mailing address…home phone…cell phone…email address

Trustworthy and Reliable. Trusted to work alone while volunteering at the high school store for one semester in Grade 10. Accountable for all cash on hand and store assets, including computer equipment and inventory. Relied upon to submit daily deposits to school office.

Math and Cash Handling Skills. Comfortable and skilled with math. Consistently maintained at least a B in all math and algebra classes. Processed cash and bank card transactions and calculated change while working in the school store last year.

Customer Service Experience. Developed customer service skills as a school store volunteer in Grade 10. Accustomed to up-selling and problem-solving. Often described as having an upbeat, outgoing personality that is suitable to sales and customer service.

Inventory Management Experience. Gained inventory control skills while working in the store. Completed daily and weekly inventory counts and investigated discrepancies. Placed new product orders. Letter of recommendation available from Entrepreneurship teacher.

Safety-Oriented. Completed Metalwork 10 and Woodwork 10 this past school year. Learned basic first aid, safety in the workplace, and handling hazardous materials in both courses.

Sports Background. Played in youth soccer league for 4 seasons. Played organized baseball for 3 seasons and placed 3rd in provincial tournament. Athletically inclined. Also enjoy golf, basketball, hockey, volleyball, snowboarding, and skiing.

Excellent Physical Condition. Comfortable working long shifts and standing for long periods of time. No health problems that would interfere with ability to perform the job. Willing and able to work in all weather conditions.

Open Availability for Scheduling. Able to work any day or shift needed including mornings, afternoons, late evenings, weekdays, weekends, and holidays. Available to work the entire summer; no vacation plans that would conflict with scheduling availability.

Joanne Hamilton • Airline Flight Attendant
Mailing Address • Home Phone • Cell Phone • Email Address

- Diploma in Travel and Tourism
- Relevant Workplace Certifications
- Professional Career Development Plan

- 4 Years' Customer Service Experience
- National and International Travel
- Fluent in English and French

EDUCATION & TRAINING

Diploma in Travel and Tourism   *Fairfield Business College, City*

Graduated in May 20XX from this 2-year, full-time industry program. Placed in the top 5% of the class with a 90% grade average while completing 18 courses, including the following:

- The Travel and Tourism Industry
- Excellence in Guest Service
- Airline and Airport Services
- Airline Reservations and Ticketing

- Destinations and Geography
- Online Travel and Tourism
- Travel Sales and Marketing
- Industry Computer Applications

Practicum Experience   *Pennington Travel Agency, City*

Completed a 3-week, full-time practicum in October 20XX. Shadowed, observed, and assisted a senior travel agent with the promotion, sale, and processing of several travel products including flights, accommodations, cruises, rail vacations, vehicle rentals, trip packages, and out-of-country travel insurance. Exceptional letter of recommendation available upon request.

Workplace Certifications   *Titan Training Institute, City*

Achieved the following industry-recognized certifications between January and May, 20XX:

- Food Production and Service Safety
- Responsible Alcohol Service

- Workplace Safety and Security
- Conflict Resolution & Communication

Career Planning   *Buckley Career Consultants, City*

Participated in a 3-week, full-time career exploration program to assist in the development of a comprehensive, attainable career development plan. Completed several assessments related to work values, personal interests, acquired skills, and personality type, with all results showing a career in travel and tourism to be the best fit. Copy of career profile available upon request.

CUSTOMER SERVICE EXPERIENCE

Cashier • Order Processor • Trainer   *Sandwich Emporium, City*

Worked part-time through high school and college since 20XX, taking and processing orders, and operating a computerized cash register. Oversaw all new hire cash training as of May 20XX. Selected "Employee of the Month" on 5 occasions, from among a team of 40.

TRAVEL HISTORY

Travelled throughout Canada and the northeast and southwest sectors of the United States, as well as the United Kingdom, France, Germany, Italy, the Netherlands, and Australia.

DISHWASHER • BUS PERSON • PREP COOK • LINE COOK

HOME PHONE
CELL PHONE

Kyle Steward

MAILING ADDRESS
EMAIL ADDRESS

1½ Years Experience as a Dishwasher and Prep Cook in a Specialty Restaurant
Certified in Safe Food Handling Level 1 and Occupational First Aid Level 1
Earned an A in Grade 11 Food & Nutrition Course

WORK EXPERIENCE

COMPASSION EATERY, City   **March 20XX – September 20XX**
Local franchise of the largest vegan restaurant chain on the West Coast, with 27 locations.
Famous for their breakfast buffet, as well as their wraps, sandwiches, pizzas, kebabs, soups,
salads, cabbage rolls, breads, and vegetable dishes. Also serve a wide variety of desserts.

Dishwasher, Prep Cook

- Worked part-time 24 hours a week while in school and full-time during the summer.
- Cleaned dishes, glassware, flatware, pots, and pans with an industrial dishwasher.
- Stored dishes, glassware, and flatware in their proper locations; kept kitchen organized.
- Divided and weighed rice, beans, lentils, and vegetables, and put into individual bags.
- Prepared and cooked pan-fried dishes; prepared and baked pizzas.
- Made wraps and sandwiches to order.
- Cleaned and sanitized all counters and sinks.
- Swept and mopped floors, cleaned bathrooms, and emptied garbage containers.
- Assisted with bussing tables when needed.
- References available from the owner and manager.

JIMMY FEAST, City   **April 20XX**
Buffet-style family restaurant specializing in quality ingredients and an extensive selection of
ethnic dishes including Vietnamese, Thai, Japanese, Russian, Italian, and German.

Dishwasher

- Completed a 30-hour work experience placement organized through Zenith High School.
- Worked with 2 other employees in the operation of an industrial dishwasher.
- Cleaned and sanitized hundreds of plates, bowls, utensils, glasses, and mugs, as well as
  pots, pans, serving trays, mixing bowls, and kitchen equipment.
- Maintained a clean working area; praised by the Kitchen Manager for neatness.
- Performed a variety of closing duties including equipment cleaning and shutdown.
- Written reference available from the Kitchen Manager.

EDUCATION

Enrolled in Grade 12 at Zenith High School; expect to graduate in June of 20XX.
Currently completing Food & Nutrition 12 course.

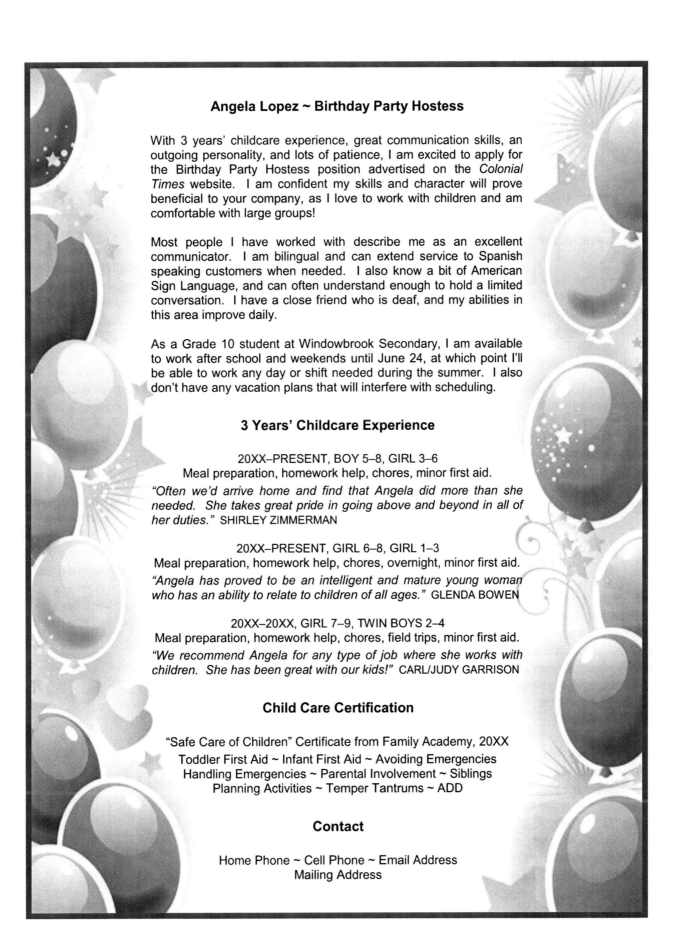

Angela Lopez ~ Birthday Party Hostess

With 3 years' childcare experience, great communication skills, an outgoing personality, and lots of patience, I am excited to apply for the Birthday Party Hostess position advertised on the *Colonial Times* website. I am confident my skills and character will prove beneficial to your company, as I love to work with children and am comfortable with large groups!

Most people I have worked with describe me as an excellent communicator. I am bilingual and can extend service to Spanish speaking customers when needed. I also know a bit of American Sign Language, and can often understand enough to hold a limited conversation. I have a close friend who is deaf, and my abilities in this area improve daily.

As a Grade 10 student at Windowbrook Secondary, I am available to work after school and weekends until June 24, at which point I'll be able to work any day or shift needed during the summer. I also don't have any vacation plans that will interfere with scheduling.

3 Years' Childcare Experience

20XX–PRESENT, BOY 5–8, GIRL 3–6
Meal preparation, homework help, chores, minor first aid.
"Often we'd arrive home and find that Angela did more than she needed. She takes great pride in going above and beyond in all of her duties." SHIRLEY ZIMMERMAN

20XX–PRESENT, GIRL 6–8, GIRL 1–3
Meal preparation, homework help, chores, overnight, minor first aid.
"Angela has proved to be an intelligent and mature young woman who has an ability to relate to children of all ages." GLENDA BOWEN

20XX–20XX, GIRL 7–9, TWIN BOYS 2–4
Meal preparation, homework help, chores, field trips, minor first aid.
"We recommend Angela for any type of job where she works with children. She has been great with our kids!" CARL/JUDY GARRISON

Child Care Certification

"Safe Care of Children" Certificate from Family Academy, 20XX
Toddler First Aid ~ Infant First Aid ~ Avoiding Emergencies
Handling Emergencies ~ Parental Involvement ~ Siblings
Planning Activities ~ Temper Tantrums ~ ADD

Contact

Home Phone ~ Cell Phone ~ Email Address
Mailing Address

ALTERNATIVE RESUMES FAQ//
HOW SHOULD I FORMAT MY RESUME?

It is essential that your resume appears clean, organized and consistent in order to get the reader's attention.

There are several aspects of formatting including page margins, fonts, paragraphs, bullets, and text enhancements. All provide an important contribution to the overall appearance.

Page Margins

Page margins should be consistent on every side and can be adjusted to expand or condense your content as needed. For example, if your margins are set at 2.5 cm (1 inch) and you're struggling to get all your information on one page, reduce them to 1.9 cm (0.75 in.). Or, if you can't fill up the page, increase them to 3.2 cm (1.25 in.). Ideally, page margins should be between 1.9 cm and 3.2 cm to provide adequate white space.

Fonts

Fonts are an important consideration as well. Use common, easy-to-read fonts like Arial, Tahoma, Franklin Gothic, or Microsoft Sans Serif, and avoid anything that's rare, hard to read, or distracting. Widely used fonts are preferred because there is a better chance the recipient will be able to view your resume properly in MS Word. To avoid any font conflicts, email your resume in PDF format whenever possible.

You can also experiment with font types and sizes to improve the appearance of your resume. If it's too packed or you run out of room, a smaller size of the same font or a smaller font type will create space. Or, if there's extra room left at the bottom, a larger font or size will make the page look full and complete. Print your resume to ensure the font type and size are appropriate, even if you're not applying in person. Hiring managers still print resumes to use in interviews.

Paragraphs and Bullets

Paragraphs and bullets are both acceptable, as long as you don't overuse either one. Paragraphs should be fairly short, as big blocks of text are daunting to a reader who needs to skim lots of resumes quickly. Long lists of bullet points can also be overwhelming and should be limited to seven. If that's not possible, add a small space between each one to make it easier on the eye. You can incorporate paragraphs with bullets on your resume too. For example, paragraphs are effective for explaining the scope, responsibilities, and duties of past jobs. Bullets are great for listing accomplishments.

Text Enhancements

Text enhancements such as **bold**, *italics*, underline, and UPPERCASE can draw attention to a name, heading, word, or title. Bold is best because it's easier to read than italics and it stands out more. Underlining works, but if you have other lines on the page it can be confusing to the eye. Uppercase is more difficult to read than lowercase, and should only be used for short phrases or single words. Remember, these features are used to make it easier for the reader or to attract their attention. If you overuse them, nothing will stand out.

LEO WATSON
Line Cook
Home Phone • Email • Mailing Address

KITCHEN TRAINING

Chef Training Program, Harbour Tradeworks Academy, City   20XX-Present
- Currently enrolled in the second year of this 2-year, full-time, post-secondary program.
- Completed courses: Food & Beverage Basics, Menu Preparation, Culinary Careers, Kitchen Sanitation Practices, Pastry Basics, Organic Ingredients, and Nutrition Fundamentals.
- Received a glowing performance assessment for a 2-week work placement with Le Maison. Assisted with pastry prep, salad prep, and line cooking. Scored 88% for "technical skills" and 95% for "professional attitude" on written evaluation; copy available upon request.
- Earned Food Safe Certificate Level 2: Kitchen Management. Placed in top 10% of class.

Culinary Arts Career Prep Program, Bakerstown Senior High School, City   20XX-20XX
- Completed this industry-recognized high school program during Grades 11 and 12.
- Completed courses: Nutrition & Wellness, Creative Meal Planning, Baking Essentials, Line & Prep Cooking, Raw Food Preparation, Kitchen Management, and Culinary Career Planning.
- Worked 5 hours per week in the school cafeteria as part of the Culinary Arts Program. Baked, cooked, and prepared a variety of lunch dishes including wraps, burritos, pitas, sandwiches, enchiladas, pizza, spaghetti, lasagne, soup, salads, bagels, and desserts.

Food Safety Certificate, Bakerstown Junior High School, City   20XX-20XX
- Completed the Food Safety Certificate Level 1: Kitchen Operations.
- Maintained an A average in Home Economics 8, Food & Nutrition 9, and Food & Nutrition 10.
- Earned First Aid and CPR Level A and Safety in the Workplace certificates.

COOKING EXPERIENCE

Line Cook, The Galleria at the Atlantic Exhibition, City   Summers 20XX-20XX
- Employed full-time during the summer fairs, assisting with all kitchen operations. Sliced and prepared fruits and vegetables for the chefs; cooked hot dishes on the breakfast grill; baked pastries, breads, and desserts; and maintained a clean and organized kitchen.

REVIEWS

Jason Cotterill, Kitchen Chef, Le Maison:
- "We have been pleased to have Leo on our team for the past two weeks. He has blended in well with our staff, he has shown the necessary skills to function effectively in our kitchen, and most of all he has shown an enthusiastic approach to learning and contributing. His performance is very good advertising for Harbour Tradeworks Academy."

Barbara Pottering, Chef Training Instructor, Harbour Tradeworks Academy:
- "Leo is performing extremely well in our Chef Training Program. He takes his work seriously and has demonstrated the desire, skill, and creativity for a successful career in this field."

Carter Smith, Instructor, Bakerstown Culinary Arts Career Prep Program:
- "His ability to work as part of a team has really improved. He understands that a successful and efficient kitchen team depends on the individual people working as a unit."

BONNIE MARCIL
Food Service • Customer Service

1 Year Customer Service and Food Handling Experience
Multilingual – Fluent in English and Italian; Conversant in Spanish
Certified in Food Safety Level 1 and Service Excellence

WORK EXPERIENCE
Experience working with people of all different ages, backgrounds, and cultures!

- Worked lunch hours in the cafeteria at Fisher Heights Secondary from Sep 20XX to Jun 20XX. Prepared a variety of lunch dishes including wraps, burritos, enchiladas, sandwiches, pasta, salads, and desserts. Worked as part of a team with 5 other students and 2 supervisors.
- Volunteered with Eastside Community Food Bank from Feb 20XX to Aug 20XX. Unpacked and stored donations, organized food shelves, interacted with patrons, completed paperwork, and cleaned and organized the 5,000 square foot warehouse.
- Babysat for neighbourhood families from April 20XX to March 20XX. Cared for children of all ages, often up to 4 at a time. Supervised play activities, prepared snacks and meals, helped with homework, mediated disputes, and maintained a clean and safe home.

EDUCATION & TRAINING
Learning centres encourage students to work while finishing their education!

- Currently completing Grade 10 at Huntsville Learning Centre; expect to begin Grade 11 in September 20XX. Earned Food Safety Level 1 and Service Excellence certificates in June of 20XX. Completed 2 Food and Nutrition courses while attending regular high school.

WORK AVAILABILITY
Attending a Learning Centre means I have better availability for work!

• Monday	1:00 to Close	• Friday	Open to Close
• Tuesday	1:00 to Close	• Saturday	Open to Close
• Wednesday	3:00 to Close	• Sunday	Open to Close
• Thursday	1:00 to Close	• Holidays	Open to Close

TECHNICAL SKILLS
Having taught myself all my computer skills, I am sure I can learn your systems quickly!

• Windows and Mac operating systems	• 45 wpm keyboard speed
• MS Word, Excel, PowerPoint and Access	• Basic file and disk management
• Internet browsing and research	• Email etiquette; Outlook; web-based email

WORK CHARACTERISTICS
A professional attitude and cheerful personality – perfect for customer service work!

- Quick learner who is maintaining a B average in school; able to follow directions quickly and easily. Proven reliable and punctual; haven't missed a single day of school all year. Regarded as multicultural; comfortable communicating with people from all walks of life.

MAILING ADDRESS • EMAIL ADDRESS • HOME PHONE • CELL PHONE

Attention: Susan Kessler, Restaurant Manager, Garden Café

As a new bus person in your restaurant, I would demonstrate a professional, customer-oriented attitude and a cheerful, enthusiastic personality. I am also highly motivated – I don't let anything stop me from achieving my goals. May we meet and discuss in person how I can benefit your business?

To prepare for working in this field, I knew I needed as much knowledge of full-service restaurants as possible. Therefore, I visited and researched both your restaurant and your competitors. I watched all the front-line, hosting, bussing, and serving staff and noted their duties and responsibilities. I also analyzed and compared your menus. Having completed this research, I feel prepared to step into an entry-level position with your restaurant and master it quickly and easily.

As an example of my research, I am including a Menu Comparison Chart to show how favourably your prices rank in the following common categories. A more in-depth report containing all my research can be provided upon request.

VEGGIE CLUBHOUSE	
1. **GARDEN CAFÉ**	**$8.99**
2. JERRY'S PLACE	$9.49
3. MARTHA'S ON THIRD	$9.89
4. THE STANLEY HOUSE	$10.49
5. BLACK DOG CAFÉ	$11.99
6. THE ROUNDHOUSE	$12.99

SOY CHEESEBURGER	
1. MARTHA'S ON THIRD	$9.49
2. **GARDEN CAFÉ**	**$9.99**
3. THE STANLEY HOUSE	$10.99
4. JERRY'S PLACE	$11.49
5. BLACK DOG CAFÉ	$11.89
6. THE ROUNDHOUSE	$11.99

BEAN BURRITO	
1. JERRY'S PLACE	$9.49
2. **GARDEN CAFÉ**	**$9.99**
3. MARTHA'S ON THIRD	$10.19
4. THE STANLEY HOUSE	$10.29
5. THE ROUNDHOUSE	$10.99
6. BLACK DOG CAFÉ	$11.99

BEAN SALAD	
1. JERRY'S PLACE	$7.49
2. **GARDEN CAFÉ**	**$7.99**
3. MARTHA'S ON THIRD	$8.39
4. THE STANLEY HOUSE	$8.99
5. THE ROUNDHOUSE	$9.59
6. BLACK DOG CAFÉ	$9.99

SPINACH SALAD	
1. THE STANLEY HOUSE	$6.49
2. MARTHA'S ON THIRD	$6.99
3. JERRY'S PLACE	$7.79
4. **GARDEN CAFÉ**	**$7.99**
5. THE ROUNDHOUSE	$8.59
6. BLACK DOG CAFÉ	$8.99

SOUP OF THE DAY	
1. JERRY'S PLACE	$4.19
2. **GARDEN CAFÉ**	**$4.99**
3. MARTHA'S ON THIRD	$5.49
4. BLACK DOG CAFÉ	$5.89
5. THE ROUNDHOUSE	$6.59
6. THE STANLEY HOUSE	$6.99

The most important thing I learned is that front-line employees need to have an overwhelming desire to make the customer's visit a pleasant one. I had the opportunity to witness two complaints and realized how important problem-solving skills are in resolving disputes. Fortunately, I do understand the relationship between customer satisfaction and business survival, and my references will confirm that my problem-solving skills are my greatest strength.

As a Grade 12 student, I am available to be scheduled every night and weekend. In addition, I live within a short walking distance, have two phone numbers so you can contact me easily, and have no problem coming in on short notice when needed. My reliability and punctuality can also be confirmed by my references.

Ms. Kessler, I am confident I have the skills and attitude to be a valuable member of your team. I will contact you next Tuesday, between 2:00 and 4:00pm so it doesn't conflict with your lunch or dinner period, to see if we can arrange an interview. Thank you in advance for your time and consideration.

Sincerely,

Glen Singer
Mailing Address
Home Phone · Cell Phone · Email Address

ELEANOR CASSIDY
Hotel Front Desk Clerk

QUALIFICATION PROFILE	TRAVEL EXPERIENCE
Travel & Tourism education from a recognized accredited college.	Travelled to Germany, Austria, France, England, Italy, and Greece at the age of 19 for 3 months.
3 years' progressive experience in customer service as Assistant Manager and Server in a high-volume downtown café.	Visited most major Canadian cities including Victoria, Vancouver, Calgary, Edmonton, Toronto, Ottawa, Montreal, and Halifax.
Accurate cash management skills including computerized register operation, terminal reconciliation, and bank deposit preparation.	Journeyed through much of the western and northern US on family road trips, visiting such cities as Washington DC, Cleveland, New York, Boston, Detroit, Chicago, San Diego, San Francisco, and LA.
Fluent in English; conversant in Spanish and German.	Performed youth missionary work in Rio de Janeiro for 3 weeks.
Extensive experience travelling and communicating with people of all cultures, ages, and backgrounds.	

EDUCATION & TRAINING		WORK EXPERIENCE
TRAVEL & TOURISM CERTIFICATE	May 20XX	THE COFFEE GRIND, City
Corning Business and Technical College, City		*A 1200 square foot café with a prime downtown location, a staff of 18 to 20, and annual sales of $3 million.*
Completed a 2-year, night school program with these courses:		
Introduction to Travel & Tourism · Travel Management & Planning Meeting and Convention Management · Ticketing & Reservations Travel Geography · Hospitality Operations · Cruise Sales & Booking Travel Industry Information Technology Systems		Assistant Manager, 20XX to Present
		Oversaw staffing, training, sales, service, and cash management. Created monthly promotional events that grew sales 18%. Took workshops on hiring, training, and performance management. Earned $2000 bonus for helping café reach top 10% in sales.
HIGH SCHOOL DIPLOMA	June 20XX	
St. Thomas Senior Secondary, City		Server, 20XX to 20XX
Graduated with honours and a focus on business and computers:		Promoted from Stock Person after just 1 month with the company. Designed a feedback form that was well received by customers. Nominated for Server of the Year in 20XX.
Accounting 11 and 12 · Entrepreneurship and Small Business 11 Marketing 11 and 12 · Computer Systems in Business 11 and 12		

CAFETERIA CASHIER • FULLERTON COLLEGE

Cash Handling Skills

Over 3 years' experience in cash handling and the operation of computerized cash register systems.

Processed credit card and bank card payments using bank terminals. Skilled at trouble-shooting, operating and maintaining terminals, and communicating with financial institutions when necessary.

Experienced with processing sales, refunds, voids, exchanges, coupons, vouchers, and credit notes.

Processed transactions and calculated customer change accurately. Reconciled cash, credit slips, and bank card receipts to register and terminal printouts at the end of shifts. No cash or receipt variances greater than $1.00 in 3 years.

Prepared bank deposit slips and presented them to managers for authorization.

Cash Handling Achievements

Cashier and Sales Associate at Scott's Sporting World from September 20XX to August 20XX.

Regarded as head cashier by managers; operated the cash desk during all peak sales periods.

Trained 8 new staff members on cash handling and reconciliation duties.

Received scores of "excellent" or "above average" in all categories on last performance evaluation.

Assisted with receiving and processing shipments, putting out new stock, and merchandising product displays in addition to cash and customer service.

Achieved highest personal sales in the store during a 2-month "spiff" promotion over Christmas 20XX.

Additional Experience

Grill Cook at Burger Haven during summer of 20XX.

Initially hired for the summer but requested to stay on afterwards by the owner/manager. Declined due to simultaneous offer from Scott's Sporting World.

Statement of Interest

"Having just started my post-secondary education and experiencing a heavy workload, my scheduling conflicts prevented me from being able to stay with Scott's Sporting World. I am attracted to your advertisement for a part-time cashier in part because I have extensive experience in cash handling, but also because there are no weekends involved. I am seeking a stable position where I can remain through the duration of my post-secondary career, which will be 3 more years. In return, I am confident my cash handling and customer service experience will contribute to the success of your cafeteria."

Additional Qualifications

Excellent communication skills. Fluent in verbal and written English and Hindi with limited German skills.

Completed one-day "Excelling at Customer Service" Certificate in March 20XX.

Regarded as honest and trustworthy. Trusted by last employer to reconcile cash trays and bank terminals, and prepare bank deposits.

Participated in numerous customer service and sales workshops including "The Seven Steps of Selling" and "Bringing Customers Back" as part of continuous training with Scott's Sporting World.

Education

Enrolled in first year general studies at the downtown campus of Fullerton College.

Currently taking Western European History, Business Communications, International Studies, and German Language classes.

Graduated from Spencer High School in May of 20XX with a B average and a focus on business, language, and computer courses.

Manu Karamchand

MANU KARAMCHAND • MAILING ADDRESS • HOME PHONE • CELL PHONE • EMAIL ADDRESS

ALTERNATIVE RESUMES FAQ//
IS IT ACCEPTABLE TO USE GRAPHICS ON A RESUME?

Using graphics on a resume is a hotly debated subject among resume writers and Human Resource professionals.

Some say a resume should never contain a graphic, regardless of the situation. Others question the status quo, asking "Why not?" Other advertising tools such as business cards and letterhead often contain photos, illustrations, or designs to attract attention and portray competency. Why can't a resume? The real answer is that adding a graphic will help in some cases and hurt in others.

Know Your Audience

Clearly, graphics on resumes are not for every situation, so only use them when they add value to your resume, and you think the recipient will react positively. How would you know? The more youthful, creative, or "alternative" the industry, the more receptive they will be to seeing graphics on a resume. If they are traditional or conservative, they likely won't react as well. Therefore, if you apply for a job in a funky store, café, or tattoo shop, there's a good chance the manager won't be offended by the graphic on your resume, and may even be impressed by your creative approach. However, if you're seeking a job in an accounting office or medical practice, stick with a conventional resume without the graphics.

Types Of Graphics

In most cases, graphics should be subtle and support the overall message of the resume rather than overpower it. This can be done with a simple clipart or design next to your name or job title, like Prudence Skyler uses on the following page. This projects an image of expertise and elevates the reader's confidence in your skills, the same way it does on business cards or letterhead. Graphics can also be used as a background or watermark on your resume. Just be sure it doesn't distract the reader. If the image in the background isn't light enough, it may be difficult to read the text. If it's too light, the reader may not know what the image is.

Although several of the resume samples in this book contain some type of graphic, they are certainly not necessary on every resume. However, they can make a positive impression if used properly. When in doubt, design two versions of your resume, one with the graphic and one without. Compare the impact of the graphic on screen and in print and solicit the opinions of family and friends before sending it to a company.

BARISTA & RESTAURANT EXPERIENCE

Gaston's
Opening Barista
Location
20XX–20XX

Sherry's Delicatessen
Barista, Hostess
Location
20XX

The Corner View
Barista, Lunch Server
Location
20XX–20XX

The Good Luck Club
Pastry Attendant
Location
20XX–20XX

Marcus House
Barista, Baker, Server
Location
20XX

The Third Cup
Barista, Baker
Location
20XX

The Daily Grind
Opening Manager, Barista
Location
20XX–20XX

Shepherd's Coffee
Barista, Roaster
Location
20XX

PRUDENCE SKYLER

mailing address…email address…home phone…cell phone

*5 years' experience in multicultural cities such as Newville and Oldville.
Food Safe Certified. Able to start immediately with open availability.*

BARISTA SKILLS

Preparing and serving all usual coffeehouse drinks including brewed coffee, espresso, cappuccino, latte, mocha, and tea. Limited bartending experience.

Baking dessert and pastry items including cakes, scones, brownies, muffins, tarts, and bars, as well as pizza and breads. Preparing and serving standard bistro items such as wraps, sandwiches, soups, and vegetable plates.

Training new staff members in all areas of restaurant operations including customer service, cash handling, drink and food preparation, serving, baking, opening and closing, dishwashing, and general maintenance.

Assembling, disassembling, cleaning, operating, and maintaining espresso machines, coffee roasters, brewers, juicers, blenders, electric mixers, graters, food processors, and convection and pizza ovens.

Operating and maintaining a wide variety of computerized cash registers as well as PC and Mac computers, printers, and copiers. Programming and operating CRS and POS machines, including bank terminals.

Managing all aspects of inventory control including purchasing and ordering, vendor relations, shipping and receiving, stocking, visual presentation, loss prevention, and conducting manual inventory counts.

TESTIMONIALS

"Prudence was our floor leader during the two years she worked here and I can tell you the customers still miss her today. She had a warm and engaging personality that really appealed to our patrons, and she always put their needs first. She knew all our regulars on a first-name basis and she always made sure their morning visit was a convenient and rewarding part of their daily schedule. I would highly recommend her for any job in this industry."
GASTON BOURQUE, CHEF, GASTON'S

"Prudence was an absolute joy to have working with us. She is a very hard working individual with the ability to learn anything new extremely quickly. And she wasn't shy about using her skill and knowledge to better the rest of the team around her. She is a natural leader with exceptional communication and service skills. I would gladly rehire Prudence if she ever wanted to come back. She is a delightful employee and I wish her all the best!"
SHERI MANLEY, OWNER, THE CORNER VIEW

"I would undoubtedly recommend Prudence Skyler for any job she feels qualified for. She was a star performer for my business!
FRANCO BRIERE, GENERAL MANAGER & CHEF, THE GOOD LUCK CLUB

Additional letters of recommendation available upon request.

Call Me!

BILLY SHEARS
Home Phone • Cell Phone
Mailing Address
Email Address

JOB TARGET	Grill Cook • Dishwasher • Bus Person • Host Cashier • Maintenance Worker
EXPERIENCE	Paper Carrier, *Barnston Review* August 20XX – March 20XX Delivered over 150 newspapers 6 mornings per week, meeting every 6:00am deadline. Earned "Carrier of the Month" award 4 times.
CHARACTER	Reliable – missed only 1 day of school in the last 3 years due to illness. Punctual – never missed a paper route deadline. Work Ethic – delivered newspapers for over 18 months in all weather conditions.
EDUCATION	Currently enrolled in Grade 10 at Susan Banfield Secondary School in Barnston. Maintaining a B course average. Earned certificates for outstanding attendance in Grade 9 and service to the school in Grade 8.
AVAILABILITY	Monday to Friday – 4:00 pm to close. Weekends and holidays – open to close.
REFERENCES	2 references available from route customers. 1 reference available from route supervisor. 1 reference available from an English teacher.

YOKO JANDANA
MAILING ADDRESS • TELEPHONE • EMAIL

Certified Travel Agent
Diploma in Hospitality and Tourism
3 Years' Customer Service Experience
Fluent in English and Japanese

Diploma in Hospitality and Tourism • Travel Agent Certificate
Turner School of Business and Technology, City, 20XX–20XX

- Tourism Sales and Marketing
- Tourism and the Law
- Ground Transportation
- Hotels and Resorts
- Business Communications
- Adventure Travel
- International Travel
- Computers in Tourism
- Geography and Culture
- Service Excellence
- Cruise Booking
- Careers in Tourism
- Ticketing
- Tour Booking
- Air Travel

Travel Experience

- CANADA: Drove across the country with family at the age of 14, visiting most major cities including Vancouver, Calgary, Edmonton, Winnipeg, Toronto, Ottawa, and Montreal.

- UNITED STATES: Visited many western and south-western states during family road trips, including WA, OR, CA, NV, AZ, NM and TX. Also travelled to NY, NJ, PA, and DC.

- SOUTH AMERICA: Travelled with family on a 3-week business trip last spring, visiting parts of Brazil, Columbia, and Venezuela.

- EUROPE: Travelled alone to Vienna, Austria to visit extended family last summer. Also journeyed through Germany, France, England, Italy, and Greece.

- AUSTRALIA: Travelled to Australia with family at the age of 13, visiting prominent cities such as Sydney, Melbourne, Brisbane, and Perth.

- NEXT: Japan and Southeast Asia, hopefully within the next 3-5 years!

Customer Service Experience

- CASHIER – The Yellow Submarine, City   June 20XX – Present
Worked part-time through school at a fast food restaurant; averaged 25 hours per week. Operated a computerized cash register and processed cash and bank card payments. Reconciled cash/receipts to computer totals at shift-end, consistently balancing to the penny. Resolved customer complaints within authority levels. Trained 4 new cashiers.

My favourite thing is to go where I have never gone.
DIANE ARBUS, PHOTOGRAPHER, 1923-1971

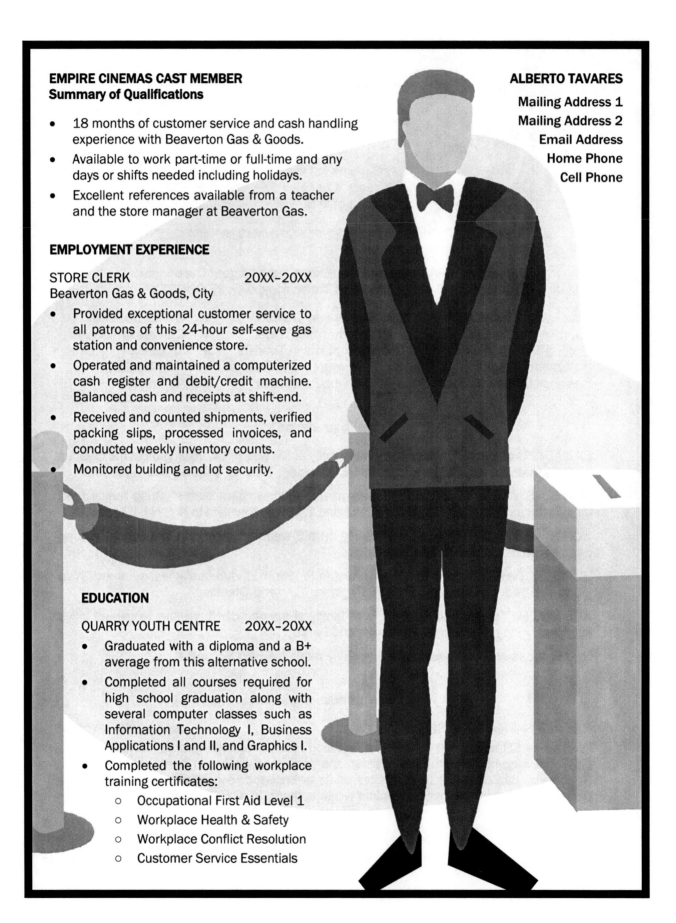

EMPIRE CINEMAS CAST MEMBER
Summary of Qualifications

- 18 months of customer service and cash handling experience with Beaverton Gas & Goods.
- Available to work part-time or full-time and any days or shifts needed including holidays.
- Excellent references available from a teacher and the store manager at Beaverton Gas.

EMPLOYMENT EXPERIENCE

STORE CLERK   20XX–20XX
Beaverton Gas & Goods, City

- Provided exceptional customer service to all patrons of this 24-hour self-serve gas station and convenience store.
- Operated and maintained a computerized cash register and debit/credit machine. Balanced cash and receipts at shift-end.
- Received and counted shipments, verified packing slips, processed invoices, and conducted weekly inventory counts.
- Monitored building and lot security.

EDUCATION

QUARRY YOUTH CENTRE   20XX–20XX

- Graduated with a diploma and a B+ average from this alternative school.
- Completed all courses required for high school graduation along with several computer classes such as Information Technology I, Business Applications I and II, and Graphics I.
- Completed the following workplace training certificates:
    - Occupational First Aid Level 1
    - Workplace Health & Safety
    - Workplace Conflict Resolution
    - Customer Service Essentials

ALBERTO TAVARES

Mailing Address 1
Mailing Address 2
Email Address
Home Phone
Cell Phone

Home Phone Number • Cell Phone Number • Email Address
Mailing Address

PROFILE

Eager and motivated young woman seeking a part-time, entry-level position with a catering company. Almost 1 year of food & beverage service experience in a very popular and busy athletics club.

EMPLOYMENT EXPERIENCE

GYMNASTICS GYM, City • Aug 20XX – Jul 20XX
A 10,000 square foot gymnastics club with recreational and competitive programs for more than 350 students of all ages and 2 large party rooms capable of catering to over 50 children.

Birthday Hostess. Hosted 2-hour birthday parties for 5-30 children ranging in age from 2 to 14. Supervised games in the party room and gymnastics area. Monitored the children's safety, especially around the other gymnasts. Prepared and served food and drinks such as wraps, veggie dogs, cake, and juice. Cleaned the rooms after each party including sweeping, mopping, wiping tables, and taking out the garbage. Assisted with office reception when needed including answering phones, explaining drop-in times, describing the birthday parties, and helping visitors to the club. Sold snacks and drinks at a concession stand for a gymnastics competition. Worked most weekends, typically hosting 4 parties in an 8-hour shift. Earned a raise after just a few months.

MARBLEHEAD WATER, City • Jan 20XX – Jul 20XX
A local distributor of bottled water and related equipment.

Maintenance Worker. Cleaned the entire office once a week after school or on weekends, including 3 individual offices, a kitchen, and a bathroom. Wiped and cleaned desks, tables, counters, sinks, walls, and windows. Swept and mopped floors, vacuumed carpets, cleaned the fridge, washed and dried dishes, sanitized toilets, emptied garbage bins, cleaned computer monitors, and watered plants.

CHILD CARE. Babysat for multiple families since 20XX, caring for up to 3 children at a time, including infants. Completed a Red Cross course in child care and infant first aid in April 20XX.

VOLUNTEER EXPERIENCE

CENTRAL HUMANE SOCIETY, City • Summers 20XX and 20XX
Local non-profit animal shelter and advocacy organization.

Junior Camp Counsellor. Volunteered with the week-long summer day camp programs at this busy shelter. Helped staff and senior counsellors supervise groups of 20+ children aged 7 to 12. Assisted with leading animal-themed activities such as games, crafts, skits, and other projects. Monitored children's safety when spending time with the animals. Learned about pet care, wildlife, farm animals, and animal welfare issues. Supervised groups of children on field trips to Central Park. Assisted with envelope stuffing in the office when needed.

ADDITIONAL INFORMATION

Good computer skills including knowledge and experience with MS Word and the Internet.
Completed basic keyboarding course in Grades 9 and 10; maintaining a speed of 40-50 wpm.
Currently enrolled in Grade 11 at Tommy Jamieson High School.
Interests and hobbies include art, drawing, painting, horseback riding, and physical fitness.

paul regan

home phone • cell phone • email address
mailing address line 1
mailing address line 2

PIZZA DELIVERY DRIVER

- 18 months' driving experience with full-time access to a 20XX hatchback.

- Clean driver's abstract; no accidents or tickets of any kind.

- Great with math and performing manual calculations; capable of securing cash payments and credit receipts.

- Trusted to work independently with little or no direct supervision.

- Professional appearance with competent presentation and service abilities.

- Excellent communicator; fluent in verbal and written English.

employment experience

Montgomery Produce, City   Summers 20XX–20XX
Lead Processor/Packer

Processed customer orders including picking products, recording weights, labelling packages, preparing boxes for shipment, and completing packing slips. Worked as part of a team of 8 to 10, but also worked independently when needed. Promoted to Lead Processor/Packer last summer; oversaw the work of 3 other employees.

education

Dermott Business and Technical College, City   20XX–Present
Currently enrolled in a business program with such courses as Accounting, Sales and Marketing, Business Communication, Statistics, and Economics.

Sheridan Senior High School, City   20XX–20XX
Graduated with a High School Diploma. Chosen leader of the yearbook committee in Grade 12 out of 6 candidates. Member of the math and photography clubs.

available seven nights a week, including holidays

MAGGIE BISHOP
Housekeeping Room Attendant

Exceeding the expectations of each and every guest!

2 Years' Hotel Housekeeping Experience

West End Villa Suites, City   20XX – Present
Housekeeping Room Attendant

- ✔ Sweep, mop, wash, wax, and polish floors.
- ✔ Vacuum carpeting and area rugs, draperies, and upholstered furniture.
- ✔ Make beds; change sheets; distribute clean towels and toiletries.
- ✔ Clean, disinfect, and polish bathroom fixtures and appliances.
- ✔ Pick up debris and empty trash containers.
- ✔ Wash windows, walls, and ceilings.
- ✔ Immediately attend to any specific guest requests.
- ✔ Accept laundry shifts when short-staffed in that department.

Completely Open Availability

Available to start immediately and work all days and shifts needed including early mornings, afternoons, evenings, overnights, weekends, and holidays. Prefer full-time but happy to accept part-time as well. Driver's licence with access to a reliable vehicle. Willing to work on short notice when required.

Contact Information

EMAIL ADDRESS   ▫   PHONE NUMBER
MAILING ADDRESS

ALTERNATIVE RESUMES FAQ//
HOW SHOULD I HANDLE REFERENCES?

Should I put "References Available upon Request" at the bottom of my resume?

No. Including the generic statement "References Available upon Request" at the bottom is outdated and most professional resume writers don't do it. It lacks detail, wastes a line on your resume, and indicates to the reader that you either used a template or your job search skills are behind the times. In some cases it is beneficial to state on your resume that you have references, especially for young job-seekers who might not be expected to have them. If so, provide more detail with a sentence such as, "Contact information and letters of recommendation available from high school math teacher and volunteer supervisor."

Should I make a reference list?

Yes. A reference list is a separate document from your resume and should only be submitted to an employer when it is requested. Since this typically occurs at the end of an interview, you need to prepare this list in advance and bring it with you to all appointments. Also include it in a portfolio if you job search in person, since you never know when a hiring manager will want to interview you. Contact information for your references usually does NOT go on the resume itself because the hiring manager does not need it until after the interview when you have both decided to proceed. Contact information should be treated confidentially and only given out when necessary.

Your reference list should contain three to five professional contacts, not family or friends, who can speak to your character, skill, experience, and achievements. Most often that means managers from past jobs but it can include volunteer supervisors, co-workers, clients/customers, professors, instructors, teachers, counsellors, and community professionals. Always ask people if they will be a reference before adding them to your list. Once you have their approval, include their first and last name, job title, company

or organization, city and province/state if located out of town, phone number and/or email address. Centre this information on a separate page with your contact information at the top and you will have a professional reference list to submit to employers.

Should I ask for letters of recommendation?

Yes. In addition to asking references if you may add them to your list, it's also a good idea to ask if they will write a letter of recommendation for you. This way you will still have a written record of the recommendation in case you lose contact with them. When an authority figure in your career is willing to praise your character or skills in writing, it becomes a testimonial for you. Keep these original letters in a safe place, such as a job search portfolio, and provide copies for interviewers.

Another way of using letters of recommendation, in addition to presenting them at interviews, is to quote them in your resume, as Colin Stipe has done on the next page. He realizes his targeted employers will already know what he did in his previous jobs, so it's more important to show how well he did it. Even though hiring managers may still contact his references to verify the authenticity of the letters or to ask more questions, these testimonials can still make a positive first impression.

It's very important to have both your reference list and letters of recommendation ready when asked, so prepare early and don't get caught off guard!

COLIN STIPE, Restaurant Manager Trainee

20XX university graduate with a Bachelor's Degree in Business Administration and 4 years of progressive experience in restaurant operations. Fluent in English; conversant in French.

Customer Service
"Colin received a score of 'Exceeding Expectations' on his Aug 20XX performance appraisal for the customer service component. In the three years he was with us, we never had a single recorded complaint about the level of service he provided."
- KEVIN HOLLOWAY, RESTAURANT MANAGER, DOMINIQUE'S

Time Management
"His ability to prioritize is one of his strongest assets. When he was promoted to Lead Server, he earned additional responsibilities over and above his regular duties. He was successful at juggling all of it while keeping an eye on the big picture. His ability to manage his time efficiently rubbed off on our other staff."
- KAREN CHANDLER, SERVICE MANAGER, DOMINIQUE'S

Organization
"The structure of this course demands that students have superior organizational skills. There are several facets to the Small Business Module, all of which require equal attention. Not all students have the ability to stay organized and not miss anything or fall behind. Colin did."
- ED BARNES, LAWSON CITY UNIVERSITY PROFESSOR, SMALL BUSINESS MODULE

Staff Supervision
"I believe Colin developed excellent supervisory skills during his time as a Lead Server. With this position came the responsibility for supervising servers and bus staff during low volume periods. His ability to communicate with co-workers in a thoughtful, considerate manner assisted him in this role."
- KAREN CHANDLER, SERVICE MANAGER, DOMINIQUE'S

Financial Control
"Colin performed admirably through the three levels of Financial Management, earning a B average over two years. He demonstrated a knack for accounting and taxation which will serve him well during his business career."
- SUE SHIELDS, LAWSON CITY UNIVERSITY PROFESSOR, FINANCIAL MANAGEMENT

FULL LETTERS OF RECOMMENDATION AVAILABLE UPON REQUEST

EMPLOYMENT EXPERIENCE

DOMINIQUE'S, Lawson City	20XX–20XX
Lead Server	20XX
Server	20XX–20XX
Host	20XX
THE WILD HORSE CAFÉ, Kent	20XX
Bus Person	
EARTH FIRST CAFÉ, Kent	20XX–20XX
Cook / Cashier	

AFFILIATIONS

Attended several meetings of the Association of Public Speakers in 20XX. Overcame fear of public speaking and a minor stutter to deliver a 10-minute speech in front of 1,000 people.

Member of Millennium Business Leaders at Lawson City University from 20XX until 20XX.

Volunteered with United Brothers from 20XX to 20XX. Served as role model for a young man experiencing peer pressure in school.

HOME PHONE · CELL PHONE · FAX NUMBER · EMAIL ADDRESS · MAILING ADDRESS

Pepper Ward

PHONE NUMBER • EMAIL ADDRESS

Grade 10 student at Columbus Secondary School seeks a stable, part-time position as a cashier or drive-thru service person in a fast food restaurant. Strong desire to gain work experience in food and customer service. Qualifications include:

- **Sales and Customer Service Experience.** Sold chocolates and seasonal cookies door-to-door as part of the Mount Haven Youth Group from 20XX to 20XX, and to raise money for lung cancer in 20XX and 20XX.

- **Outgoing Personality.** Acted in 3 school plays in junior high, including the female lead in *Romeo and Juliet* in Grade 9. Won 2nd place for singing and playing piano in front of 600 students in the Grade 10 talent show.

- **Teamwork Skills.** Played in the Harrison Youth Soccer League for 6 seasons as a child and teenager. Active member of the Mount Haven Youth Group for 3 years.

- **Leadership Skills.** Elected captain of soccer team for the 20XX season. Currently completing the Leadership & Entrepreneurial Skills 10 course in high school.

- **Dependability.** Babysat for 3 different families over the course of 4 years. All will provide telephone or written references if needed.

- **Communication Skills.** Fluent in verbal and written English; conversant in French.

PERSONAL STATEMENT

I am confident I would be a valuable addition to your team because I have always excelled in high pressure, stressful situations and I know that will help me provide exceptional service to your customers. I work well as part of a team, and I am quick to learn and master new skills. My goal is to find a part-time job that will last through the rest of my school career; with my post-secondary plans that means I hope to contribute to the success of your business for the next few years. Thank you for your time and consideration of my application!

EMPLOYMENT QUALIFICATIONS

- Earned a B+ with 88% in hospitality and tourism course at Dundas Learning Centre in May 20XX.
- Completed Service Excellence Level 1 and Food Safety Level 1 certificates in November 20XX.
- Letter of recommendation available from work experience employer in the hospitality industry.
- Very reliable and punctual; earned the Outstanding Attendance Award during Grade 9.
- Excellent availability; attend school part-time and available to work more than most students.
- Strong computer skills including Word, Excel, Outlook, Simply Accounting, and Internet research.
- Team player; worked as part of a team of 6 at Haven Resorts; member of basketball team in school.
- Physically fit; exercise regularly, not afraid of frequent heavy lifting or standing for long hours.
- Able to follow written and verbal instructions quickly and easily.

AVAILABILITY

Mon   12:30–Midnight

Tues   12:30–Midnight

Wed   12:30–Midnight

Available to work any shifts from 12:30pm Thursday to midnight on Sunday.

Available to start today.

LUKE FISHER

Mailing Address Line 1
Mailing Address Line 2
Home Phone • Cell Phone
Email Address

Hostel Clerk

EDUCATION

Recently completed all Grade 10 courses and requirements at Dundas Learning Centre. Now enrolled in Grade 11.

Attend M–Th from 8:45 to 12 noon.

Improved grades from a C– average in regular school to a B+ average at Dundas.

WORK EXPERIENCE

Front Desk Clerk   Haven Resorts, City   Feb 20XX
- Completed a 4-week, full-time work experience placement organized by Dundas Learning Centre.
- Assisted with all front desk operations including registering visitors, processing payments, arranging transportation, responding to guest and telephone inquiries, and promoting local tourist attractions.
- Worked in the laundry and housekeeping departments for 2 days each to learn their job functions.

Office Assistant   Corrigan & Fisher, City   Dec 20XX
- Assisted with various year-end duties at a family accounting practice for 3 weeks.
- Answered telephone inquiries on a 4-line system, booked appointments, and relayed messages.
- Entered data in Excel and Simply Accounting programs, batched invoices, and assisted with filing.

Child Care Provider   Various Families, City   20XX–20XX
- Cared for numerous neighbourhood children, up to 4 at a time, ranging in age from newborn to 10.
- Planned meals and snacks, organized activities and outings, and oversaw homework completion.
- Assisted with housekeeping duties including laundry, vacuuming, dusting, and organization.

sadie dawson

RIDE ATTENDANT

Volunteer Experience
Volunteered as a referee for high school volleyball tournaments and wrestling meets. Worked independently. Trusted to demonstrate fairness and integrity while ensuring the safety of participants. Accustomed to dealing with difficult and challenging situations, particularly when coaches and athletes disagree with decisions.

Trained in First Aid and CPR
Completed an emergency first aid course for junior high school students. Capable of assisting guests who are feeling nauseous.

Reliable / Punctual
Able to get a ride to work; don't need to rely on public transit. Didn't miss a single day of school in Grade 9; copy of report card available.

Able To Work All Summer
Fully available from June 24 until September 5. No vacation plans that will interfere with work availability.

Open Scheduling Availability
Willing to work any day/shift needed including mornings, afternoons, late evenings, weekdays, weekends, and holidays. Able to work as many hours as needed during the fair.

Excellent Health and Physical Condition
Comfortable standing for long periods of time. Capable of operating heavy machinery. Willing and able to work in all weather conditions.

References
Recommendation letters and contact information available from high school science teacher and head of athletics department.

Contact
Sadie Dawson • Mailing Address
Home Phone • Cell Phone • Email Address

THEATRE USHER	Rex Schindler
OBJECTIVE	To Provide Exceptional Service to Patrons of the Royal Sapphire Theatre
AVAILABILITY	All Evening and Weekend Performances
EMPLOYMENT	Paper Carrier, 20XX – 20XX *Wellington Citizen* Newspaper 6 Mornings per Week
EDUCATION	Currently Enrolled in Grade 10 Sir Lionel Drake Secondary, City
TEAM EXPERIENCE	High School Football, 2 seasons Community Soccer, 3 seasons Little League Baseball, 5 seasons
INTERESTS	Feature Films / Documentaries Anime / Drawing / Painting
FUTURE GOALS	Novelist / Screenwriter Stand-up Comedian
REFERENCES	Supervisor, *Wellington Citizen* High School Career Prep Teacher High School Football Coach
CONTACT	Mailing Address Line 1 Mailing Address Line 2 Home Phone / Cell Phone Email Address

RESTAURANT	POSITION	SCOPE	SUCCESS
THE CAVERN Location / City	General Manager 20XX – Present	Accepted full P&L and operational accountability for a 180-seat casual restaurant and 45-seat patio with $4.5M in annual revenue. Provide leadership, guidance, and support to over 40 front-of-house staff and 20 kitchen employees. Report to the restaurant owner.	Improved annual revenue from $3.4M in first year to $3.9M and then $4.5M. Exceeded projections by an average of 9% each year. Reduced labour costs by 10% through efficient staff scheduling and wage management. Lowered employee turnover 6% by designing a new-hire orientation and training program. Cut operating expenses by 7% in 2 years.
PICCOLO Location / City	Restaurant Manager 20XX – 20XX	Planned, opened, and managed first year front-of-house operations for a new 150-seat Italian restaurant that recorded $2.8M in first year revenue. Recruited, hired, trained, and managed a team of 40. Reported to the restaurant owner.	Exceeded overall revenue projections by $600K and wine sales targets by 13% in the first year. Operated first year at 4% under budget for labour expenses. Developed and implemented several programs for staff recruitment, orientation, training, and leadership development.
TAPS GRILL Location / City	Restaurant Manager 20XX Assistant Manager 20XX – 20XX	Oversaw front-of-house operations for a 140-seat casual restaurant and 40-seat patio generating $2.4M in annual revenue. Maintained and led a team of 25. Reported to the Regional Manager.	Increased revenues from $1.9M to $2.4M, surpassing annual sales objective by 7%. Reduced employee turnover by 8%. Created a leadership development program that resulted in 7 staff earning promotions to positions of greater responsibility.

JUDE PRIESTLEY
Prep Cook • Service Associate • Cashier • Trainer

2 YEARS' EXPERIENCE · FOOD SERVICE CERTIFICATION · AVAILABLE EVERY DAY, EVERY SHIFT

Marchant Café & Bakery, City, 20XX–20XX
LETTER OF RECOMMENDATION AVAILABLE UPON REQUEST

FOOD SERVICE

- Prepared several breakfast, lunch, and dinner items including sandwiches, enchiladas, pizza, burritos, wraps, soups, salads, breads, muffins, pastries, and desserts.
- Served beverages such as soft drinks, cappuccino, lattes, espresso, tea, and fruit juices.
- Replaced expired stock with new product during the graveyard shift; counted perished items.
- Assisted in the bakery department as needed, preparing breads, muffins, and bagels.
- Performed detailed cleaning on various machines, such as cappuccino and coffee makers.

CUSTOMER SERVICE

- Consistently provided first-rate customer service at both the counter and drive-thru positions.
- Earned company "Top Service Award" and bonus for receiving positive customer feedback.
- Achieved an "A" on last performance evaluation for communication skills with customers.
- Received second highest score on "Staff Incentive Promotion" for up-selling menu combos.
- Used problem-solving skills to handle customer complaints in a professional manner.
- Answered telephone and responded to questions about location, hours, products, and policies.

CASH HANDLING

- Operated and maintained a computerized cash register and scanning system.
- Used a bank terminal to accurately process credit and bank card payments.
- Processed store and vendor coupons; performed transaction voids, refunds, and exchanges.
- Reconciled cash and receipts to register totals at shift-end; regularly balanced to the penny.
- High level of computer knowledge; able to troubleshoot most system and printer problems.

ADDITIONAL RESPONSIBILITIES

- Often worked the graveyard shift with just one other staff member, with complete responsibility for the security, contents, and operation of the entire café/store.
- Promoted to Staff Trainer position after eight months; trained 5 new employees on customer service, food preparation, cash handling, computer systems, and cleaning/maintenance.
- Received new supply and product deliveries; verified packing lists and authorized invoices.
- Maintained organization and cleanliness of entire café/store, including outside parking lot.

EDUCATION and TRAINING

Food Care Health & Safety Certificate
Customer Service Skills Certificate

Lottery Terminal Operator Certificate
High School Diploma

LABOUR AND TRADES

Chapter 3

Entry-level positions in labour often require few skills and little or no experience.

Apprentice and assistant positions in a trade may require more qualifications, but also offer the potential for rewarding careers. These are just a few of the reasons teens and young adults enjoy working in labour-oriented jobs. This chapter starts with the deconstruction of a Labourer/Landscaper resume, and continues with three FAQ tips and 22 sample resumes.

DESIGNING MY ALTERNATIVE RESUME//
KEN MCKAY : LABOURER/LANDSCAPER

Ken McKay has two years experience as an auto technician. Now he wants to make the transition to a new career where he can work outdoors and utilize his additional skills and interests.

He heard about an opportunity for a labourer/landscaper with the municipal government through his contacts who work there. Since he doesn't have direct employment experience in this field, Ken has designed his resume to market his transferable skills and accomplishments towards this new opportunity. Ken's resume can be viewed on the following page.

1. Personal Profile

Ken uses his personal profile to respond directly to the list of qualifications indicated by the employer. Because it's a "jack-of-all-trades" type of position with an emphasis on landscaping, Ken summarizes his well-rounded skill set at the top and follows it with a point-by-point list of his key selling features. He includes his background as an auto technician, but he doesn't focus on it. Once the hiring manager realizes from the profile that Ken meets the basic requirements of the position, the manager will continue to the next section for a more in-depth analysis of Ken's experience.

2. Accomplishments & Skills

Since the majority of Ken's relevant achievements come from his personal interests rather than his employment, he devotes a large part of his resume to an Accomplishments & Skills section rather than the traditional Work Experience. He demonstrates his talents through detailed descriptions of major labour and landscaping projects he has worked on at home or in the community to convince the reader he has the required skills for this position.

3. Employment

Just as he did in the Personal Profile section, Ken includes the basic information about his work in auto mechanics, but he doesn't expand on it. He knows the reader will understand what an auto technician does, and it's not directly relevant to the job he is seeking. He leaves off two completely unrelated jobs in a fast food restaurant and furniture store that he held as a teenager.

4. References

Although reference names, phone numbers, and email addresses should not be listed on a resume in most cases, Ken has included this information with the approval of his contacts. All of his references work in the government department he is applying to, and all of them know the exact person who will be reviewing resumes and hiring for this position.

KEN MCKAY
Municipal Park Services
Labourer/Landscaper

Home Phone Number
Cell Phone Number
Fax Number
Email Address

Mailing Address Line 1
Mailing Address Line 2

❹ REFERENCES

Barney Turnbull
Landscape Technician
Municipal Park Services
Phone / Email

Marcia Spurling
Registration Clerk
Municipal Park Services
Phone / Email

Jan Candlewood
Recreation Coordinator
Municipal Park Services
Phone / Email

PERSONAL PROFILE ❶

- Experienced in a variety of trades and labour work including landscaping, construction, woodwork, metalwork, and painting.
- Mechanically inclined, including BCTC certification and 2 years' experience as an Automotive Technician.
- Skilled with most hand and power tools.
- Physically fit; capable of working in all weather conditions.
- Comfortable with frequent heavy lifting and working at heights.
- Class 5 driver's licence; preparing to obtain a class 3 licence.
- Experience driving a wide range of motor vehicles.
- Willing to work weekdays, evenings, weekends, and holidays.

ACCOMPLISHMENTS & SKILLS ❷

- Designed and built a 26' x 26' wood garage with a concrete foundation. Performed all installations including wiring, drywall, windows, drainage, roofing, and siding. Painted the exterior.
- Repaired and eventually replaced a 6' x 30' wood porch/stairs. Designed and built a 64' x 75' fence and a backyard deck.
- Installed a school playground. Laid landscape ties and pea gravel, built a border for a 60' x 100' lot, and assembled and installed 10-12 metal playground equipment pieces.
- Removed and disposed of a 25' tree, planted various shrubs and plants, trimmed and pruned trees, applied fertilizers and pesticides, and operated manual and power mowers.
- Painted the interior/exterior of a 2200 sf, 4-bedroom house, a 26' x 26' garage, and several homes for friends and family.
- Paved a shopping mall parking lot. Constructed a sidewalk with interlocking brick pavers.
- Performed minor welding of exhaust pipes and other projects as an auto mechanic.

EMPLOYMENT ❸

- Auto Technician, Russell-Meyer Motors   20XX–20XX

EDUCATION

- Autobody Estimating Program   20XX
- BCTC Automotive Repair Certification   20XX
- Completed numerous continuing education workshops related to gardening, landscaping, carpentry, and deck building.

Loredana Ricci 🚲 Bike Mechanic

"Loredana was a great addition to our bicycle mechanics program. She applied herself well and had a natural grasp for the concepts taught. She is definitely a mechanically inclined young woman with a passion for the bike industry. She also proved she could work well as part of a team, showed respect for her fellow students and instructors, and demonstrated an eagerness to improve. I highly recommend her as I feel she would be a welcome addition to any bike shop. Feel free to call me if you have any questions or concerns."

RAY DAVIS, HEAD INSTRUCTOR – SUNWOOD YOUTH EMPLOYMENT CONNECTION, PHONE NUMBER

CERTIFICATE IN BICYCLE MECHANICS, 20XX
Bicycle Mechanic Program – Sunwood Youth Employment Connection

Completed a 3-month bicycle mechanic program that fully prepared students to work in a bike shop. Program included practical experience, theoretical teaching, and daily homework assignments. Life skills training classes such as time management, career planning, money management, team building, and conflict resolution were also included.

CAPABILITIES

- Assembling new bicycles that are received from the manufacturer.
- Verifying safety and proper assembly of bicycles before they go on the sales floor.
- Servicing and repairing bicycles brought to the shop by customers.
- Safely using tools such as hand drills, grinders, spanners, and wheel tuning equipment.
- Advising customers about repair or replacement options, parts and accessories.
- Maintaining and updating parts and other stock inventories.
- Discussing purchasing options with customers and closing sales.
- Answering the phone, opening and closing the shop, and performing administrative work.

WORK EXPERIENCE

Self-employed community bicycle mechanic for the past 2 years. Assembled and repaired approximately 20 bicycles for both adults and children. Built one bike entirely from spare parts. 2 letters of recommendation available upon request.

AVAILABILITY

Available to start immediately and work any day or shift needed including early mornings, afternoons, evenings, weekdays, weekends, and holidays. Comfortable with either a full-time or part-time schedule. Easy to contact via cell phone if needed on short notice.

CONTACT

Mailing Address • Home Phone • Cell Phone • Email Address

EMPLOYMENT HISTORY

Farm Labourer
Barrington Farms, City

Installed and removed irrigation pipes, transported pipes using a tractor, oversaw operation of two irrigation pumps, performed minor repairs on piping and equipment. Worked alone in all weather conditions. 20XX–20XX

Vineyard Labourer
Calm Ridge Vineyard, City

Provided support for grapevines using wooden poles. Assisted with preparing equipment to spray fields. Usually worked unsupervised. Summer 20XX

Bus Person
The Broiler Room, City

Prepared tables and assisted servers with delivering food and beverage orders. Set up dining room for banquets. 20XX–20XX

Farm Labourer
Kramer Farms, City

Worked weekends and holidays for one year, often 12 hours a day. Used hand and power tools to plant, cultivate, fertilize, and irrigate. Harvested and stored crops and grains. Performed minor repairs on tools/equipment and handled other maintenance duties. 20XX–20XX

WORK PLACEMENTS

Landscape Assistant
Reynolds Designs, City

Worked full-time for three weeks during Grade 12 work practicum. Built trails and ponds, paved a driveway, detailed & maintained lawns and gardens, and set-up a fountain pump system. 20XX

Maintenance Worker
Evergreen Fairways, City

Worked full-time for two weeks during Grade 11 work practicum. Detailed & maintained pathways and lawns. Used rakes, edgers, and other gardening tools and equipment. 20XX

LETTER OF REFERENCE

"Max was a tremendous asset to our business during the summer of 20XX. In fact, we wanted to offer him a permanent job but he moved to the coast. While he was here, he showed that he was a mature young man who wasn't afraid of hard work. He was always on time and reliable. Any job we asked him to do – he was up to the task! We wouldn't hesitate to recommend him for any type of work you feel he's qualified for!"

Henry Stiles, Owner
Calm Ridge Vineyard

MAX KITE
Farm Labourer

Mailing Address
Telephone · Email Address

2 years' labour experience

Completely open availability

Safety footwear and clothing

Driver's licence and truck

LETTER OF REFERENCE

"Max Kite worked for us from October 20XX until May 20XX. He was a full-time employee in good standing with us. For the most part, he worked steadily on the irrigation piping, but we often counted on him to pick up the slack in other areas as well. He was a very hard worker who didn't mind the long hours and heavy labour that comes with the job. He gets the job done without needing someone to look over his shoulder all day long. I'm sure you will be happy with him on your team. Please call me with any questions."

Tom Barrington, Owner
Barrington Farms

WORK QUALIFICATIONS

Physically Fit

Exercise regularly to maintain the best possible physical condition. Comfortable with frequent heavy lifting, standing for long hours, and working at great heights. Accustomed to working long days. Very high energy level.

Mechanically Inclined

Natural ability to fix mechanical items, including tools, equipment, and vehicles. Performed minor maintenance and repairs in most jobs. Skilled with a variety of hand and power tools. Able to drive automatic and standard transmissions, including tractors, pickup trucks, and vans.

Independent Worker

Accustomed to working alone without direct supervision. Able to look at the "big picture" and make appropriate decisions. Former employers have been very pleased with work ethic, attitude, reliability, and maturity. References available.

Quick Learner

Graduated high school on the honour roll. Consistently able to learn quickly by watching a task being completed and then doing it after. Learned the concept of "WorkSmart" and the benefits of batch work.

Strong Communicator

Fluent speaker, reader and writer in English; conversant in French. Maintained cooperative working relationships with all employers.

EDUCATION & TRAINING

Cactus Secondary School, City

Graduated with a high school diploma in 20XX. Earned honour roll status three semesters in Grades 11 and 12. Completed a variety of shop courses, including Woodworking 11/12, Metalwork 11/12, Auto Mechanics 11/12, and Drafting 11.

JESSICA HARRISON
Commercial Truck Driver

Home Phone • Cell Phone • Email Address
Mailing Address

DRIVER'S LICENCE

Upgraded to an unrestricted Class B licence with full air brakes certification in March 20XX. Over 4 years' driving experience with a Class C licence, with no tickets, fines, or warnings. Driving report and copy of licence available upon request.

EMPLOYMENT EXPERIENCE

Furniture Delivery Driver
Russell's Home and Furniture Warehouse, City
October 20XX – January 20XX

Operated a 5-ton truck to deliver furniture and home accessories to customers throughout the district. Maintained a perfect driving record with no safety incidents, accidents, or vehicle damage.

Shipper/Receiver; Order Picker
CNC Bottling Depot, City
October 20XX – September 20XX

Operated forklifts, cherry-pickers, and lift trucks and earned training certificates for all three. Oversaw shipping & receiving, return-to-vendor processing, and order picking in a 20,000 square foot depot.

EDUCATION

Graduated from Stanfield Secondary School with a high school diploma in May 20XX.

OTHER QUALIFICATIONS

Extensive travel experience throughout Canada, the United States, and Mexico.

Excellent physical condition; exercise every day to achieve and maintain optimum health.

DRIVER TRAINING

COMMERCIAL TRUCKING LICENCE PREPARATION PROGRAM
Island Driving School, City, Feb 20XX

Completed a 180-hour driver training program over 6 weeks, including 120 hours of in-cab training and 60 hours in-class learning. Topics included:

Introduction to Trucking

Pre-trip and Post-trip Inspections

Canada / US Border Regulations

Log Book Regulations

Safe Driving Practices

Multiple Trailers

Professional Driver Image

Electrical Systems

Fuels and Fuel Systems

Brakes and Braking Techniques

Trip Planning, Routes, and Maps

Load and Weight Distribution

Transporting Hazardous Materials

Extreme Weather Conditions

Mountain Driving

Transmissions and Differentials

Frames, Suspension, and Axles

Cooling and Lubrication Systems

RODNEY WEXLER
Mailing Address • Home Phone • Cell Phone

ATTENTION SHOP MANAGER:

Having completed the first year of my training program, I would like to meet with you and discuss an **Automotive Collision Technician Apprenticeship** with your shop. I have one year automotive experience and can provide excellent references. Please review the following qualifications:

AUTOBODY EXPERIENCE

* Reviewed damage reports and estimates with a senior technician and planned work.
* Repaired and replaced doors, front end components, and body/underbody components.
* Hammered out dents, buckles, and other defects with blocks and hammers.
* Used soldering equipment and plastic filler to fill holes, dents, and seams.
* Removed damaged fenders, panels, and grills using wrenches and cutting torches.
* Bolted, welded, and glued replacement parts into place.
* Straightened bent frames using frame and underbody pulling and anchoring equipment.
* Filed and sanded body surfaces using hand and power tools.
* Applied primer and repainted vehicle surfaces with spray guns.
* Repaired or replaced glass components, including windows, windshields, and mirrors.
* Repaired or replaced interior components such as seat frames, carpets, and floorboards.
* Inspected and test drove vehicles to ensure safe operation.

AUTOBODY TRAINING

AUTOMOTIVE COLLISION TECHNICIAN PROGRAM, East Technical School   20XX–20XX
Completed the 1st year of a 3-year apprenticeship program with an average grade of 88%.

"Rod demonstrated a natural ability for autobody work. He is mechanically sound and has been a great addition to our class. His safety attitude is high, and I gladly recommend him!"
GEORGE PELLETIER, PROGRAM INSTRUCTOR

AUTOMOTIVE EMPLOYMENT

FARLEY MOTORS   20XX
Completed a 2-month work experience placement in the bodyshop, working closely with 2 senior technicians in all areas of automotive bodywork.

"If we didn't already have an apprentice in our shop, Rodney would be on board today. With his quality workmanship and determination, he will no doubt have a great career in this field."
STAN JACKSON, GENERAL MANAGER

CAMPBELL'S CARS   20XX–20XX
Worked closely with the owner of this shop, performing minor repair and maintenance tasks including fluid changes, tune-ups, oil changes, tire changes, and radiator flushes.

"Rod is a hard-working employee who always cared what the customer thought of his work. He isn't afraid to go the extra mile to make sure they leave happy. He has a bright future."
TOM CAMPBELL, OWNER/MANAGER

CAPABILITIES

Stable Work

Picking Stalls

Cleaning Paddocks

Spreading Sawdust

Sweeping

Cleaning/Polishing Tack

Operating Hay Elevators

Stacking Hay

Repairing Fences

Controlling Pests

Horse Work

Feeding Grain and Hay

Watering

Turning Out

Blanketing

Brushing and Clipping

Tacking Up

Lunging Exercises

Ground Work

Riding

tori moss

MAILING ADDRESS • CELL PHONE • EMAIL ADDRESS

HORSE STABLE WORKER

- 6 months' experience working in a large boarding stable with up to 20 horses at a time.

- 7 years' horseback riding experience, including 2 years of English and 5 years of Western.

- Familiar with the proper use, care, and maintenance of Western and English saddles and bridles, as well as halters and blankets.

- Excellent physical condition; member of high school track and field team in Grades 10, 11, and 12, and girl's rugby team in Grades 10 and 11.

- Earned a First Aid Level 1 Certificate in high school.

STABLE EMPLOYMENT

- DEVON STABLES   Summers 20XX–20XX
  City

  Worked full-time in July and August for each of the last 3 summers. Assisted with the cleaning of 20 stalls and 6 outdoor paddocks, AM and PM feedings, and general horse care and exercise. Performed basic construction and repair work to fences, barns, and an outdoor ring.

EDUCATION

- EDINBURGH HIGH SCHOOL   20XX–20XX
  City

  Graduated with a high school diploma and certificates in first aid, CPR, and conflict resolution. Received a certificate of merit for outstanding attendance.

Home Phone
Cell Phone

Mailing Address
Email Address

PHIL MCKENZIE
Freelance Construction Worker

PROFILE

- 3 years' construction experience on numerous residential, commercial, and industrial worksites throughout the region.

- Skilled in a variety of construction and labour work such as painting, carpentry, window framing, drywall, concrete, rubbish removal, roofing, and bricklaying. Experienced with most hand and power tools.

- Excellent physical condition and overall health. Capable of frequent heavy lifting and working long days. Comfortable working at heights and in all weather conditions.

- Available 24/7 and on short notice for assignment to any construction site in the region.

- Driver's licence with a reliable late-model vehicle.

- Own basic hand tools, safety vest, safety gloves, steel-toe boots, and a hard hat.

RESIDENTIAL PROJECTS

- Constructed 14 wooden backyard decks in 3 months in a new housing development in Trent as a contractor for Morelli's Carpentry Services.

- Framed windows in a new 32-storey condominium tower in Benton Heights for 3 months as a contractor for Crowder and Young Building Construction.

- Painted home interiors in a new 110-unit townhouse complex in Crofton for 2 months as a contractor for Russell and Sons Painting Services.

- Cleared a 3,500 square foot bulldozed residential lot in Trent in 1 week as a contractor for Wallace Garvin Contractors.

COMMERCIAL PROJECTS

- Painted the interior of a new 30,000 square foot Book Town store in Crowder for 2 weeks as a contractor for Russell and Sons Painting Services.

- Replaced a tar and gravel roof on a 70,000 square foot grocery store in Benton Heights for 10 days as a contractor for Kinney Roofing Specialists.

- Performed drywall work for 2 weeks in a renovated 15,000 square foot bank in Yorktown as a contractor for Tupper Construction Ltd.

INDUSTRIAL PROJECTS

- Poured concrete for the foundation of a manufacturing plant in Thompson Business Park for 2 weeks as a contractor for Browning & Johnston Concrete Ltd.

- Cleared a 2-acre bulldozed lot in Thompson Business Park in 3 weeks as a contractor for Powell Brothers Construction Corporation.

CERTIFICATIONS

First Aid Level 2 & CPR, 20XX Expiry • Workplace Health & Safety Level 1, 20XX Expiry • Hazardous Materials Systems, 20XX Expiry

ALTERNATIVE RESUMES FAQ//
SHOULD I INCLUDE INTERESTS AND HOBBIES ON MY RESUME?

Interests and hobbies should only be included on your resume if they support your overall message.

This normally occurs when your particular interests are related to the job you're applying for, such as an avid cyclist applying at a bike shop. You can also include them if your targeted industry, such as teaching, simply prefers candidates with a broad range of knowledge. Interests and hobbies may seem harmless but if they are used inappropriately, your resume may be rejected. Here are three steps to follow to make the most of your interests and hobbies:

1. Make sure the interests are relevant.

If you're applying for a job in a sporting goods store, they will appreciate that you enjoy playing hockey but they won't care that you like photography. Conversely, if you want to work in a camera store, they will be thrilled that you like photography but won't care that you play hockey. Make sure your interests and hobbies are relevant to your job target. Otherwise, they will diminish the overall impact of your resume.

2. Make sure the interests are not offensive.

This can be difficult because we don't know what offends everyone. Avoid controversial and highly personal topics such as religion or politics, and common interests that may be viewed negatively such as rap music or hunting, unless you're applying for a related job. Hiring managers with lots of resumes to go through will find any reason to reject an applicant.

3. Don't use an Interests and Hobbies section.

Since hiring managers see thousands of resumes with completely irrelevant information in an Interests and Hobbies section, naming it that is almost like calling it Unrelated Filler. When the reader sees it, they won't have high expectations. Instead, use your suitable interests to help prove your soft skills or character traits, or make new

sections as Heidi Blanchett has done on the following page. She enjoys woodworking at home but rather than categorizing it under Interests and Hobbies, she created more interesting sections called Woodworking Accomplishments and Tool and Equipment Experience.

Look at the following examples of two job-seekers applying for a job in a video store. One candidate uses an Interests and Hobbies section, while the second takes a more creative approach:

CANDIDATE 1
INTERESTS AND HOBBIES

- Movies
- Music
- Mountain Biking
- Camping
- Travelling
- Canoeing

CANDIDATE 2
MOVIE KNOWLEDGE

- Own over 1,000 DVDs from all genres and eras.
- Broad knowledge of drama, crime, thriller, and suspense genres, with a particular emphasis on 1970 to the present day.
- Strong knowledge of actors, directors, box office records, and awards.
- Skilled at researching movies using print and online resources.

Candidate 2 clearly appears to possess more movie knowledge. However, Candidate 1 may have the same knowledge but because the individual used a more traditional section, they couldn't expand on it. And because the Movie Knowledge heading will be much more eye-catching to a video store manager than Interests and Hobbies, Candidate 2 comes out well ahead.

CARPENTER'S ASSISTANT

PERSONAL PROFILE

Mechanically inclined, physically fit young adult seeking an entry-level carpentry position. Completed all available woodworking courses while in high school, and gained experience with hand and power tools. Worked in retail for two years before pursuing long-term career path. Completed vocational assessments that verified a carpentry career is an ideal match for personal skills, interests, and values.

WOODWORKING TRAINING

Graduated from Kensington High School in 20XX. Focused on industrial arts courses and completed Introduction to CADD, Metalwork 11, and Auto Mechanics 11, in addition to these relevant classes:

- Woodworking 11. Taught the basics of woodworking tools, clamping and fastening, project planning, and finishing, and included a heavy emphasis on mathematics and proper measuring.
- Woodworking 12. Expanded on the fundamental skills and included in-depth training on tools, clamping and fastening, project planning, and finishing. It also introduced the concepts of joinery.

WOODWORKING ACCOMPLISHMENTS

Designed and built these items either in woodworking class or as personal projects at home:

- Bookshelf, 5' x 8'
- Shed, 8' x 12' x 10'
- Hope Chest
- Fence, 30' x 5'
- Display Shelf
- Toy Box
- Coat Rack
- Bird Feeder
- End Table
- Bookends
- Gift Box
- Toy Car

TOOL AND EQUIPMENT EXPERIENCE

Gained school and personal experience with the following tools and equipment:

- Table Saw
- Bench Grinder
- Jig Saw
- Belt Disc Sander
- Bench Drill Press
- Bench Vise
- Miter Saw
- Band Saw
- Router
- Lathe
- Nail Gun
- Hand Saw

CAREER EXPLORATION

Completed a 3-week career exploration program that included numerous assessments to match skills, interests, work values, and personality type with suitable career choices. All results pointed toward trades occupations as being most appropriate, particularly carpentry.

ADDITIONAL QUALIFICATIONS

- First Aid Training. Hold a certificate in Emergency First Aid with CPR; expires in March of 20XX.
- Workplace Safety Training. Achieved two certificates in "Workplace Safety" and "Violence in the Workplace" from The Health & Safety Society as part of a career preparation program in Grade 12.
- Excellent physical condition. Able to stand for long periods of time and capable of heavy lifting. Run 20 miles every week. Member of track and basketball teams in high school.
- Work Experience. 2 years' experience as a cashier at Whole Foods from January 20XX to present.

CONTACT INFORMATION

Heidi Blanchett • Home Phone • Cell Phone • Email Address • Mailing Address

INTERIOR PAINTER ◆ RESIDENTIAL/COMMERCIAL

Two years' experience as a freelance interior painter and subcontractor. Skilled in the preparation of walls, ceilings, woodwork, and floors and the application of primer and latex paint. Some knowledge of faux finishes. Comfortable working alone or as part of a team.

Extensive residential experience including houses, townhouses, condominiums/apartments, and mobile homes.

Moderate commercial experience including individual offices, building common areas, boutique stores, big-box stores, full service restaurants, and fast food mall outlets.

Testimonials

"We absolutely loved the work that Gurmeet did in our two bedrooms. They hadn't been painted in at least 20 years and were looking awful. We didn't attempt to do them ourselves because of our antique furniture, but Gurmeet took great care of it all, and the rooms looks amazing!"
R. UNDERWOOD, CITY

"Gurmeet, thank you so much for the beautiful job you did on our condo. We can't believe you got the whole place done so quickly – and it looks great!"
K. SCHULLER, CITY

"I'd like to say that I would highly recommend Gurmeet Singh for any painting jobs you may have. He is very talented and did a wonderful job on my office. His service is exemplary."
C. WHATLEY, CITY

"We hired Gurmeet Singh to paint the lobby and common rooms in our apartment building, including the washer/dryer room and the meeting room. His fee was fair, his service was quick, and the quality of his work was exceptional. We would hire him again."
J. CARRINGTON, CITY

Contact

Gurmeet Singh
Cell Phone ◆ Email Address

Available for small and large projects throughout the region.

JAYNE PARKER • LANDSCAPER

MAILING ADDRESS – HOME PHONE – CELL PHONE – EMAIL ADDRESS

Freelance residential landscaper since 20XX. Performed work for over 50 different homeowners in the area. Own tools, vehicle, and some equipment. Full project portfolio and letters of recommendation available upon request. Accomplishments include:

- Pruned shrubs and trees throughout a 120-unit housing complex for 3 months.
- Planned and constructed a backyard water feature incorporating a 10'x14' pond and a 3' high waterfall with a circulating pump.
- Maintained a 200 square foot greenhouse for an entire summer.
- Designed and built a 60' brick path from a house to the street.
- Created a 10' circular flower bed with a wide variety of perennials.
- Erected a 4' x 16' wooden retaining wall on a concrete foundation.
- Assisted with the design and construction of a 12' x 8' wooden backyard deck.

TOOL EXPERIENCE

Power Mowers – Electric Chippers – Chain Saws – Hand Pruners – Landscape Edgers
Loppers/Spreaders – Lawn Shears – Pruning Saws – Garden Forks – Snow Blowers
Cultivating Hoes – Landscape Rakes – Wheelbarrows – Hedge Trimmers

EDUCATION • CERTIFICATES • LICENCES

Pesticide Operator's Licence – Continuing Education, City   September 20XX
High School Diploma – Frankfurt Secondary, City   June 20XX
First Aid Level One Certificate – The Care Centre, City   January 20XX

Knowing trees, I understand the meaning of patience.
Knowing grass, I can appreciate persistence.

SKILLS

Weeding Gardens

Mowing Lawns

Pruning Shrubs & Trees

Designing & Building Paths

Installing Water Features

Maintaining Greenhouses

Laying Sod

Planting Flowers, Grass, Shrubs, & Trees

Maintaining Flower Beds

Fertilizing & Watering Lawns

Spreading Top Soil

Clearing Gutters & Drains

Raking Leaves

Clearing Snow

RICKY P. MORTENSEN

Home / Cell Phone
Email Address

MECHANIC'S ASSISTANT

Mailing Address
Mailing Address

Attention: Craig Newman, Shop Manager

As a pending high school graduate with advanced automotive technology training from Andover High School, I am excited to apply for a Mechanic Assistant or First Level Apprentice position in your shop. I will complete all my Grade 12 courses by June 15, 20XX and will then be able to work any time. My practical and theoretical automotive training comes from the following 3 high school courses:

- **Automotive Technology 11**
  Automotive Fundamentals: Tools & equipment, safety procedures, mechanical operations
  Engine Components: Engine component identification and operational understanding
  Chassis: Suspension systems, steering and alignment, brake replacements, tire repairs

- **Automotive Technology 12**
  Automatic Transmissions: Replacement of transmissions and transaxles, component identification
  Manual Transmissions: Service and adjustments to clutches, drive lines, drive axles, differentials
  Fuel Systems: Service of filters, supply lines, fuel gauges, tanks, and air induction systems

- **Advanced Automotive Technology 12A**
  Engine Reconditioning: Engine overhaul diagnosis, removal, installation, and disassembly
  Automotive Electronics: Distributors, alternators, starters, lights, climate control
  Advances in Automotive Technology: Emission controls, computerized fuel injection, electronics

I come from a family of auto mechanics and am considered mechanically inclined. Under the supervision of my father and uncle, I have performed repairs and maintenance on several vehicles. This includes catalytic converter replacements, brake lining and caliper replacements, radiator repairs, tire repairs, muffler installations, battery replacements, engine tune-ups, and oil changes.

Automotive mechanics is definitely the right career for me. Not only have I proven to have the basic skills and aptitude for the work, but I have also completed a career planning course in high school that showed how my skills, interests, values, and personality are a strong fit for this field. My shop teacher agrees, as shown here in this excerpt from his letter of recommendation:

- **"Ricky will benefit any employer he works for. He has a knack for auto mechanics and he is very teachable. He listens well, respects his educators, and always strives to do his best. He has the talent and attitude to excel and I wish him much success."**
  WALTER KINNEALY, HEAD AUTOMOTIVE INSTRUCTOR, ANDOVER HIGH SCHOOL

With almost 2 years' experience in a fast food restaurant, I have also proven I work well as part of a team, am comfortable in fast-paced environments, and have experience talking with customers. I am also fluent in verbal and written English, have very neat hand-writing, and excellent computer skills.

I have grown up around car repairs and look forward to a long and rewarding career in this field. I will contact you a week from today and perhaps we can arrange a meeting to discuss this further. Thank you in advance for your time and consideration.

Ricky Mortensen

EILEEN NEWELL
Telephone • Email

Mailing Address
Mailing Address

CONSTRUCTION FLAGGER QUALIFICATIONS

Traffic Control Certification. Successfully completed the government-sponsored, two-day training course in August 20XX through Moss Training Services, and received a Certificate in Traffic Control that doesn't expire until August 20XX. Scored 94% on the course exam.

Excellent Safety Record. Maintained a perfect safety record for over two years as a vehicle inspector at the Clean-Air Inspection Station, with no injuries, accidents, or safety incidents of any kind. Served on the station's health and safety committee for six months.

Experience with Irate Motorists. Gained considerable experience with irate motorists as a Clean-Air inspector. Used a firm approach and calm tone while defusing potentially volatile situations, explaining policies, and listening to complaints about test procedures and results.

Additional Qualifications. Own steel-toe boots and safety gloves. Possess a valid driver's licence and a reliable vehicle. Earned dual certificates in Occupational First Aid Level 1 and Workplace Health and Safety in 20XX through Baker Alternative Education.

EMPLOYMENT EXPERIENCE

VEHICLE INSPECTOR, F/T   **20XX–20XX**
Clean-Air Inspection Services, City

- Conducted vehicle emissions tests on all types of cars and light trucks. Entered vehicle identification information into the computer system. Communicated with motorists and processed cash, credit, and debit payments.

- Identified potential safety concerns or other reasons for halting testing such as excessive exhaust leaks, inaccessible exhaust systems, excessive smoke, tire concerns, fuel leaks, overheating, engine stalls, or lack of brake or steering control.

- Tested gas caps for emission leaks. Positioned vehicles for testing using appropriate safety procedures and equipment. Escorted drivers to waiting rooms. Drove vehicles on a dynamometer at speeds of up to 90 km per hour.

- Selected by the station manager to test vehicles on a new dynamometer system due to excellent personal safety record.

- Elected by peers to serve as their health and safety representative for six months and as acting shop steward for three months to cover an illness period.

ALTERNATIVE RESUMES FAQ//

WHAT QUALIFICATIONS ARE DESIRED FOR MANUAL LABOUR JOBS?

Many teens and young adults work in manual labour because they like physical work or enjoy being outdoors.

Sometimes they believe it requires fewer skills or less training. Opportunities can be found in construction, painting, warehousing, distribution, rubbish removal, roofing, landscaping, maintenance, manufacturing, and more. Here are common qualifications that hiring managers in these industries look for:

1. Physical Conditioning

Labour jobs require a certain level of strength, endurance, or other physical capability, such as working at heights as a roofer or crawling through small spaces as an HVAC (heating, ventilation, and air conditioning) assistant. Working in challenging weather conditions, frequent heavy lifting, walking or moving for long periods, or operating heavy machinery are also common. Demonstrating your awareness of these conditions and your physical ability to handle them may move your resume to the top of the list.

2. Safety Training

Labour work can be dangerous and managers may need employees with previous training, certification or experience in workplace health and safety, occupational first aid and CPR, or handling/transporting hazardous materials. Highlighting these qualifications on your resume will help you get noticed. Employers may also want you to supply your own steel-toe footwear, hardhat, gloves, or other safety equipment, so include those as well if you have them.

3. Transportation

A driver's licence and reliable transportation are frequently required by employers in these fields. Many of these companies and job sites are not located in residential areas or on bus routes, and sometimes these positions involve working at different sites or delivering supplies. If you have a driver's licence and own or have access to a reliable vehicle, state it on your resume.

4. Own Tools

Many jobs in the trades require employees to provide their own hand tools. If you own common hand tools that you are willing to use on the job, include that on your resume. If you have taken training courses that involved hand or power tools, add these as well to demonstrate your skills and abilities.

5. Availability

Many labour companies, such as warehouses and manufacturing plants, are in operation for long hours each day, sometimes 24 hours a day. Therefore, they need employees with great availability who can be scheduled or called in for morning, afternoon, evening, overnight, weekend, and holiday shifts.

Landscaping

Painting

Construction

Labour

Carpentry

Janitorial

Roofing

Paving

Assembly

Woodworking

FRED ROBBINS
Maintenance Worker, Residential Complex

MAILING ADDRESS • HOME PHONE • CELL PHONE • EMAIL ADDRESS

Employment Qualifications

- First Aid Level One & CPR certificate. Hazardous Materials Certificate.
- Clean driver's licence with a late-model, reliable pickup.
- Experienced with most hand and power tools, including band saws, planers, skill saws, blow torches, compressors, table saws, scroll saws, drill presses, screw guns, lathes, nail guns, and chainsaws.
- Own hand tools, safety footwear, vest, gloves, and hardhat.
- Comfortable working at heights and using safety equipment.
- Physically fit and capable of frequent heavy lifting.
- Completed several shop courses in high school, such as Woodworking 9-10, Metalwork 10-11, Drafting 10-11, and Auto Mechanics 11-12.

Labour Skills & Projects

- Designed and built a 12' x 8' x 10' shed of wood and vinyl siding; insulated interior, painted interior and exterior, and wired electricity.
- Painted exterior of two-level detached houses, including staircases and carports; stained sundecks and gazebos.
- Painted interiors of homes, including basements, bathrooms, kitchens, bedrooms, and hallways.
- Designed, planted, and maintained lawns and gardens, including trees, shrubs, flower beds, hedges, vegetable gardens, and pathways.
- Pressure-washed driveways, sundecks, and houses.
- Repaired a leaky roof on a two-story home.
- Paved a 40-foot driveway.
- Designed and constructed various wooden products, including a coffee table, coat rack, bookshelves, storage unit, and dog house.

Contract Employment

- Order Picker and Shipper/Receiver, Suburban Grocers   20XX
- Machine Operator, Bennington Steel   20XX
- Residential Painter, Sunshine Painting   20XX
- Construction Assistant, Bonds Contracting   20XX
- Landscape Assistant, Bartlow's Lawn & Garden   20XX

Availability

- Available to start immediately and work any day/shift needed, including early mornings, afternoons, evenings, weekends, and holidays.
- Comfortable with full-time, part-time or temporary work.

SELENA MARTIN
Automotive Fluid Technician
Mailing Address • Home Phone • Cell Phone • Email Address

Capabilities

- Changing automatic transmission fluid, including replacing filters and pan gaskets.
- Changing manual transmission fluid.
- Changing differential fluid and cleaning drain plugs.
- Changing transfer case fluid on four-wheel drive vehicles.
- Cleaning fuel systems, including fuel injectors, intake valves, and combustion chambers.
- Inspecting the under hood fuel system and air intake system.
- Inspecting the radiator, hose and heater core, pressure testing the system, and radiator cap, and changing the radiator fluid.
- Replacing headlights, tail lights, turn signals, and brake lights.
- Inspecting and replacing PCV valves and fan belts.
- Changing air filters and wiper blades.

Education

- DOWNTOWN TECHNICAL SCHOOL, 20XX–20XX
  Graduated with a focus on automotive and other shop courses. Completed Automotive 11 and 12 and finished with the 3rd highest mark in Grade 12 out of a class of 22.

Recommendation

- "Selena showed a tremendous interest while in my class. She was always eager to learn and did so quickly and easily. She also demonstrated patience and aimed to finish the job correctly, even if it meant she didn't finish first. Safety was always a priority with her."
  - Anthony Butterfield, Automotive Teacher, Downtown Technical School

Work Experience

- FOSTER MOTORS, Summer 20XX
  Worked full-time in an uncle's auto shop for 10 weeks. Cleaned and organized the shop, helped with minor repairs, and ordered parts when needed.

- URBAN CHRONICLE NEWSPAPER, 20XX–20XX
  Delivered newspapers in the community twice a week. Managed a route ranging from 225 to 275 papers, and met every deadline.

CELL PHONE
EMAIL ADDRESS
MAILING ADDRESS

DYLAN MCCARTNEY
Apprentice Roofer

PROFILE

6 months' summer experience as a full-time roofing assistant. Gained skill and experience in the installation, repair, and replacement of residential flat roof and sloped roof systems. Knowledge of single-ply and built-up roofs. Completed approximately 50 homes.

Skilled in the application of a variety of roofing materials including tar and gravel, asphalt shingles, dimensional shingles, engineered rubber, sheet metal flashings, and galvanized steel. Applied waterproof coatings as required.

Maintain excellent physical condition; comfortable with frequent heavy lifting and working at heights. Experienced with most hand and power tools. Able to provide own hand tools.

Available for scheduling on a full-time or part-time basis. Able to work any days needed including weekends and holidays. Comfortable with long hours.

RECOMMENDATIONS

"Dylan was a terrific help to us over the past two summers. He's very dependable; he was never late for jobs and didn't miss a single day of work. He's got a great work ethic; he was always willing to work overtime to complete a job. And the quality of his work improved quite quickly; the customers were very happy. If I wasn't retiring this year, I would have offered him a permanent position with us."   - PROJECT MANAGER, GARRISON ROOFING SERVICES

"Thank you so much for the wonderful job you did on my roof! I was a bit worried about the potential for mess and noise, but John and Dylan were very professional and considerate. They kept the mess to a minimum, warned me before they made a lot of noise, and finished the job sooner than expected. I was extremely pleased with their service and work, and I will gladly recommend your company to my neighbours."   - SATISFIED CUSTOMER

EMPLOYMENT

Roofing Assistant • Garrison Roofing Services   Summers 20XX / 20XX

Dishwasher • Blue Shores Seafood Restaurant   20XX–20XX

EDUCATION

High School Diploma • Courtenay Senior Secondary School   20XX–20XX

WAREHOUSE WORKER

16 Months' Warehouse Experience • Cherry Picker Licence • Own Safety Boots

Sheri Mansfield • Mailing Address • Home Phone • Cell Phone • Email Address

Milton Labour Services, 20XX–Present

Completed 50+ temporary placements ranging from 1 day to 1 month for this local employment agency specializing in construction, warehouse, and light industrial staff.

✓ **Essence Organic Food.** Fulfilled a 1-month assignment to cover for an injured warehouse worker. Sorted and packed a variety of fruits and vegetables and prepared for shipping. Handled containers weighing up to 11 kg each.

✓ **Home and Garden Superstore.** Participated in the setup of a 55,000 square foot retail store and warehouse prior to opening. Worked as part of a large crew to install a 24-foot pallet rack system over the course of 3 weeks.

✓ **Food-Valu Grocery Corporation.** Worked for 2 weeks in a cold storage facility loading and unloading pallets of packaged food products. Handled 20 kg boxes. Received letter of appreciation from the warehouse manager.

✓ **National Auto Parts.** Completed a 3-week assignment to batch-pick orders of auto parts in a 50,000 square foot warehouse using cherry pickers and powered pallet jacks. Earned cherry picker forklift licence in the first week.

✓ **Monster Media Source.** Picked DVD and CD orders in a 15,000 square foot warehouse while covering a 2-week vacation. Selected to return later in the year and cover for an injured warehouse worker for an additional week.

✓ **Gemini Restoration Services.** Performed general clean up and restoration work for 10 days in a 30,000 square foot warehouse damaged by flooding. Used industrial-strength vacuum pumps, air movers, air scrubbers, and dehumidifiers.

✓ **National Inventory Auditors.** Completed a 1-day assignment counting stock with a handheld scanner at a dry goods warehouse, and subsequently asked to come back for several more day jobs in warehouses throughout the region.

✓ **Furniture Emporium.** Assisted in the setup of a 20,000 square foot distribution centre for this national retailer. Worked as part of a 25-person crew for 1 month to install racking and shelving, and receive and unload merchandise shipments.

Available 24/7

RINGO SCULLY
Home Phone: 555.555.5555
Cell Phone: 555.555.5555
Mailing Address Line 1
Mailing Address Line 2
Email Address

Dear Mr. Marley:

With over 2 years' experience performing a variety of general labour duties for my father's company, including residential window washing, I feel qualified and excited to apply for the part-time window washer position as advertised on the website of *The Daily Record.* I am comfortable working at heights and using ladders, and have a perfect safety record. My work experience and skills are as follows:

SCULLY HOME & LAWN SERVICES, June 20XX – Present

Worked part-time around my school schedule to provide the following home labour services, mostly to the residents of our 155-unit housing complex:

- Hand-washing windows
- Pressure-washing houses and driveways
- Hand-washing vehicles
- Painting fences and decks
- Mowing lawns
- Clearing gutters and drains
- Raking leaves
- Shovelling snow

I am currently a part-time student at Dickerson Regional Alternative School where I am enrolled in Grade 11 courses Monday to Thursday mornings from 8:30 to 12:00. Therefore, I am available for work anytime after 12:30 from Monday to Thursday, and anytime on Fridays, Saturdays, Sundays, and holidays.

Part of my career development at Dickerson School included taking training courses to prepare me for employment. I completed a 7-hour course in first aid and a 4-hour course on handling dangerous materials, and earned the following certificates:

- First Aid Level 1 with CPR – expires December 31, 20XX
- Workplace Hazardous Materials Management – expires June 15, 20XX

I just recently passed my driver's licence exam and have access to a reliable vehicle for work. I have never been late for a job, and I have 3 letters of recommendation from residents in my complex that were extremely happy with the quality of my work.

Mr. Marley, I am confident I can be an excellent window washer for your company. Thank you for considering my application, and I look forward to hearing from you.

Sincerely,

Ringo Scully

ALTERNATIVE RESUMES FAQ//
SHOULD I INCLUDE A JOB FROM WHICH I WAS FIRED?

Getting fired is nothing to be ashamed of. It happens to many people and can be a learning experience.

Although being fired does present some challenges for your job search, it doesn't mean that no one will interview you. You will have to give some thought to how you handle this experience on your resume, but with hard work and perseverance, you will find success in a new job.

If you were fired from a job, you need to decide if you want to include it on your resume. Although you should never actually state on your resume that you were terminated, expect interviewers to ask why you left all your previous jobs. Therefore, if you decide to include a job you were fired from, be prepared to explain the details.

Advantages and Disadvantages

If you include the job on your resume, you can claim the skills and experience you gained there and don't have to minimize or hide any of your qualifications. However, you will probably have to explain the nature of your departure in the interview. If you leave the job off your resume, you don't have to answer questions about the termination, but you also can't claim the experience you gained. Ask yourself whether the upside of the employer knowing you have that experience outweighs the downside of having to explain why you left. Most likely, that will depend on what other experience or qualifications you have.

If you held three short-term jobs and you were fired from one, and it's not relevant to the job you're applying for now, it may be best to leave it off. The hiring manager will see the relevant experience from your other jobs, and you can avoid discussing why you were fired. However, if you were let go from the only job you've had, and you were there for two years, leaving it off would be detrimental. You would appear to have no work experience at all, and you'd have a difficult time marketing your skills if you can't say where you developed them.

Resumes vs. Application Forms

Resumes and application forms are different. Resumes are a job-seeker's tool used to advertise qualifications in order to secure an interview. That means you can choose what to include and what not to – whatever markets you most effectively. Application forms are an employer's tool used to bring consistency to their hiring practices. You need to include all past employment on application forms and agree at the bottom that the information is complete. If you don't, and the employer finds out, you may get fired again.

Deciding whether to include a terminated job on your resume is a difficult decision and there is no right or wrong answer. Just remember you have nothing to be embarrassed about and don't automatically feel like you have to hide it or no one will hire you. Focus on proving to your next employer that you learned from your mistakes and you'll do everything you can to not let them happen again.

| Mailing Address | **DAVID TANAKA** | Home Phone |
| Email Address | **Residential & Commercial Furniture Mover** | Cell Phone |

KEY QUALIFICATIONS

Driving and Delivery Experience

- Delivered pizzas and beverages on a full-time basis for Lombardi's Pizzeria from March to December in 20XX. Accustomed to ensuring items arrived in perfect condition.
- Over 2 years' experience driving standard and automatic transmission vehicles. Earned a Class C driver's licence in May 20XX; currently studying for a Class B licence.
- No restrictions added to driver's licence. No tickets, fines, or warnings.

Customer Service Skills

- Served up to 40 customers per shift at their homes while employed as a delivery driver with Lombardi's for 10 months. Consistently strived for customer satisfaction.
- Rated as "above average" for communication and "excellent" for customer service by the General Manager of Lombardi's on an October 20XX performance evaluation.
- Letter of recommendation from the General Manager of Lombardi's states, "I didn't get a single complaint about David's service the entire time he was here."

Knowledge of the Region

- Lived in several different parts of the region. Went to school in the Hayfield, Gratton, and Seaside districts, gaining excellent geographic knowledge of the area.
- Delivered pizzas for 10 months in a 10-km radius of Lombardi's Pizzeria.
- Comfortable using handheld GPS units to navigate directions.

Excellent Physical Condition

- Participated in the Andrea Rowland Run for Human Rights the last 2 years, successfully completing the 10-mile marathon each year. Active in long distance running for 4 years.
- Member of school football team in Grades 11 and 12, and wrestling team in Grade 11.
- Played organized soccer in the Hayfield Youth Soccer Association for 5 seasons.

Reliable and Professional

- October 20XX performance review from Lombardi's shows no lates or absences.
- Letter of recommendation from the General Manager of Lombardi's states, "He was very reliable and always acted in a professional manner." Full copy available upon request.
- Grade 12 report card from Hayfield Secondary School shows no lates or absences.

EMPLOYMENT

Delivery Driver, FT	Lombardi's Pizzeria, City	20XX

EDUCATION

High School Diploma	Hayfield Secondary School, City	20XX

Lucy Griffith
Cell Phone • Home Phone • Email Address
Mailing Address

SHEET METAL WORKER: Apprentice/Assistant

Motivated and determined high school graduate seeking an apprentice or assistant position in a sheet metal shop. Completed the Introduction to Sheet Metal course at TTI with a grade of 96%, highest in the class. Mechanically inclined with top marks in several trades courses. Excellent physical condition; member of school track and field team in Grades 11 and 12. Clean driver's licence with access to a reliable vehicle. Perfect attendance record at school for the last 2 years.

EDUCATION

TRADES TRAINING INSTITUTE, City   January 20XX – May 20XX

- Selected from among 1,000 high school trades students in the region to join a class of 20 in the Advanced Trades Learning Program (ATLP) for the spring semester. Selection criteria included success in previous trades courses, suitable results from a school career exploration program, references from trades teachers, and a personal interview with the TTI instructor.
- Attended Trades Training Institute 4 mornings per week to take the post-secondary course Introduction to Sheet Metal, while completing other academic requirements for high school graduation in the afternoons and on Fridays.
- Researched the current structure, scope, and demands of the industry while learning to fabricate basic sheet metal products such as j-hooks, tool trays, and 90-degree elbows. Learned the safe and appropriate operation of brake presses, plate rolls, and plate shears. Developed the ability to read blueprints and prepare orthographic drawings.
- Earned the top grade in the class, 96%, with the second highest being 89%. Simultaneously maintained a B+ average in all other Grade 12 classes.

HOOVER SENIOR SECONDARY SCHOOL, City   June 20XX

- Graduated with an Honours Diploma and an average grade of 89%. Completed every trades course, including Metalwork, Woodwork, Drafting, and Auto Mechanics, as well as computer classes such as Information Technology, Business Applications, and Graphic Design.
- Participated in a comprehensive career exploration program as part of a Planning 10 course. Completed self-assessments related to skills, interests, work values, and personality type to determine suitable career choices. All indicators pointed to a career in trades.

REFERENCE

"Lucy proved to be a very conscientious, dedicated, and bright student during my Introduction to Sheet Metal class. She takes her career planning and training very seriously and I am confident that will benefit her tremendously. She is also a very gifted learner, isn't afraid to ask questions, and strives to do all tasks to the best of her ability. She has a bright future ahead."
        - BRAD STENOWICH, TTI INSTRUCTOR (FULL LETTER AVAILABLE UPON REQUEST)

EMPLOYMENT

PALLADIUM CINEMAS, City	Cashier	February 20XX – Present
GEORGIO'S CAFÉ, City	Cashier	June 20XX – September 20XX

STEVE ROBERTSON, HVAC Technician
Mailing Address • Home Phone • Cell Phone • Email Address

CAPABILITIES

- Installing complete HVAC systems in residential, commercial, and industrial facilities.
- Disassembling, repairing, and replacing parts such as valves, compressors, seals, belts, motors, gaskets, evaporators, bearings, condensers, air filters, and electronic controls.
- Conducting tests and measurements to detect gas leaks and analyze chemicals, and taking action to correct the situation.
- Adjusting system controls and equipment to maintain required environmental conditions.

CLASSROOM TRAINING

HVAC Technician Certificate
Thompson Regional Trades Academy, City, Sep 20XX – Jun 20XX

- Completed all 8 required courses and graduated in the top 10% of the class with an average final grade of 88% and a letter of recommendation from the course instructor.
- Studied all aspects of installing, repairing, and maintaining electric, oil, gas and propane heating, ventilation, air conditioning, and refrigeration systems.
- Developed knowledge of carbon monoxide detectors, combustion analyzers, refrigerant detectors, digital clamp meters, digital multimeters, thermometers, and manometers.

WORK EXPERIENCE PRACTICUM

HVAC Assistant
Frederickson HVAC Services, City, May 20XX

- Completed a 2-week, 80-hour work experience practicum organized through Thompson Regional Trades Academy as part of the HVAC certificate program.
- Performed routine repair and maintenance tasks under the supervision of a Senior HVAC Technician at commercial and industrial sites such as stores, offices, and warehouses.
- Received a rating of "excellent" on performance review and a letter of recommendation signed by the Senior HVAC Technician and the General Manager.

EMPLOYMENT HISTORY

Restoration Worker
Browning Restoration Services, City, Jun 20XX – Present

- Provided disaster restoration services in residential and commercial buildings affected by fire, smoke, and water damage. Worked on teams ranging from 3 to 15.
- Operated all relevant equipment including vacuum pumps, air scrubbers, air movers, and dehumidifiers. Removed damaged materials and performed light demolition work.
- Worked full-time in the summers and part-time on weekends while attending high school and Thompson Regional Trades Academy.

EMPLOYMENT QUALIFICATIONS

Excellent Knowledge of Downtown – Delivered pizza throughout the region for almost 1 year. Accustomed to reading maps and locating obscure addresses. Capable of locating most downtown streets and areas without assistance.

10 Years' Biking Experience – Serious biker with a passion for mountain and long-distance biking. Own a Reynolds RZ-40 city sport bike and a Whistler M-6500 mountain bike.

Physically Fit – Lift free weights and cardio exercise 3 times a week. Excellent stamina, strength, and conditioning. Willing and able to work in all weather conditions.

Able to Work Independently – Succeeded in both previous delivery positions while working alone. Self-motivated to work hard and beat deadlines. Trusted with cash and receipts.

Safety-Oriented – No accidents or safety incidents in two previous delivery jobs.

- - - - - - - - - - - - - - -

ABBEY WATTS
Mailing Address Line 1
Mailing Address Line 2
Postal / Zip

BIKE COURIER
Home Phone Number
Cell Phone Number
Email Address

- - - - - - - - - - - - - - -

EMPLOYMENT EXPERIENCE

Delivery Driver, Pizza Station   20XX – 20XX

Delivered pizzas to businesses and residences within a 10-km radius of the restaurant. Navigated downtown traffic to deliver within specified time frames. Constantly monitored by company management with customer surveys and a clock in/out system to ensure deliveries were made on time and service was acceptable. Accepted cash, credit card, and bank card payments. Used personal cell phone to keep in contact with restaurant management.

Route Carrier, *West Coast Chronicle*   20XX – 20XX

Delivered early morning newspapers before school 6 days a week. Route varied in size from 90 to 140 homes, requiring anywhere from 1 to 2 hours. Consistently met delivery deadline of 7:00am. Earned written commendation from the Regional Route Manager after covering for another carrier during an extensive illness. Received 2 letters of recommendation from customers and several thank-you cards and tips during each holiday season.

ASSEMBLY · SET-UP · FACTORY · STOCK ROOM · WAREHOUSE

ROOFING · CONCRETE · CONSTRUCTION · WOODWORKING · CARPENTRY

PREM NEHRU
General Labourer

2 years as a General Labourer with specific experience in painting, concrete, construction, roofing, rubbish removal, and maintenance. Available to start immediately and work any hours and days needed. Flexible with a full-time or part-time schedule. Perfect safety record on the job. Valid driver's licence with a reliable late-model vehicle and an excellent driving record.

WORK CHARACTERISTICS

STRONG WORK ETHIC – Frequently worked overtime when needed, often up to 14-hour shifts.
VERY RELIABLE – Only missed 1 day of work in 2 years; references will verify dependability.
PHYSICALLY FIT – Comfortable with frequent heavy lifting and standing for long periods.
ABLE TO WORK AT GREAT HEIGHTS – Experienced with 12-foot ladders and rooftop work.
MECHANICALLY INCLINED – Skilled with most hand and power tools.
SAFETY CONSCIOUS – Never had an accident, incident, or injury on the job.

WORKPLACE CERTIFICATION

OCCUPATIONAL FIRST AID LEVEL 2 – First Responder Society   Jun 20XX
CPR LEVEL 2 – First Responder Society   Jun 20XX
WORKPLACE HAZARDOUS MATERIALS – Workplace Safety Board   Mar 20XX
OCCUPATIONAL FIRST AID LEVEL 1 – Avis Medical Training   Nov 20XX
CPR LEVEL 1 – Avis Medical Training   Nov 20XX
WORKPLACE CONFLICT RESOLUTION – Keller Alternative School   Oct 20XX

EMPLOYMENT HISTORY

RESIDENTIAL EXTERIOR PAINTER – Tupper Painting   May 20XX – Sep 20XX
GENERAL LABOURER, CONCRETE – Dennis Boyd Contracting   Mar 20XX – May 20XX
RUBBISH REMOVER – That's Rubbish!   Aug 20XX – Mar 20XX
ROOFING ASSISTANT – Roofing Experts   Jun 20XX – Aug 20XX
GENERAL LABOURER, CONSTRUCTION – Marvin Contractors   Oct 20XX – Jun 20XX
MAINTENANCE WORKER – Kiel Auto Parts Ltd.   Aug 20XX – Oct 20XX

Mailing Address   Telephone / Email

MARLA BAUSTON
16 Months' Experience in Order Picking and Shipping/Receiving

EMPLOYMENT HISTORY

Order Picker, Shipper/Receiver
SUNSET DISTRIBUTION, 20XX–20XX

- 60,000 sf. warehouse with 24-foot racking
- Primary products: apparel and accessories
- Operated forklifts, reach trucks & power jacks
- Earned forklift and reach truck licence
- Member of Health & Safety Committee
- Participated in a government safety inspection
- Earned Emergency First Aid Level 1 certificate
- Perfect personal safety record

Order Picker, Shipper/Receiver
FRANCIS FOODS, 20XX

- 50,000 sf. warehouse with 24-foot racking
- Operated cherry pickers and pallet jacks
- Assisted with cold storage shipping/receiving
- Participated in a manual inventory count
- Used a baler to recycle flattened cardboard
- Rearranged product lines to reduce old stock
- Earned WHMIS certificate

Stock Clerk
FOOD BARN, 20XX–20XX

- Worked in grocery and produce departments
- Merchandised products using planograms
- Assisted customers with locating items
- Used pallet jacks to transport skids
- Trained 3 new stock clerks
- Used balers and box-cutters on a daily basis

Sales Clerk
TRENDSETTERS, 20XX

- Hired on a temporary basis for Christmas
- Assisted customers with locating and selecting clothing, footwear, and accessories
- Merchandised wall and floor product displays
- Operated a cash register and bank terminal
- Listened to customers and resolved concerns

ADDITIONAL QUALIFICATIONS

- **Physically fit.** Exercise regularly to keep in excellent physical condition. Former track and field champion in school. Comfortable with frequent heavy lifting and working at heights.

- **Proven team player.** Member of school basketball team for 2 seasons and track and field for 1. Played organized softball for 5 years. Get along well with all team members, coaches, co-workers, and supervisors.

- **Enjoy manual labour.** Experienced in order picking, shipping and receiving, warehouse and stock work. Mechanically inclined; able to learn the proper use of tools, equipment, and machinery quickly and easily.

- **Excellent leadership skills.** Completed leadership courses in Grades 10, 11, and 12. Selected to train new staff members at Food Barn. Elected captain of basketball team.

- **Strong communication skills.** Fluent in English and Dutch. Conversant in German, having completed up to Grade 10. Capable of following instructions easily.

- **Open availability.** Able to start immediately and work any days or shifts needed, including mornings, afternoons, evenings, graveyards, weekends, and holidays. Willing to accept either a full-time or part-time position.

- **High school diploma.** Graduated from Buchanan High School in 20XX. Earned a Certificate of Outstanding Attendance in Grade 11. Completed several shop courses such as Woodworking, Metal Work, and Drafting.

- **Driver's license.** Valid Class B driver's license with 2 years' driving experience and a clean record. Own a reliable vehicle.

MAILING ADDRESS · **EMAIL ADDRESS** · **PHONE NUMBER**

OFFICE AND TECHNICAL

Chapter 4

This chapter provides resumes for common entry-level office jobs such as Receptionist, File Clerk, and Office Administrator.

This chapter also includes related positions such as Medical Office Assistant, Cash Office Clerk, and Accounting Clerk. Technical jobs such as Website Designer, Network Developer, and Social Media Consultant are also represented here. The chapter begins by examining the resume of a Temporary Office Administrator, and goes on to provide another fifteen resumes and two FAQ tips.

DESIGNING MY ALTERNATIVE RESUME//

SUNITA CHAWDRA : TEMPORARY OFFICE ADMINISTRATOR

Sunita Chawdra has sixteen months' work experience as a temporary office administrator through a local employment agency that provides contract office staff to companies and non-profit organizations.

She performed admirably for this placement agency and has excellent computer skills. She did not graduate from high school. Her goal is to secure a permanent position in an office. Sunita's resume can be viewed on the following page.

1. Objective

Sunita gained experience in administration, reception, and accounting while employed with Werner & Lowe, and she is targeting a position in any of these areas. Rather than appearing old-fashioned by using a conventional objective statement, or limiting herself to one position by stating a job title as an objective, Sunita uses these three job functions to best represent her flexibility and expertise.

2. Experience

Since she essentially had several employers over the last sixteen months, and it isn't feasible to list them all with complete details, Sunita focuses her work experience section on the placements where she received written praise for her performance. She selects the top five and briefly outlines the scope of the position, her accomplishments, and the recognition she received.

Describing the scope of her position is important because the reader will likely know little or nothing about the environment she worked in. Using actual numbers whenever possible provides a framework for the reader to visualize her capacity and judge her competence. Her achievements and recognition are equally valuable because they show the reader that she worked hard, added value to the company, and impressed her supervisors.

3. Computer and Language skills

Sunita gained knowledge and experience with several operating systems and software programs through employment, school, and self-study. She knows that current computer skills are critical for office administrators and must be included on her resume. In addition to listing them at the bottom, Sunita integrates her technical expertise into her work achievements to emphasize her proficiency.

Advanced language skills are in demand by many employers. Sunita is fluent in three languages. Although she doesn't know whether a particular employer requires fluency in two or more languages unless they state it in a job ad, she includes it on her resume regardless of the company or position she targets because it is a universally appreciated qualification.

WHAT'S MISSING?

Her lack of a high school diploma may concern potential employers, so Sunita leaves the education section off and focuses her resume on her impressive experience. The topic will likely come up in an interview but Sunita feels she can handle the high school question better in person.

SUNITA CHAWDRA
❶ **Administration • Reception • Accounting**

Home Phone • Cell Phone • Fax Number • Email Address • Mailing Address

WERNER & LOWE TEMPORARY PERSONNEL ❷   20XX–Present
Fulfilled a variety of temporary assignments with businesses and non-profit organizations throughout the region including, but not limited to, the following:

- **National Cancer Society**   **2 weeks**
  Managed the reception area at a national head office with 65 staff. Greeted up to 50 visitors per day, operated a 10-line telephone system, and routed up to 400 calls per day.

  Sunita was a standout – thank you! She stepped into a high-pressure role with little support due to a wave of influenza that plagued our office, and she proved to be extremely competent and professional. We would welcome her back in a heartbeat! - VICE PRESIDENT OF OPERATIONS

- **Bower McCaffrey Insurance Corporation**   **1 week**
  Supported an 8-person accounting department with year-end invoice preparation, distribution, and filing. Generated and mailed over 1,000 invoices, and reorganized the entire filing system.

  Not only was she punctual and reliable, she was also very organized and detail-oriented and we really needed that for this job. Thank you for sending her and we hope that we can work with her again in the near future. - CONTROLLER

- **Harrison Region Humane Society**   **10 days**
  Provided reception and administrative services for an office with 35 staff and a board of directors. Managed a 4-line phone system that received 150 calls per day. Prepared several Excel reports.

  We were really pleased with the performance of Sunita Chawdra, who covered for our receptionist during her vacation. She demonstrated excellent service and communication skills, and we even received two compliments from visitors. She would be welcome back anytime. – FACILITY MANAGER

- **Stern and Goldberg, Environmental Consultants**   **2 weeks**
  Utilized PowerPoint skills to develop a complex and technical 120-page presentation for the Managing Partner. Created and included over 50 multifaceted graphs and charts.

  I appreciate you assigning Sunita Chawdra to our office to assist me with a very important PowerPoint presentation. Not only did she have the technical skills I required for this project, but she also displayed superior patience during a very stressful time. – MANAGING PARTNER

- **Compassion International**   **1 week**
  Co-managed the reception area for an office with over 100 staff. Operated a 12-line phone system, routing 300 calls per day. Coordinated the pickup of over 100 packages each day.

  Sunita was the best contract staffer you have ever sent us. She stepped into a challenging situation and performed admirably. We were most impressed with her presentation skills, as she really made our guests feel welcome in our office. –MANAGER OF OPERATIONS

❸ COMPUTER SKILLS

80 wpm • Windows, Mac • MS Office Suite: Word, Excel, PowerPoint, Publisher, Access, Outlook
Internet Explorer, Firefox, Opera, Safari, Chrome • Dreamweaver, FrontPage • Lotus Notes

Fluent in English, Hindi, and Farsi.

DALE GREENWOOD
OBJECTIVE: Office Administrator, Bowen & Green Corp.

EMPLOYER NEEDS	CANDIDATE QUALIFICATIONS
Two years' experience in office administration.	20XX–20XX JENSEN, HOLMES & RUTHERFORD Employed as a full-time billing clerk in the six-person administration department of a large legal firm. Managed all aspects of billing including reviewing time sheets, entering information in customer databases, preparing and mailing itemized invoices, and answering client questions. Also provided daily reception relief. 20XX HORIZON LEASING INC. Worked as a full-time, temporary receptionist and administrator in a five-person office. Answered telephones and relayed messages, coordinated mail and courier deliveries, drafted correspondence, ordered office supplies, and entered data in the computer system.
Diploma or certificate in office administration.	20XX–20XX DIPLOMA OF GENERAL STUDIES Graduated from a two-year, full-time diploma program through Greg Stanton Community College. Completed several business courses, including Financial Management, Marketing, Business Technology, Management Accounting, Micro Economics, Macro Economics, and Business Communications.
Excellent computer skills with 60 wpm keyboard speed.	Completed workshops in Word, Excel, Access, and PowerPoint at Stanton College. Took computer classes in high school, including Keyboarding 11/12 and Information Technology 11/12. Current keyboard speed is 65 wpm, as tested in March 20XX.
Database experience.	Used Maximizer software on a regular basis with Jensen, Holmes & Rutherford. Limited experience with an in-house database system with Horizon Leasing. Trained in MS Access.
Ability to work in a high-stress environment.	Consistently met firm semi-monthly and monthly deadlines with the law firm. Worked closely with the rest of the administration team to ensure team deadlines were met. Received praise from a senior partner for ability to succeed in a high-pressure environment.
Ability to work with confidential information.	Accustomed to handling highly sensitive and confidential customer information with both previous employers. Trusted to maintain the integrity of the company.
Bilingual an asset.	Fluent in verbal and written English and French.

MAILING ADDRESS   ·   HOME PHONE   ·   CELL PHONE   ·   EMAIL ADDRESS

MELISSA BARCLAY
Website Developer/Designer

WEB DESIGN

HTML / XHTML

CSS

ASP – VBScript

SQL

PHP

Dreamweaver
Programming
Language

ColdFusion

IIS/Unix Servers

APPLICATIONS

Adobe Dreamweaver

Adobe Fireworks

Adobe Flash

Adobe Photoshop

Adobe Illustrator

Adobe Acrobat

Corel Draw

QuarkXPress

MS Office

Lotus SmartSuite

FTP

CuteFTP

FileZilla

SmartFTP

FREELANCE

WEBSITE DESIGNER, 20XX–Present

- Develop websites of varying scopes and sizes for corporate and non-profit clients. Create and implement enhancements for existing sites.
- Plan site structures and navigation layouts.
- Utilize XHTML and CSS coding, complying with all current established standards.
- Focus on search engine optimization and browser compatibility.
- Design Flash presentations.
- Plan and create email newsletters.
- Provide ongoing site management as needed.
- Full project portfolio available upon request.

GRAPHIC DESIGNER, 20XX–20XX

- Provided graphic design services for corporate clients, most notably several weekly community newspapers including *Real Estate Review*, *Auto Seller*, and *The Compton Leader*.
- Collaborated with the production teams on the layout and design of all advertisements.
- Met strict weekly deadlines.

COMPUTER TECHNICIAN, 20XX–20XX

- Setup and configured new PC systems, installed and upgraded hardware and software, tested systems and applications, diagnosed problems, setup wired and wireless local area networks, and provided technical guidance to clients.

TRAINING

Diploma in Web Design and Development, 20XX
Art & Design Technical Institute

Certificate in Graphic Design, 20XX
Art & Design Technical Institute

BROWSERS

Internet Explorer

Mozilla Firefox

Opera

Google Chrome

EMAIL

Outlook

Outlook Express

Web-based Email

OPERATING SYSTEM

Windows 95–>

Mac OS 7–>

Linux

HARDWARE

RAM

CD / DVD Drives

Hard Drives

Multimedia Cards

Sound Cards

Video Cards

USB Ports

Printers

Scanners

External Drives

DWIGHT SANDERS / Cash Office Clerk

Mailing Address • Home Phone • Email Address

CASH MANAGEMENT SKILLS & EXPERIENCE

Cash Office

- Replace cash office associate at Shop Mart for vacation relief and other occasions as needed.
- Count and prepare all cash register trays prior to the start of cashier shifts.
- Reconcile previous day's cash, bank receipts, cheques, and coupons to computer totals.
- Research and correct, or provide explanations for, all cash or paper discrepancies.
- Total all cash and receipts and prepare bank deposits; calculate and call in coin orders.
- Verify identity of armoured car staff and complete secure exchange of deposits for coin orders.
- Monitor employee access to cash office; follow all store security policies and procedures.
- Maintain stock of bank deposit forms, register tape, and cashier float authorization sheets.
- Verify total cash and coin in store safe and sign off with a member of management.

Cashier

- Over 2 years' cash handling experience as a cashier in both high and low-volume retail outlets.
- Operate computerized cash register systems, accepting all tender types as payment.
- Perform line/transaction voids, refunds, exchanges, discounts, and tax exemptions accurately.
- Reconcile cash and receipts to computer and bank terminal printouts at the end of each shift.
- Accurate history of balancing to the penny; largest variance in 2 years has been 75¢.

FINANCIAL EDUCATION

Post-Secondary

- Completed Financial Management and Managerial Accounting classes at Caulfield College.
- Placed in the top 5% of the class, with final grades of 91% and 96% respectively.
- Plan to begin the Certified Financial Accountant's night school program beginning Sep 20XX.

High School

- Graduated in June 20XX from Dr. Nicholas Brayer Senior Secondary.
- Successfully completed Accounting 11 and 12, Advanced Accounting 12, Marketing 11 and 12, Computers in Business 11, and Entrepreneurship 12.
- Oversaw the accounting and reporting functions of a hypothetical company during a 3-month group project in Entrepreneurship 12.

COMPUTER SKILLS

- Experienced with Windows and Mac systems up to and including the latest versions.
- 2 years' experience with MS Office, including Word, Excel, Access, Outlook, and PowerPoint.
- Trained in Simply Accounting and MYOB business accounting software.
- Skilled in Internet research, email etiquette, and file management.

EMPLOYMENT HISTORY

- Cashier / Cash Office Associate, Shop Mart, City   December 20XX – Present
- Sales Associate, Footwear Factory, City   November 20XX – December 20XX

Medical Office Assistant Diploma, Harrington Technical College, City   20XX

Graduated 2nd in the class from this 9-month, full-time program. Earned recognition for high academic achievement in Medical Transcription and Medical Terminology courses. 1st in the class to secure a 3-week practicum placement with a medical clinic. Courses included:

Intro to Pharmacology	Medical Clinical Assistance	Laboratory Procedures
Medical Administration	Office Management	Medical Transcription
Medical Terminology	Medical Disorders	First Aid with CPR

Business Administration Certificate, Barker School of Business, City   20XX

Graduated 4th in a class of 20. Developed intermediate-level skills in MS Word and Excel. Delivered a 10-minute PowerPoint presentation to the school faculty. Courses included:

Intro to Accounting	Intro to MS Office	Small Business Management
Credit Management	Business Law	Intro to Marketing

Maryelle Woodward
MEDICAL OFFICE ASSISTANT

Home Phone   •   Cell Phone   •   Email Address   •   Mailing Address

---

Jefferson Gateway Medical Clinic, City   20XX

Completed a 3-week practicum in this busy walk-in clinic. Gained experience in patient service, clinical assistance, medical billing, hospital communications, and general office management. Received letter of recommendation from the Office Manager:

"Maryelle demonstrated exceptional communication skills when dealing with our patients in the often stressful atmosphere here in our clinic. She was warm, patient, and caring even during the busiest periods. In addition, her computer skills were called upon to troubleshoot minor concerns. Overall, Maryelle has the personality, attitude, and intelligence to make a great Medical Office Assistant and we wish her well in her career."

Reynolds & Carrington Insurance Brokers, City   20XX–20XX

Employed for 18 months prior to the managing partner's retirement. Started as the part-time receptionist and promoted to full-time office administrator after 2 months. Operated a 6-line computerized telephone system, designed an electronic scheduler for appointments, utilized ACCPAC to maintain accounts payable/receivable, developed a customer database using Access, and liaised with insurance companies. Excerpt from letter of recommendation:

"...her maturity and high level of professionalism were appreciated by the entire team. Maryelle was reliable, always anxious to help out in any area, and always skilled enough to do so successfully. She is extremely organized with a strong eye for detail. Maryelle will definitely be an asset to any company that hires her, and we wish her much success!"

ALTERNATIVE RESUMES FAQ//
WHAT SHOULD I INCLUDE ABOUT MY WORK EXPERIENCE?

Work experience is usually the most important qualification on a resume. Nothing else shows your ability to succeed at a job more than the fact that you've done it before.

However, a consistent problem with resumes is the lack of significant detail when describing past employment. Most people focus on their job title and duties. But there are, in fact, seven types of information that can be included, as Kerry Turnbull shows on the following page:

1. Company Name and Description

Although you're familiar with the companies you worked for, the reader may not be. And if they don't have a clue what your former employer does, it can be hard to understand your resume. What do they do? What are their products or services? Are they local, regional, national, or international? What are their annual sales? Are they a division of a larger company? What location did you work at?

2. Employment Dates

Include start and end dates for each job on your resume. If you held more than one position with a company, include the overall start and end dates by the company name and add the dates for each individual position beside the job title. This makes it clear how long you were employed by the company. State years or months/years, and be consistent throughout the resume.

3. Job Title

Include every job you held with the company. Showing past promotions is a terrific way of demonstrating your value to an employer.

4. Scope

Simply stating "Assistant Manager" isn't enough, because the Assistant Manager of a fifteen-person store with $2 million in sales is very different from the Assistant Manager of a five-person store with $500 thousand in sales. Think about what you were accountable for, and explain the size and scope of that accountability using actual figures.

5. Duties and Responsibilities

What did you do? What job functions were you responsible for? Include duties you performed regularly and those that were less frequent. Focus on tasks that are relevant to your job target.

6. Accomplishments

This is one of the most important parts of a resume. It's fine that they know you're a call centre supervisor, but how great a call centre supervisor are you? This will tell them. Think of examples that demonstrate how well you did your job and what impact you had on the company. Consider key performance indicators for your job and include actual figures if possible. How much did you grow revenues or cut costs, and how did you achieve it?

7. Awards and Recognition

Similar to accomplishments, describing how your performance was regarded by your company or industry can reveal how well you did your job. These can be significant because rather than you stating how great you did, a third party is confirming it. Consider awards and contests you won, testimonials you received, bonuses you earned, and major projects you were selected for. Always put the recognition in context. Rather than stating "Won district award," expand on it by stating, "Won district sales award for generating the highest sales in 20XX out of 35 eligible associates."

KERRY TURNBULL
Call Centre Supervisor

MAILING ADDRESS • HOME PHONE • CELL PHONE • EMAIL ADDRESS

MAVERICK COMMUNICATION CORPORATION, City   **20XX–Present**
Global leader in the call centre industry with $800M in annual revenues, approximately 6,000 employees, and inbound and outbound operations throughout North America and Europe.

Supervisor of Customer Care, Computer Town • 20XX–Present
Oversee the operation of a 26-agent inbound customer care department servicing the Computer Town account. Manage all aspects of staff and team development including the coordination of new-hire training programs and ongoing workshops for skill upgrading. Monitor calls and liaise with mystery service contractors to evaluate service levels. Track and analyze key performance indicators. Coach individual agents as needed to address performance issues. Prepare and conduct quarterly performance assessments.

- Increased calls per hour 9% by lowering average hold time 12% and talk time 8%.
- Raised the caller access rate from 74% to 85%; lowered abandoned calls by 3%.
- Improved call quality from mystery service evaluations and call monitoring by 27%.
- Reduced customer complaints and negative feedback by 11%.
- Voted 3rd runner-up for "Supervisor of the Year" in 20XX out of 16 candidates.
- Awarded "Supervisor of the Month" in November 20XX.
- Recognized by the Vice President of HR for excellence in workshop development.

Team Leader, Subscriptions • 20XX–20XX
Directed the training, development, productivity, and performance of a team of 12 telephone agents in an outbound department. Monitored team and individual performance indicators, analyzed productivity and efficiency, conducted weekly coaching sessions, and prepared and delivered quarterly performance evaluations.

- Exceeded monthly team sales goal by an average of 14%.
- Increased annual sales revenue by 8% over 20XX.
- Reduced customer complaints and negative feedback by 11%.
- Awarded "Team Leader of the Year" in 20XX out of 21 eligible employees.
- Earned the highest annual bonus in the subscriptions department in 20XX.
- Received 3 consecutive top-score performance reviews.

Telephone Agent, Subscriptions • 20XX
Placed an average of 34 calls per hour in an outbound telemarketing department, promoting and selling subscriptions from a list of over 50 magazines and other periodicals.

- Surpassed daily sales targets by an average of 38%, with a call quality rating of 94%.
- Promoted after just 5 months based on exceptional sales performance.

Bachelor of Arts in Communications, Central University, 20XX

JULIANNE HALL
Accounting Clerk

Accounting Knowledge

- Managing complete accounting cycles including posting journal entries, reconciling general ledger accounts, and preparing period-ending income statements and balance sheets.
- Maintaining accounts payable/receivable systems. Preparing and distributing invoices.
- Reconciling bank accounts and petty cash boxes.
- Administering payroll processes. Overseeing complex filing systems.
- Utilizing widely accepted accounting software applications.

Accounting Training

- CRAWFORD COMMUNITY COLLEGE, City   20XX–20XX
  Successfully completed several 1st and 2nd level general business courses including Financial Accounting 1, Management Accounting 1, Finance 1, Economics 1 and 2, Marketing 1 and 2, Business Communications 1 and 2, Administrative Management, and Business Statistics. Achieved an average grade of 90% on all courses completed.

- T.G. HUFFINGTON SENIOR SECONDARY SCHOOL, City   20XX
  Graduated with an honours diploma after completing a variety of accounting and business courses including Accounting 11 and 12, Advanced Accounting 12, Marketing 11 and 12, Computer Applications 11 and 12, Information Technology 11, and Entrepreneurship 11.

Career Planning

- OPTIONS CAREER EXPLORATION PROGRAM, Sinclair Community Services, City   20XX
  Completed a 3-week career exploration and planning program that included self-assessments of work values, skills, interests, and personality, as well as research on specific job markets and overall career development. All assessments and research showed personal aptitude and suitability for a career in accounting.

- PROFESSIONAL ACCOUNTING CERTIFICATION PROGRAM
  Currently accepted for enrolment in level 2 of the accounting program based on achievement in prior accounting coursework. Will begin Management Accounting 2 course in September 20XX, followed by Finance 2 in December. All courses will be through distance education.

2 Years' Office Experience

- RECEPTIONIST, Thompson & MacDonald Environmental Consultants, City   20XX–Present
  Oversee all aspects of reception, front office management, and client service for a 30-person consulting practice. Manage a 6-line switchboard that averages 300 calls per day. Greet and serve up to 40 visitors per day. Coordinate courier and postal shipments. Liaise with outside service providers on office maintenance issues. Prepare and distribute a variety of reports.

- FILE CLERK, Kerrigan Accounting & Tax Specialists, City   20XX–20XX
  Organized and managed a file room containing over 50,000 current and archived client files. Filed correspondence, receipts, reports, invoices, and other documents. Located information from files for colleagues and managers. Restructured fixtures and revised file flow to provide additional space. Created and implemented colour-coding systems.

JAMES VAN RYAN

1 year experience as a Telecommunications Technician and 2 years' experience in Information Technology. Excellent communication skills with experience in telephone support, group facilitation, and training.

TELECOMMUNICATIONS TECHNOLOGY

EDUCATION

Electronic Engineering Technical Diploma   20XX
Telecommunications Option
Turner Technical Institute, City

EMPLOYMENT

Telecom Technician   20XX-Present
Capital Electronic Corporation, City

SKILLS

Troubleshooting and repairing computers, printers, fax machines, cell and cordless phones, GPS units, and audio products.

Troubleshooting hardware issues with respect to RF, power, and signal processing circuits.

Utilizing oscilloscopes, ohmmeters, voltmeters, and spectrum analyzers.

Designing tuned amplifiers, clippers, clamps, timer circuits, switching power supplies, differential and op-amp circuits, and active analog filters.

ACCOMPLISHMENTS

Designed and evaluated matching RF circuits, LP, HP, BP and BR filters, stub matching circuits, small signal amps using Y & S parameters, light-wave transmission systems, RF power amps, microstrip circuits, and wideband transformers/amplifiers.

Wrote software and designed hardware for a temperature sensor with audible notification. Incorporated temperature transducer, Assembly Language software, electronic circuit design, and a micro-controller. Displayed Fahrenheit & Celsius. When temperature changed, product emitted an audible alarm that could be toggled.

Created a power supply incorporating three voltage output terminals: +5 volt, -15 volt, and variable 15 volt. Designed PCB layout and chassis. Soldered electrical and surface mount components.

INFORMATION TECHNOLOGY

EDUCATION

Network Administrator Certification   20XX
Systems Analyst Certification   20XX
Turner Technical Institute, City

CONTRACT EMPLOYMENT

Network Administrator   20XX-Present
JVR Consulting, City

Systems Analyst   20XX
Jackson and Hillier, City

Systems Developer   20XX-20XX
Carlton Community Services, City

SKILLS

Thorough knowledge of Windows/Mac operating systems, MS Office, Lotus Notes, QuickBooks ACCPAC, and other business application software, as well as programming languages C++, Assembly, and Matlab. Moderate Java experience.

Creating, implementing, and troubleshooting Local Area Network systems. PC troubleshooting and repair. Designing serial communication interfaces.

Encoding, modulation techniques, error detection, control methods, and protocols in a variety of data communication systems.

ACCOMPLISHMENTS

Contracted p/t services as a network administrator to several companies including Cameron Holdings, Fullerton Optical, Madison and Walker Consultants, Hannah Schaeffer Catering, and Blackbird Tattoos.

Designed, implemented, and maintained several LAN and Proxy configurations ranging from 3 to 18 workstations with different operating systems.

Developed and maintained websites for Jantzen and Crawford Consulting, Home Maids Inc., Docker Home Improvement, and Mobile Motorsports.

Elizabeth Parker

MAILING ADDRESS · HOME PHONE · CELL PHONE · EMAIL ADDRESS

POSITION DESIRED: **OFFICE FILE CLERK II**	RELEVANT EXPERIENCE: **LIBRARY CIRCULATION CLERK**
File large quantities of correspondence, invoices, receipts, and other records in alphabetical and/or numerical order, and perhaps by subject matter.	Shelved large quantities of returned or misplaced books, magazines, newspapers, video, and audio according to numerical and alphabetical systems.
Locate information contained in files and provide data for co-workers and managers.	Assisted visitors with searching for hard-to-find or misplaced books and other materials.
Shift, plan, and revamp complete filing systems according to physical limitations of file room.	Shifted book aisles and audio/video shelves due to incoming shipments and rotating stock levels.
Read incoming material and sort according to filing system. Colour-code material to be filed to reduce errors. Date-stamp new material.	Received book and magazine shipments. Verified orders and authorized invoices. Prepared new catalogue labels and book jackets.
Prepare labels and index information for folders using a computer and printer.	Prepared and attached new endcap signs and directories, as well as individual shelf labels.
Purge filing system of old and/or obsolete files in accordance with established timelines.	Searched for, located, and evaluated condition of old/obsolete books scheduled for sale.
Maintain records of documents removed and files purged; investigate and retrieve missing files.	Maintained accurate accounting records of all books removed from floor and put in sale bin.
Verify accuracy of documents and reports to be filed. Enter information on records.	Shelf-read catalogue numbers in all book aisles to ensure accuracy of filing.
Provide regular and timely break relief for the receptionist. Greet visitors and clients, answer questions, operate a computerized switchboard, and coordinate mail and courier deliveries.	Assisted visitors with locating and using all library resources. Performed administrative duties such as registering visitors, answering the phones, recycling waste, and operating office equipment.
Operate office equipment such as computers, fax machines, photocopiers, printers, and scanners. Investigate and troubleshoot technical problems.	Operated and repaired computers, scanners, readers/printers, coin-op photocopiers, and audio and visual equipment.

EMPLOYMENT	**EDUCATION**
Crestview Public Library 20XX–Present LIBRARY CIRCULATION CLERK	Middle Rock University 20XX BACHELOR OF ARTS DEGREE

GARRY RHODES
Home Phone • Cell Phone • Email Address
Mailing Address

FEDERAL GOVERNMENT INTERNSHIP

High school graduate with strong computer skills and training in business and accounting seeks a federal government internship in an office administration role. Additional qualifications include 60 wpm keyboard speed and work placement experience in an office environment. Regarded as mature and highly organized. References from teachers and supervisors available upon request.

Academic Achievements

- Graduated with a high school diploma from Brian Thatcher Senior Secondary in June 20XX.
- Completed several business courses including Accounting 11 and 12, Advanced Accounting 12, Business Communication 11, Marketing 11 and 12, and Entrepreneurship 12.
- Earned place on the school's honour roll every semester in Grades 11 and 12.
- Awarded Certificate of Merit for outstanding academic achievement in Entrepreneurship 12.
- Member of graduation committee in Grade 12; volunteered 5-15 hours per week for 4 months.
- Served as campaign manager for student body presidential nominee in Grade 11.
- Nominated for graduating class valedictorian in Grade 12.

Technical Skills

- Proficient with Windows systems, up to and including newest version; beginner Mac skills.
- Trained and experienced with business application software including MS Word, PowerPoint, Excel, Access, Outlook, and Lotus Notes.
- Completed computer courses such as Information Systems and Computer Applications.
- Experience using office equipment such as photocopiers, fax machines, and postal machines.
- Knowledge of graphic imaging equipment and software, including scanners and Photoshop.

Practicum Experience

- Completed a 2-week, full-time practicum in the administration and accounting departments of Bowler-Wheeling Inc. as part of Advanced Accounting 12 class.
- Used accounting software to reconcile invoices, post journal entries, and audit accounts.
- Designed an Excel spreadsheet to list and monitor outstanding and bad debts.
- All scores on final performance review were either "Excellent" or "Above Average."

Community Involvement

- Assisted with the office set-up of the East End Women's Shelter in 20XX.
- Active participant in the annual West Coast Run for Cancer since 20XX.
- Raised funds door-to-door for the Cystic Fibrosis Foundation in 20XX.

Career Goal

- To attend City University in September 20XX and study accounting and commerce.
- Long-term goal is to become a Certified Financial Accountant and open a private practice.

ALTERNATIVE RESUMES FAQ//
WHAT SHOULD I INCLUDE ABOUT MY EDUCATION?

Education is an important section on a resume for someone without much of an employment history, like Penny Mirren on the next page.

Many job-seekers only list their diploma or degree, and don't feature all the skills, experience, training, recognition, and accreditation they gained in school. Consider the following aspects of high school or college for your resume:

1. Degree / Diploma / Certificate

Did you graduate? What is the exact name of your degree, diploma, or certificate?

2. Work Experience

Did you complete any internships, practicums, or work experience placements? Describe these as completely as you would for a regular job by adding company details, duties, responsibilities, and accomplishments. Consider adding excerpts from positive performance evaluations.

3. Volunteer Experience

Did you volunteer in the school library, cafeteria, or computer lab? Were you on the graduation committee or involved with student government? Did you work on the yearbook or serve as a peer tutor? Volunteering with your school is just as valuable as volunteering outside of school.

4. Awards and Accomplishments

Were you awarded any school or industry certificates of merit for outstanding achievement? How about leadership, attendance, or volunteer service? Did you win any scholarships or attain high academic status such as honour roll, top student, or dean's list? These successes help demonstrate your character, dependability, work ethic, and commitment to a future employer.

5. Sports or Academic Involvement

Were you on the basketball team or in the science club? This demonstrates teamwork skills, a strong work ethic, and the ability to balance priorities. Don't forget leadership skills gained from coaching or serving as team captain. Include awards to show you're a high achiever.

6. Specific Courses

Did you complete any courses that are relevant to your job target? What about courses that don't seem relevant but may demonstrate your character or capabilities, such as Peer Tutoring or Entrepreneurship? You can also list exceptional grades and major projects.

7. Computer Training

Did you take computer courses? Include knowledge of operating systems, software packages, and the Internet, as well as keyboard speed and troubleshooting skills if they are relevant.

8. Workplace Training

Did you complete any workplace training workshops? Many schools offer industry-sponsored or recognized certification in such areas as customer service, first aid and CPR, safe food handling, workplace safety, conflict resolution, workplace harassment, and handling hazardous materials.

9. Night School

Did you take any night school, continuing/adult education, professional development workshops, correspondence, or other part-time courses? These may also be important to employers.

PENNY MIRREN
Junior Receptionist / Administrator

Home Phone • Cell Phone • Email
Mailing Address

Waterfield Senior Secondary School, City   20XX–20XX
Graduated with a high school diploma, maintaining a B average throughout Grades 9 to 12.

Office Reception Experience

- Provided administrative and service support to the full-time receptionist at Allied Motors while completing an 80-hour work experience placement organized through the Business Communications 12 course.
- Greeted visitors, operated a 6-line telephone system, responded to basic inquiries, and transferred calls to 4 different departments and over 30 employees.
- Prepared, maintained, and distributed a variety of reports, correspondence, and other documents using MS Word and Excel.
- Coordinated mail pickups and deliveries with 2 different courier companies.
- Maintained a clean and organized reception desk.

Office Administration Experience

- Completed a 70-hour work experience placement in the accounting department at Dayton Office Equipment to satisfy the practicum requirement in Accounting 11.
- Provided break coverage on reception when needed. Co-managed a 15-line telephone system, routing calls to over 80 employees in 9 different departments.
- Restructured the flow of 15,000 files in a large filing room to maximize available space.
- Assembled, packaged, and addressed over 600 customer mailings.

Computer Skills

- Completed several computer courses including Information Technology 10, Keyboarding 9–12, Computer Applications 10–12, and Graphic Arts 11–12.
- Proficient in the use of MS Office software including Word, Excel, PowerPoint, Access, Publisher, and Outlook. Trained in both Windows and Mac systems.
- 70 wpm keyboard speed.

Leadership and Teamwork Skills

- Collaborated with a team of 8 on production of the yearbook as part of Graphic Arts 11 and 12. Selected by the teacher to serve as team leader the final year.
- Volunteered to work in the library with 3 librarians and another student assistant for both Grade 11 semesters. Shelved books and helped students locate and use resources.
- Member of the math club from Grades 9 to 12. Elected captain in the final year.
- Awarded a "Certificate of Merit for Outstanding Leadership" in Grade 12.

"We have had several work experience students from your school over the years, and I can honestly say that Penny Mirren was the very best. If we had a suitable position available today, we would offer it to her."
                                          - HAROLD RIDGE, BUSINESS MANAGER, ALLIED MOTORS

SHAWN WELLAND
Marketing Representative

Phone • Email
Mailing Address

EDUCATION / TRAINING

Marketing Management Diploma • Central Business Institute   May 20XX
- Graduated from the advertising option of this two-year, full-time business program.
- Completed such courses as Marketing, Advertising Budgets, Advertising Principles, Graphic Design, Accounting, Business Communication, Economics, Statistics, and Advertising Media.
- Developed a complete business plan for a hypothetical company, including an annual budget, marketing plan, and print advertising materials. Placed in the top 5% of the class.
- Prepared and delivered a presentation on advertising trends and earned a grade of 92%.
- Researched and wrote a paper on "Ethics in Advertising" and received a grade of 90%.

High School Diploma • Charles Thurmond Secondary School   Jun 20XX
- Graduated with honours, completing several business courses such as Marketing, Accounting, Advanced Accounting, Business & Consumer Math, and Computers in Business.
- Participated in the Peer Tutoring Program, assisting students with English, French, and Math.
- Earned a Certificate for Outstanding Attendance each semester in high school.
- Developed strong teamwork skills as a member of the basketball team and science club.

COMPUTER / LANGUAGE SKILLS

Skilled in Windows, Mac, and Linux business and graphics applications including MS Word, Excel, Access, PowerPoint, and Publisher. Moderate knowledge of Corel Draw and Adobe Photoshop. 60-70 wpm. Fluent in English and French, with limited skills in German and Spanish.

EXPERIENCE / ACCOMPLISHMENTS

Customer Service Representative • Wilderness World   Mar 20XX – Present
Employed in the apparel and footwear department. Assist customers with finding and selecting merchandise, ensure stock levels on the sales floor are maximized, organize the stockroom, change price signs and tickets, and maintain a clean department.

Webmaster • www.website.com   Feb 20XX – Present
Developed and continue to maintain a website featuring the local tourist community. Research attractions, upload images, correspond with readers, and market the site through search engines.

Youth Worker • Central Youth Corps   Nov 20XX – Jan 20XX
Volunteered to work alongside the Youth Support Leader, planning and organizing fund-raising events, charitable activities, and wilderness adventures. Counselled youth on an individual basis.

Project Portfolio Available for Viewing

Eva Balfour
Mailing Address
Phone Number • Email Address

JOB OBJECTIVE: **OFFICE ASSISTANT, SUMMER**

WORK EXPERIENCE:

Completed a 120-hour work experience practicum in the administration office at Dover Bay Secondary School during the spring 20XX semester. Performed data entry, batched and reconciled invoices, reorganized the filing room, counted and ordered office supplies, called vendors, answered phone enquiries, and scheduled appointments. Gained experience with photocopiers, fax machines, printer/scanners, computers, and shredders.

WORK CHARACTERISTICS:

Organized. Received a score of "excellent" for organizational skills on the work experience evaluation report. Completed a one-day workshop on time management as part of a life skills class in Grade 10.

Determined. Overcame many obstacles and adhered to grueling practice schedules during 3 years of competitive tennis. Reached the regional championships in 20XX.

Hard Worker. Demonstrated a strong work ethic by balancing school and homework priorities with athletic and other commitments for 3 years.

ADDITIONAL QUALIFICATIONS:

Available Anytime. Can work either full-time or part-time for the summer. No vacation plans in the summer to interfere with availability for work. Able to work in the fall if Grade 12 class schedule can be accommodated.

Computer Literate. Completed classes in data management, information processing, MS Word, and MS Excel. Self-taught MS PowerPoint, MS Publisher, and Corel Draw. 55 wpm keyboard speed with 96% accuracy.

Multilingual. Fluent in English and German. Conversant in verbal and written French, having studied up to and including Grade 11.

BRANDON HUNTER
Network Developer / Administrator

MAILING ADDRESS   HOME PHONE   CELL PHONE   EMAIL ADDRESS

SKILLS

Computers/Networking
- Mac and Windows operating systems, up to and including current versions.
- MS Office – Word, Excel, PowerPoint, Access, Publisher, and Outlook.
- Simply Accounting, MYOB.
- Built entire systems from parts.
- Installed all hardware components.
- Set-up a LAN with 5 computers.
- 55 wpm keyboard speed.

Teamwork
- Worked as part of a 6-member team during a 4-week work placement with Elementary Toys.
- Employed as a crew member with Goody Foody for 16 months, working closely with up to 12 other staff.

Leadership
- Supervised youth group for 2 years, overseeing activities of 15 kids.
- Elected captain of school rugby team.

Communication
- Fluent in spoken and written English.
- Conversant in spoken French.

EDUCATION

Certificate – LAN Basics
Continuing Education, 20XX
- Completed a 3-month night course on the basics of networking systems.
- Achieved a grade of 92%, 2nd highest in the class of 18.
- Learned wiring and electrical safety.

High School Diploma
Eastern Secondary School, 20XX
- Completed business courses such as Accounting, Computer Applications, Marketing, and Communications.
- Achieved honour roll in Grade 11 and one semester in Grade 12.
- Received a Certificate of Outstanding Attendance in Grade 11.
- Received a Certificate of Merit for high marks on performance review at work experience placement.
- Completed a 3-month group project, including a group presentation, on advertising and consumerism.
- Member of rugby team for 2 years, reaching provincials both seasons.
- Member of wrestling team for 1 year; won bronze medal in 20XX.

EXPERIENCE

Administrative Assistant
Elementary Toys, City, 20XX
- Completed a 4-week, full-time work placement in the sales administration and accounting departments.
- Entered month-end journal entries and met all deadlines.
- Compiled and organized weekly and monthly sales analysis reports.
- Calculated and verified monthly sales commissions; maintained Excel report.
- Performed other data entry, filing, and organizing duties as needed.

Cashier / Cook
Goody Foody, City, 20XX–20XX
- Took customer orders and accepted cash/debit payments on computerized system; operated bank terminal.
- Reconciled cash and bank receipts to register; completed daily reports.
- Assisted with calculating, preparing, and delivering daily bank deposits.
- Performed closing duties for 3 shifts in the absence of the Assistant Manager.
- Trained new staff on all duties.
- Employee of the Month for Mar/20XX.

LAUREL KEATON
Office Reception & Administration

- 2 years' office reception experience
- Intermediate level MS Office skills
- Fluent in both English and French

SKILLS and ACHIEVEMENTS

Developed an electronic appointment book for an 18-person office using MS Excel; comfortable with both computerized and manual systems.

Reorganized the client filing system for an 11-person law office; purged and stored over 1,000 outdated files. Reorganized a filing room that contained over 20,000 files for Butterfield Industries.

Employ a professional telephone manner; skilled with managing up to 10 lines on computerized phone systems.

Highly professional with respect to staff and client confidentiality. Accustomed to working with sensitive information with the West Coast Cancer Society and various other businesses and organizations.

Covered for the Executive Assistant of a Vice President for a 3-day medical leave.

Effective working in high-pressure offices and consistently meeting strict deadlines.

Knowledge of Windows and Mac systems. Proficient with MS Word, Excel, Access, PowerPoint, Publisher, and Outlook. 65 wpm keyboard speed.

CONTACT INFORMATION

Mailing Address Line 1
Mailing Address Line 2
Home Telephone   555-555-5555
Cell Telephone   555-555-5555
Fax Number   555-555-5555
Email Address   Email Address

EMPLOYMENT HISTORY

Harper & Ross Temporary Agency
20XX to Present

Assigned to over 40 local businesses for temporary office assistance in the past 2 years. Full placement listing, as well as 3 letters of recommendation from office supervisors, available upon request.

- Harrington Munroe Mining Limited
  Reception/Administration, 4 Months

- West Coast Cancer Society
  Reception, 2 Months

- General Water Limited
  Reception, 2 Months

- Jackson, Fuller and Brown Architects
  Administration, 6 Weeks

- Western Heritage Buildings Ltd.
  Reception/Administration, 5 Weeks

- Smithson Foods Incorporated
  Reception, 4 Weeks

- Anthony, Drysdale and Clarke
  File Management, 3 Weeks

- Butterfield Industries Limited
  File Management, 2 Weeks

"We constantly received positive feedback from Laurel's placements. In the two years she has worked for us, we have never had an issue with her performance. She is a professional, reliable member of our temporary staffing pool."
JANICE ROSS, PARTNER

EDUCATION / TRAINING

Certificate in Office Administration   20XX
Bradson Business Academy

Certificate in MS Office   20XX
District Continuing Education

High School Diploma   20XX
Humboldt Senior Secondary

GEORGE TIMMINS
Online Social Media Consultant

Email Address
Website

Created, implemented, and managed a variety of social media marketing campaigns for businesses and non-profit organizations since 20XX. Developed and demonstrated significant knowledge of several Web 2.0 communication, collaboration, and multimedia tools including:

- Social Networking: Example, Example, Example
- Blogs: Example, Example, Example, Example
- Microblogs: Example, Example, Example
- Internet Forums: Example, Example, Example
- Event Management: Example, Example

- Bookmarking: Example, Example, Example
- Social News: Example, Example, Example
- Wikis: Example, Example, Example
- Video/Photo Sharing: Example, Example
- Livecasting: Example, Example

Contributions

✓ Created and implemented a marketing program using social networking and video/photo sharing tools that generated over 100,000 followers in the first 8 months for a national housing advocate.

✓ Designed and launched an online donation program that generated $20,000 in the first 6 months for a regional community living society based in Oakville.

✓ Developed and co-facilitated a live webinar that drew 300 viewers and added 800 subscribers for an educational consulting company in Marysville.

✓ Increased monthly e-newsletter subscriptions by 68% for a national health care research institute by upgrading the software, improving the formatting, and conducting a subscriber survey.

✓ Orchestrated a complete website redesign that increased traffic by 170% for a non-profit animal shelter and advocacy group based in Doughty.

✓ Created and launched 3 social networking pages that attracted over 2,500 fans and increased website traffic by 120% for a coastal waterways protection group.

✓ Developed a social bookmarking/tagging initiative that resulted in 2,000 new tags in just 30 days for an emerging ladies fashion designer in Scarborough.

✓ Launched and marketed a new blog that attracted over 1,000 subscribers in the first 3 months for a performing arts institute in Welland.

✓ Established a microblog web presence that resulted in 850 followers in 1 week for a local university radio station.

✓ Promoted a press release that received 1,500 "likes" in 3 days through 2 social news sites.

✓ Prepared and published wiki profiles for a local environmental consultant, an international poverty and human rights advocacy group, and a regional LGBT support network.

Expertise

- User Generated Content [UGC]
- Consumer Generated Media [CGM]
- Digital Advertising
- Digital Influencer Identification
- Search Engine Optimization [SEO]
- Social Media Optimization [SMO]

- Blog Guidelines / Blogger Outreach
- Integrated Communication Strategies
- E-commerce
- New Media Marketing
- Really Simple Syndication [RSS]
- Social Media Measurement

COMMUNITY SERVICE

Chapter 5

Chapter 5 covers the growing field of non-profit and community service.

In this job sector, teens and young adults find employment with organizations that help disadvantaged segments of society or contribute to the betterment of the general population. This chapter starts by dissecting the resume of Jason Lu, who is applying for a position as an Emergency Services Dispatcher, and continues with an additional fifteen sample resumes and two FAQ tips.

DESIGNING MY ALTERNATIVE RESUME//

JASON LU : EMERGENCY SERVICES DISPATCHER

Jason Lu has two years' experience in road service dispatching and is applying for a job with the municipal government as an Emergency Services Dispatcher.

This is a highly coveted position that was advertised online and in the daily newspaper and is sure to attract a large volume of applicants. Jason's resume can be viewed on the following page.

1. Objective

Jason uses a job title rather than a conventional objective because he wants to be perceived as a qualified and confident Emergency Services Dispatcher that can step in and hit the ground running. He knows that most applicants will use something like, "Objective: To obtain a full-time position as an Emergency Services Dispatcher," but he wants his resume to stand out from the crowd.

2. Summary of Qualifications

Jason uses a summary underneath his job title to match his qualifications to the list of requirements in the job ad. He begins with describing his relevant skills and employment history because the ad asked for 2–3 years of related experience. He then includes his first aid certificate, language skills, keyboard speed, and availability, all requested in the job ad. By responding directly to the list of employer needs, Jason makes it easy for the recipient to see that he meets their basic requirements.

3. Telecommunications Experience

Jason includes his telecommunications experience as a dispatcher for a road service company and as a call centre agent. He leaves off the unrelated jobs in food service he held before that time. Although there is nothing wrong with his prior experience, he recognizes those earlier jobs will not add much value to his resume, and they may actually detract from the overall impact he is trying to achieve.

He also knows that many other job-seekers with comparable employment backgrounds will apply for the same position. Simply listing his duties and responsibilities at these two jobs will not be enough because the employer will see that on most of the resumes they receive. He needs to prove that he didn't just do the job, he did it extremely well. Since his best resources for proving that are the frequent performance evaluations he received in both jobs, he uses them on his resume to attract attention and demonstrate his expertise.

4. Education and Technical Skills

Jason's Diploma of Criminology is relevant to emergency services dispatch, so he lists several of the courses he completed to demonstrate his overall knowledge of the criminal justice system. He also lists the basic software and equipment skills he gained from his experience to show his range of technical expertise.

❶ EMERGENCY SERVICES DISPATCHER

❷

- 2 years' employment experience as a dispatcher of emergency and non-emergency road services.
- Skilled at making sound decisions using all available information in high-pressure situations.
- Experience with receiving and transmitting communication over standard radio/telephone equipment.
- Knowledge of public safety classification codes, motor vehicle traffic laws, and broadcasting policies.
- Exceptional knowledge of the geographic region. Adept at reading and interpreting maps.
- Certified in Occupational First Aid Level 2 with CPR. December 20XX expiry.
- Bilingual; fluent in both English and Cantonese. Excellent verbal and written communication skills.
- 75 wpm keyboard speed. Proficient in the operation and maintenance of technical equipment.
- Available for all days and shifts including weekdays, weekends, evenings, overnights, and holidays.

❸ TELECOMMUNICATIONS EXPERIENCE

Dispatcher   **Burnside Towing and Traffic Services, City**   **20XX–Present**

Deploy tow trucks and road service crews to emergency and non-emergency traffic situations throughout the region in response to communications received via telephone and radio. Allocate resources efficiently based on priorities. Communicate with emergency response authorities and other agencies as needed. Operate and maintain computer, telephone, and radio equipment. Report to the Dispatch Supervisor.

Performance Evaluations:	Dec 20XX	Jun 20XX	Dec 20XX	Probation
Final Grade	96%	91%	84%	80%
Overall Rating	Outstanding	Outstanding	Very Good	Good

Call Centre Agent   **Global Communications Enterprise, City**   **20XX–20XX**

Placed 30–50 outbound telemarketing calls per hour using a verified contact list, marketing and selling a variety of Internet and wireless communication products and services. Followed a detailed flowchart script to demonstrate features and benefits, overcome objections, and close sales. Managed difficult customers and situations within boundaries of authority. Reported to the Account Supervisor.

Performance Evaluations:	May 20XX	Nov 20XX	May 20XX	Probation
Final Grade	92%	88%	81%	74%
Overall Rating	Exceeds	Exceeds	Meets	Meets

❹ EDUCATION

Diploma in Criminology   **Mount Leduc College, City**   **20XX–20XX**

Completed a 2-year, full-time program with a high B average in such courses as Police Administration, Criminal Justice, Legal Systems, Community Policing, Social Psychology, Youth Justice, Critical Thinking, Correctional Theory and Programs, Government and Politics, Ethics and Morality, and Computer Systems.

❹ TECHNICAL SKILLS

Windows and Mac ◆ MS Word, Excel, Access, PowerPoint and Outlook ◆ Lotus SmartSuite
CRM Software ◆ CommuniTech Multi-Line Phone Systems ◆ PBR Radio Operations Equipment

CHRISTINE THIESSEN
Special Needs Education Assistant

EMAIL ADDRESS • PHONE NUMBER
MAILING ADDRESS

EMPLOYMENT EXPERIENCE

Educational Assistant, Central School District   May 20XX – Present
- Work in two kindergarten classrooms at Cascade and Johnston schools.
- Assist two autistic students with participation in all classroom activities.
- Adapt lesson plans to meet students' needs; set social goals for students and encourage positive interaction with peers and teaching staff.
- Prepare learning materials specifically for special needs students.
- Tutor reading, writing, and math with other students.

Childcare Worker, Disability Resource Centre   Summer 20XX/20XX
- Assisted physically and mentally disabled child with personal care.
- Administered medicine. Assisted with feeding and seizure management.
- Accessed community services and resources through recreational activities.
- Followed behaviour management program and completed weekly reports.
- Established and maintained a positive relationship with the family.

VOLUNTEER EXPERIENCE

Literacy Tutor, Learning Disabilities Association   Mar 20XX – Jun 20XX
- Tutored two students one-on-one to improve their reading and writing skills.
- Taught students reading strategies for increased competency.
- Assisted students to self-correct their writing using worksheets and charts.
- Provided monthly progress reports to students and parents.
- Completed regular lesson plans and kept accurate student records.

Teacher's Assistant, Bradson Elementary School   Jan 20XX – May 20XX
- Worked in three different classrooms from kindergarten to second grade.
- Helped physically and mentally disabled students participate in activities.
- Assisted physically disabled students with mobility.

Child & Youth Care Counsellor, Youth Options   Dec 20XX – May 20XX
- Supervised recreational activities for children with physical disabilities.
- Encouraged skill development and positive interaction among peers.
- Increased integration into community resources.
- Discouraged inappropriate behaviour through consistent reinforcement.
- Assisted with mobility, toileting, and feeding.

EDUCATION / TRAINING

Autism and Related Conditions I & II   Jan 20XX / Apr 20XX
- Continuing Education Workshops

Special Needs Education Assistant Diploma   May 20XX
- Northwest Community College

Real Reading Literacy Tutor Certificate   Mar 20XX
- National Special Needs Association

"I have come to rely on and respect Christine's ability to interact with special needs kids. When challenges arise, she is calm, composed, patient, and creative."
- DAVID MORRISON
TEACHER, CASCADE
ELEMENTARY SCHOOL

"Christine is a very welcome addition to our staff. Her commitment to the students is great!"
- ELLEN ROMNEY
PRINCIPAL, JOHNSTON
ELEMENTARY SCHOOL

"Christine always demonstrated a complete and solid understanding of the fundamentals of working with special needs kids. She earned her placement on the Dean's List."
- JAMISON PACKARD
COURSE INSTRUCTOR
NORTHWEST COLLEGE

"Children in our program genuinely enjoy her pleasant personality and respond well to her leadership style."
- SUE TAFT, DIRECTOR
LEARNING DISABILITIES
ASSOCIATION

MOHANDAS KUMAR = HIGH SCHOOL MATH TUTOR

- **Math skills and knowledge.** Placed in the top 5% in all advanced placement courses in university and high school including calculus, algebra, trigonometry, statistics, geometry, and advanced mathematics. Thorough knowledge of all high school math classes.
- **High school tutoring experience.** Provided individual and group tutoring in algebra and calculus for up to 4 students at a time as part of the work experience component of a university math class. Tutored 11 high school students in total.
- **Presentation and public speaking skills.** Presented to an audience of 1,500 as part of a university technology course. Prepared and delivered multiple PowerPoint presentations for groups of 20 or more. Presented lesson plans to tutoring students.
- **Technical skills and knowledge.** Advanced MS Office skills on Windows, including Word, Excel, PowerPoint, Publisher, Access, and Outlook. Intermediate knowledge of HTML and web design. 70 wpm keyboard speed. Skilled in hardware troubleshooting.

HIGH SCHOOL TUTORING EXPERIENCE

Central University Peer Development Program, City   Mar/Apr 20XX

- Tutored 11 high school students in algebra and calculus to fulfill the work experience requirement of a Community Development course at Central University. Tutored 1 to 4 participants at a time including students with special needs.
- Presented lesson plans that were prepared by the math department, assisted students with homework and in-class assignments, prepared a group of students for the federal government exam, and reviewed in-class material with students who were absent.
- Provided 60 hours of tutoring in total, including 22 hours at Carver High School and 18 hours at Longview High School, voluntarily surpassing the required minimum of 40 hours.

ACADEMIC EDUCATION

Central University, City   Sep 20XX – Present

- Earned an A in Math I and II, Pre-Calculus, Calculus I and II, and Statistics I and II, with an average grade of 96%. Averaging 93% in a variety of technology classes.
- Completed 3 major group projects each semester that involved solving complex math problems, proving complicated theorems, and presenting and defending the analysis.
- Active member of the prestigious Central University Math Club.

Carver High School, City   Graduated May 20XX

- Completed all available math courses with an average grade of 98%.

CONTACT

Mailing Address   •   Home Phone   •   Cell Phone   •   Email Address

Mailing Address
Email Address

Home Phone
Cell Phone

MARINA GOODALL ▪ OFFICE ADMINISTRATOR
Humane Education Department, Provincial Animal Welfare Society

OFFICE ADMINISTRATION

- Two years' office administration experience in a non-profit environment.

- Provided administration and reception in a busy social services office that received up to 100 client visits per day.

- Welcomed clients in person and on the phone; explained services and confirmed eligibility; referred to other local services when needed.

- Recruited, interviewed, hired, and supervised several volunteer office assistants.

- Purchased all office supplies and equipment; collected quotes for office repairs/renovations.

- Managed petty cash and social committee funds and completed monthly reconciliations.

- Maintained extensive filing systems for active, dormant, and archived client files.

- Recorded and prepared meeting minutes and distributed to all staff members.

- Designed and maintained Excel spreadsheet for all invoices and receipts received.

EMPLOYMENT HISTORY

- Office Administrator, Senton Services Limited 20XX–Present

- Temporary Office Support, Crawford Careers 20XX

- Temporary Accounting Clerk, Feather Schools 20XX

COMMUNICATIONS

- Wrote four articles for *Companion Animals*:
  - i) "Bonding with Animals" [Jan/Feb 20XX]
  - ii) "Adult Dogs and Cats Need a Second Chance" [Mar/Apr 20XX]
  - iii) "Horse-Back Riding on a Tight Budget" [Aug/Sep 20XX]
  - iv) "Aggression in Dogs" [May/Jun 20XX]

- Participated in several workshops through the District Writers Conference, including:
  - i) Writing and Selling Articles
  - ii) Pet Writing
  - iii) How to Write Attractive Query Letters
  - iv) Submitting Non-Fiction Articles

- Researched, wrote, and published several articles in the Crawford Careers newsletter. Covered for an injured co-worker on the Newsletter Committee for two months.

- Currently completing a Bachelor of Arts in English through distance education.

- Excellent computer skills including MS Office proficiency and 70wpm keyboard speed.

- Volunteered with the annual Heart and Stroke telethon twice; utilized compassion and sensitivity when interacting with donors experiencing tremendous personal loss.

- Consistently demonstrated skill in empathy and conflict resolution while interacting with clients and counsellors in social services.

ANIMAL WELFARE

- Currently completing the Animal Welfare Certificate Program via distance education.

- Completed an Animal Assisted Therapy course which analyzed the use of animals in therapy work and the link between violence against animals and violence against people.

- Earned an A in Environmental Ethics course which compared several major advocates in animal and environmental rights.

- Attended two animal conservation lectures, including one in support of the Spirit Bear.

- Committed to personal development by staying informed through humane societies and animal organizations.

- Participate in fundraising campaigns for Pacific Spay-Neuter Association and Fur Free Society, and donate to Animal Care Society, Craw Humane Society, and Pet Lovers Club.

- Volunteered in an animal hospital for one year; assisted vets with handling patients.

- Attended conference of the Association of Professional Dog Trainers in 20XX.

- Attended two Dog Owners' Association lectures in 20XX: Dog Aggression and Understanding Dog Behaviour.

- Owned a horse for five years; active rider for 14 years. Owned many pets over lifetime.

- Completed dog obedience training; achieved the Canine Good Citizen certification.

Community-minded activist seeking a challenging position with a local non-profit agency. Experienced with fundraising and developing awareness around a variety of social conditions. Often described as a straightforward, organized team player with a constant eye on the big picture. Culturally sensitive, accustomed to working with people of different ages, cultures, classes, and backgrounds. A strong communicator who is fluent in English and conversant in French and Spanish.

JEREMY SZEPANIAK

CELL PHONE • HOME PHONE
MAILING ADDRESS • EMAIL ADDRESS

AFFILIATIONS / VOLUNTEERING

- **Young Community Leaders.** Member of local chapter for past 3 years; elected and served as secretary for the past 7 months.

- **Pacific Resources.** Provided ongoing support and a positive role model for a troubled teen for the past 4 years.

- **Family Aid International.** Travelled to Mexico in 20XX to participate in a 3-week humanitarian project. Worked as part of a 10-member team on the construction of a house for an underprivileged family.

- **Bobby Dryden Society.** Earned a Certificate of Outstanding Achievement and inclusion in their quarterly newsletter for raising $5,000 in 20XX.

- **Simon Bothwell Youth Camps.** Past member and current volunteer. Assist with chaperoning summer camps and substituting for group leaders in their absence.

- **Blood Disorder Association.** Volunteer as a fundraiser at the annual telethon.

- **Eastside Homeless Society.** Coordinated winter clothing drives from 20XX-20XX.

ACADEMICS

- Just finished 2nd year at Pacific University, majoring in social work.

- Graduated high school in 20XX, placing on the honour roll every semester. Awarded top student in Leadership 12. Earned the Simpson Scholarship for outstanding community service. Served as student council treasurer in Grade 12.

EMPLOYMENT

- Currently employed 5 hours per week as a circulation clerk at Pacific University Library, with responsibility for shelving books, shelf reading, checking books in and out, and helping students locate and use resources.

- Worked 3 summers as an office assistant with the family landscaping business, answering phones and booking projects, preparing estimates, and maintaining files and bookkeeping records.

COMPUTERS

- Proficient with Windows and Mac. Advanced level Word, Excel, and PowerPoint. Familiar with Lotus Suite, Corel Draw, Adobe Photoshop, and Dreamweaver. Competent Internet researcher; 65 wpm keyboard speed.

ALTERNATIVE RESUMES FAQ//

HOW MUCH HISTORY SHOULD I INCLUDE ON MY RESUME?

A resume is a marketing tool, not a complete record of everything you have done in your career or at school.

It should be a carefully crafted document that showcases your most relevant and impressive qualifications for a particular job, company or industry. In other words, you choose what to include and how much emphasis to put on it.

Employment

Older and more experienced workers should limit their resumes to the last ten years because that's most relevant to employers. But what if you only have five years of experience? Should you include every job you've held and dedicate equal space to each one? It depends on what will appeal to your targeted employers.

Look at the resume on the next page for example. Rachel Deneuve has three years' current experience in social services, and two years' prior experience as a restaurant server. Since she plans to continue her career in social services, she emphasizes her jobs and volunteer experience in the last three years and minimizes her previous restaurant employment.

Education

Debating whether to indicate your high school diploma if you're enrolled in or have graduated from college is the same as deciding whether to include an old job now that you have more recent employment experience. It depends on what is applicable to your job target.

There are more reasons to include high school education on your resume than simply to point out your diploma. If you're a college student or graduate, and you can't remember much about high school, leave it off because the reader will realize you graduated. However, you can expand your high school credentials by including work experience placements or internships, volunteer experience, workplace certificates, or extracurricular activities if these are relevant to your job target.

In Rachel's case, she graduated college with an Office Administration Certificate, but she decided to include her high school education as well. In addition to her High School Diploma, she completed a Workplace Safety Certificate and a First Aid Certificate, and she knew those would be relevant to her job target. If she decided to only include her post-secondary education, she wouldn't have two qualifications on her resume that may prove to be very important to an employer in her field.

RACHEL DENEUVE
Counsellor, Supporter, and Advocate for Women and Youth
MAILING ADDRESS · EMAIL ADDRESS · HOME PHONE · CELL PHONE

---

2 years' experience working with multi-barrier youth in employment programs.
1 year experience counselling and supporting women with The Family Planning Clinic.
3 years' experience in social services working with people of all cultures and backgrounds.
Familiar with local social service agencies and many issues facing women and youth today.

WORK and VOLUNTEER EXPERIENCE

WEST END YOUTH SERVICES, City   20XX–Present

Youth Counsellor. Assist in the delivery of employment interventions such as Youth Skills and Youth Internship programs. Provide counselling on all aspects of career planning and job searching, and follow-up weekly upon completion of the intervention. Teach, advise, and support clients with barriers to employment such as teen pregnancy, lack of affordable housing, difficult family and partner relationships, health concerns, and financial problems.

WOMEN'S FAMILY PLANNING CLINIC, City   20XX–Present

Volunteer Counsellor. Interview patients and provide educational materials and counselling on birth control methods, STDs, and sexual practices. Provide support to patients during medical exams. Completed a 3-month course on crisis intervention and sex education.

HUDSON HOUSE, City   20XX–20XX

Youth Worker. Supervised the behaviour and attendance of up to 8 teen girls at a time as a weekend Resident Youth Worker in a group home.

YOUTH ACTION, City   20XX–20XX

Volunteer Street Worker. Provided friendship and emotional support to street youth in the downtown area. Conducted presentations for prison inmates and performed street theatre.

Prior work experience includes 2 years as a restaurant server.

EDUCATION and TRAINING

Participated in numerous company-sponsored workshops with West End Youth Services, including Counselling Suicidal Clients, Challenges Facing Youth, Women's Issues, Drugs & Alcohol, Employment Maintenance, Job Search Strategies, and Resume/Letter Design.

Completed Office Administration Certificate program at Royal Oak College in 20XX. Courses included Computer Systems & Applications, Desktop Publishing, Introduction to Accounting, Client Relations, and Business Communication.

Graduated with a High School Diploma, Workplace Safety Certificate, and Emergency First Aid Certificate from Masterson High School in 20XX.

Roy Zeeman
YOUTH CAMP COUNSELLOR

Telephone / Email
Mailing Address

Counselling Experience
- ◄ Participated in the Grade 11 peer counselling program. Received training in counselling, listening, and empathy. Counselled 7 Grade 9 students about peer and academic pressures.

Wilderness Experience
- ◄ Avid camper, backpacker, and outdoor sports enthusiast.
- ◄ Excellent knowledge and experience with tenting, swimming, hiking, food preparation, and backpacking.
- ◄ Moderate knowledge of canoeing, kayaking, and whitewater rafting.

Child Care Experience
- ◄ 3 years' babysitting experience, with up to 4 children at once.
- ◄ Experienced with both boys and girls, aged 6 months up to 9 years.

Additional Qualifications
- ◄ Certified in Emergency First Aid Level 1 with CPR; 20XX expiry.
- ◄ Aqua level 8 swimmer. Completed 4 years of swimming lessons.
- ◄ Member of Hyack boys swim team for 3 years.

Employment Attributes
- ◄ Reliable and punctual. Missed only 1 day of school in the last 3 years due to illness.
- ◄ Team player. Played youth soccer for 4 seasons and organized softball for 2. Elected captain of swim team in 20XX.
- ◄ Quick learner. Earned honour roll standing first semester in senior high school. Referred to the peer counselling program by 2 teachers.
- ◄ Strong work ethic. Balanced schoolwork with babysitting, swim team responsibilities, and extracurricular activities for 3 years.

Availability
- ◄ Available to work anytime from June 27 until September 4, 20XX.

References
- ◄ Present babysitting employer.
- ◄ Former babysitting employer.
- ◄ Present high school guidance counsellor.

AMY MALONE
Home Phone • Cell Phone • Email Address • Mailing Address

CAREER RESOURCES COORDINATOR
Chadwick Community Services, City, 20XX–Present

CLIENT SUPPORT

- Work with a diverse client base of youth and adults on all aspects of job searching and career planning.

- Empower clients to identify needs such as changing careers, completing education, or targeting a specific job market.

- Assess barriers to employment and offer guidance regarding transferable skills and employment prospects.

- Assist clients with writing and editing resumes and cover letters, as well as completing application forms.

- Show job-seekers how to obtain a free email address and apply for jobs online in a professional manner.

- Advise novice computer users on basic file/disk management, word processing, and general computer use.

- Monitor client computer usage to ensure proper and appropriate use of the Internet and all office equipment.

- Provide job-seekers with advice on how to prepare for job interviews.

- Aid clients in clarifying their career choices; provide current labour market information and research support.

- Maintain knowledge of current trends in the labour market.

RESOURCE MANAGEMENT

- Oversee all aspects of a career resource room with 18 workstations and an average of 150 client visits per day.

- Research and compile local and online resources pertaining to specific client needs; distribute to career advisors as needed.

- Perform online searches for relevant job ads to post on the job board; remove outdated ads daily.

- Network with local employers regarding job opportunities; post ads on the job board as they come in.

- Maintain the efficient operation of all workstation equipment including hard drives, disk drives, and monitors.

- Control inventory of a large resource library that includes job search and career planning books, school calendars, self-help books, and labour market reports.

- Research and order new materials and resources for the library.

- Collect and recycle daily and weekly newspapers and other subscriptions.

- Perform minor maintenance on office equipment such as photocopiers, fax machines, and printers.

- Provide reception relief and general office support as needed.

CAREER DEVELOPMENT PRACTITIONER CERTIFICATE
Denningham Community College, City • 20XX

DOWNTOWN YOUTH CORPS, City

Manager of Recreational Programming, 20XX

- Developed seasonal recreation programs for children/youth, including team and individual sports, physical fitness, arts and crafts, and a variety of interest and hobby classes.
- Recruited, hired and trained 3 new recreation leaders; recruited 30+ facilitators for individual contract courses. Supervised a team of 10-12 recreational leaders.
- Grew child and youth program participation by 12% and added an additional 13 programs over the previous year.
- Delivered presentations to community groups and neighbouring schools to promote the Youth Corps mission and programs.

Recreation Leader, 20XX-20XX

- Facilitated a variety of recreational programs for youth up to age 19.
- Sports programs included recreational floor hockey, basketball, volleyball, and badminton; arts and crafts classes included photography, painting, and drawing.
- Organized numerous seasonal events such as Halloween haunted mansion parties, Easter egg hunts, Christmas carol trips, and national birthday barbeques.
- Coordinated and chaired a youth committee to improve communication with Youth Corps management.

Cashier, 20XX

- Registered program participants in person and over the phone; answered questions regarding courses and Youth Corps policies and procedures.
- Operated cash registers and processed cash, cheque, debit, and credit card payments.
- Reconciled cash and receipts to computer totals at the end of each shift; prepared computerized bank deposits.
- Consistently delivered outstanding front-line service to the community.

ACADEMIC EDUCATION

Bachelor's Degree in Social Services
University Of East Peninsula, City
20XX-20XX

Diploma in Child and Youth Care
East Peninsula College, City
20XX-20XX

WORKPLACE TRAINING

Certificate - Emergency First Aid Level A
Workers' Health & Safety Board, City
20XX

Certificate - CPR
Workers' Health & Safety Board, City
20XX

Certificate - Crisis Intervention
East Peninsula College, City
20XX

Certificate - Workplace Safety
Trent Senior High School, City
20XX

matthew gore

youth recreation leader

Mailing Address Line 1
Mailing Address Line 2

Home Phone: 555.555.5555
Cell Phone: 555.555.5555

Email Address

Certified Personal Care Aide – Seniors

8 Months Experience in Elderly Care • Certified in First Aid Level 2 and CPR
Clean Driver's Licence with a Reliable Vehicle

CAREGIVER TRAINING

Personal Care Aide Certificate • Maplewood Technical Institute • 20XX–20XX

Completed a 1-year, full-time program with 8 distinct courses covering all facets of personal care for seniors including basic skills, disease management, behaviour control, liaising with medical professionals, emergency first aid, legal issues, ethics and personal rights, nutrition and food safety, and personal stress. Graduated with a 91% average grade, 2nd highest in the class. Letter of recommendation from the course instructor available upon request.

COMMUNITY SERVICE

Volunteer Senior Companion • Maplewood Hospital • 20XX–Present

Provide companionship, comfort and assistance to elderly patients and their family members in the geriatric ward. Expedite food service and assist patients with meals, provide towels and linens, run errands for patients and supporters, and provide bedside visits. Respond to call alerts for simple requests, and provide feedback to hospital staff. Received a letter of reference from the head nurse and a letter of appreciation from a patient's family member.

Volunteer Care Assistant • Henderson Long-Term Care Home • 20XX

Assisted the residents and staff with daily activities and special events including providing companionship, escorting residents throughout the facility, helping them with dining and personal care, planning and facilitating bingo games and arts & crafts events, and shelving books in the library. Received a letter of recommendation from the general manager.

CAREER EXPLORATION

Participated in a 3-week career research and planning program after high school graduation. Completed several assessments to establish skills, interests, work values, and personality type, and match them with appropriate career choices. All assessments indicated suitability for a career in the social services field. Copy of assessment profile available upon request.

EMPLOYMENT

Bastion Public Library	Reference Services Clerk	20XX–Present
Marvin's Restaurant	Food Service Cashier	20XX–20XX

SIERRA LONDON • MAILING ADDRESS • HOME PHONE • CELL PHONE • EMAIL ADDRESS

ALTERNATIVE RESUMES FAQ//

WHAT CAN I INCLUDE BESIDES EXPERIENCE AND EDUCATION?

Most job-seekers have more qualifications for employment than just work experience and education.

This is particularly important for teens and young adults because they don't have an extensive work history. Experience and education are very important and should not be ignored, but unconventional qualifications can also be valuable on your resume. Examples include:

Bilingual; fluent in both English and German.

In this global and multicultural economy, almost every company can benefit from employees who are fluent in more than one language. These skills are essential to include on resumes.

Travelled throughout Europe & Southeast Asia.

Employers in many industries may be interested in your travel history. These include hospitality, travel and tourism, retail, and other fields where cultural sensitivity and experience are important.

Clean driver's licence with access to a reliable vehicle.

Some jobs require a driver's licence and a vehicle. Even if your job target doesn't, including this on your resume may convince a hiring manager that you are reliable because you have dependable transportation.

Performed in a theatre production for an audience of over 1,000 people.

Many jobs require you to "perform" a role. Acting experience is a good way of demonstrating your ability to manage stress and perform under pressure, present an outgoing personality when necessary, and "play the part" that is required of you.

Available to work any day or shift including evenings, weekends, and holidays.

Staff availability is extremely important to businesses that are open long hours or seven days a week. If you have open availability, or potentially better availability than most people who are applying for the same jobs as you, make it clear on your resume.

Physically fit; participant in 3 full marathons over the past 4 years.

Many jobs, especially those in trades and labour, require extensive physical effort and hiring managers want employees who can handle those demands. If you're applying for these types of jobs, provide examples that demonstrate your physical capabilities.

Played organized soccer for 6 seasons; elected captain 2 years in a row.

Leadership and teamwork skills are highly valued by employers, and can be important to include with examples from work or volunteer experience, school, or extracurricular activities.

On the following page you will see that Gabrielle Johansson is a graduate from an Early Childhood Education program and is seeking her first position in a pre-school or daycare. Since she doesn't have direct experience as an Early Childhood Educator, and she knows there are multiple job requirements in that field, she supported her education and experience with additional qualifications that will interest employers.

You will find examples of alternative job qualifications throughout this book. Remember that although work experience and education are very important and usually the most appropriate and compelling qualifications you will have, they aren't everything. Dig a little deeper and you will find additional features that will prove you're the best person for the job!

EDUCATION / TRAINING

Diploma – Early Childhood Education. Graduated from a 2-year, full-time program at Grafton University College with an average grade of 89%, having completed such core courses as Infant Caregiving, Programming for Special Needs, Administration of Childhood Centres, Applied Behaviour Analysis, Parent Collaboration, Nutrition and Health, and Curriculum Development. Completed a 2-week practicum in the college daycare; reference available upon request. 20XX.

Certificates. Earned Occupational First Aid Level B and CPR certificates through Care Institute. Completed certificates in food safety and customer service while in high school.

WORK EXPERIENCE

Child Care. Provided child care services for 15 neighbourhood families before and after school, as well as weekends. Cared for boys and girls aged newborn to 11, including 2 children with special needs: a 5-year-old autistic boy and a 6-year-old boy diagnosed with ADD. Supervised up to 4 children at a time. Maintained a clean home, supervised indoor and outdoor activities, assisted with homework, and disciplined according to parent instructions. 20XX–Present.

Arts & Crafts. Worked part-time as a sales associate at Touching Images Scrapbooking. Used creativity and passion for scrapbooking to assist customers with selecting supplies and tools for their projects. Facilitated nightly classes to groups of 10-15 teens and adults. Operated a cash register and processed transactions. Used communication and problem-solving skills to assist customers with their concerns and make their shopping trip enjoyable. 20XX–20XX.

OTHER QUALIFICATIONS

Bilingual. Fluent in English and Swedish. Studied French in high school from Grade 8 to 12 and earned an A in each class. Limited knowledge of Finnish.

Musical Skills. Sang in holiday festivities as a choir member for 6 years. Intermediate level piano player; completed 4 years of lessons. Played the clarinet in the high school band.

Multicultural. Lived in and visited several foreign countries including Sweden, Finland, Norway and Germany. Comfortable interacting with people of all ages, backgrounds, and cultures.

Excellent Availability. Available to start immediately and willing to accept a full-time, part-time, permanent or temporary position. Able to work any days or shifts needed.

Available to Transport. Valid class B transport driver's licence with a clean driving record and a reliable, late model vehicle. Copy of driving record available upon request.

Fully Immunized. Able to provide full immunization record, including TB test from 20XX.

Mailing Address ▪ Home Phone ▪ Cell Phone ▪ Fax Number ▪ Email Address

GABRIELLE JOHANSSON

ATTENTION: JEFF HARDING, BURNSIDE ANIMAL SOCIETY

The following letter of recommendation outlines my background, skills, and employment qualifications. My goal is to attend university and become a veterinarian, but in the meantime I want to work with animals in a government-funded animal care facility or hospital. I plan to work p/t through school.

I have owned and cared for many pets in my life, including a basset hound, a border collie, three cats, several hamsters, two rabbits, a parakeet, a cockatoo, and many fish. I respect all animals and believe I have the passion and personality for a successful career in this field.

Gene Sinclair has been a volunteer with Hampton Pet Shelter for the past three years, since he was 14 years old. In that time, I have worked closely with Gene in all aspects of his work. During the school year he volunteered 10 to 15 hours per week and during the summer holidays his dedication and enthusiasm resulted in approximately 30 hours per week. All in all, Gene has volunteered well over 1,000 hours for us!

Gene began his work with us by taking dogs on a daily walk. He quickly proved to be very reliable and his duties soon increased. During his time here he has walked, bathed, fed, and generally cared for most of the animals we have. Gene has also been involved with cleaning, building, and repairing cages, shelters, and kennels, assisting the veterinarian when needed, purchasing pet food and other supplies, answering the telephone, greeting visitors, and answering questions, posting notices, and following up with pet owners.

Gene has proven to be one of our most dedicated volunteers. His compassion for animals is immense and it shows in his work. He is flexible and always willing to chip in when needed. When caring for the animals, he demonstrates patience and a sensitive disposition but also knows when and how to be firm when the situation demands it. He definitely has the character, personality, and attitude appropriate for working with animals.

This past May, Gene was awarded the "Volunteer of the Year" Award from Hampton Pet Shelter for his tireless efforts and the enormous amount of time he has donated to our cause. After careful deliberation, Gene was selected from a group of 20 other volunteers. Once he finds a suitable job, we will surely miss his contributions to our organization.

I highly recommend Gene for any position he seeks. I am confident you will find his work ethic, reliability, professionalism, teamwork skills, and attitude are all excellent, and I am sure he will make a positive contribution to your business. Should you have any questions or concerns, please don't hesitate to contact me anytime at 555-555-5555.

Warm regards,

Kendra Hopkins - Managing Director of Hampton Pet Shelter

Currently enrolled in Grade 11 at Hampton High School, I am available to work Monday to Friday from 4:00 to close, as well as anytime on weekends and holidays. I can start immediately and work as many hours as needed. I have also proven to be an effective communicator with fluency in English and conversational skills in Spanish. My experience dealing with the general public, explaining policies and procedures, and answering all types of questions, may also prove beneficial to your organization. Thank you for your consideration, and I look forward to meeting with you about suitable opportunities.

Sincerely,

Gene Sinclair
Home Phone • Cell Phone • Email Address   Mailing Address

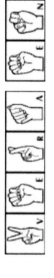

VERA ENVIK

American Sign Language Interpreter

HOME PHONE · CELL PHONE · EMAIL ADDRESS
MAILING ADDRESS

SIGN LANGUAGE INTERPRETATION DIPLOMA
Kenmont Community College, City, 20XX

A two-year, full-time program with the following core courses:

- Interpretation of Language and Culture
- Interpreting ASL I-IV
- Introduction to the Deaf Community
- Mediation in Interpretation
- Interpretation Practicums I and II
- Non-Standard ASL
- Professional Business Code of Ethics
- Advanced Issues in Interpretation

"Vera proved through her enthusiasm and dedication to be a valuable addition to our program. Her ASL skills were in the top 5% of the class and she consistently demonstrated the ethical and professional maturity necessary for a career as a Sign Language Interpreter."
- SHARON HENDERSON, KENMONT COLLEGE PROGRAM INSTRUCTOR

AMERICAN SIGN LANGUAGE CERTIFICATE
Erickson College of Communications, City, 20XX

A ten-month, full-time program teaching advanced level American Sign Language skills through the following courses:

- American Sign Language I to IV
- Public Speaking
- Deaf Culture and Community I to III
- English Skills

FIVE YEARS' SIGN LANGUAGE EXPERIENCE

- Daughter born deaf in 20XX, communicate daily with her using ASL.
- Communicate daily with the Special Needs Assistant at her school.
- Over three years' experience communicating with other special needs professionals in the educational and medical communities.
- Extensive knowledge and understanding of the deaf community.

VOLUNTEER EXPERIENCE

Donation Sorter, Regional Food Bank – 20XX to Present
Class Assistant, Meadow Elementary – 20XX to Present
Victim Services, Women's Relief Shelter – 20XX to 20XX

"Vera displays a high level of diplomacy, compassion, and tact when interacting with food bank patrons. She is a strong communicator, has high morals, and is a true humanitarian."
- JANICE THOM, DIRECTOR OF DISTRICT FOOD BANK

EMPLOYMENT HISTORY

OTC Associate, SuperSave Foods – 20XX to Present

Assist customers with locating and selecting a wide variety of over-the-counter pharmaceutical and health products. Arrange consultations with the pharmacist when needed.

ADDITIONAL SKILLS AND KNOWLEDGE

Sports, such as swimming and tennis. Arts and crafts, including photography, drawing, scrapbooking, and painting. Travelling, history, and geography. Fashion and interior design.

Viggo Bentham

Objective: YOUTH SUPPORT WORKER, THE MARCUS SUNDSTROM SOCIETY

- **Youth Work.** 2 years' experience working with male high-risk youth in probation programs, employment programs, and community projects. Accustomed to working with clients facing multiple challenges including contact with the legal system, anger management, substance abuse, mental health, violent behaviour, family/relationship, and housing/stability concerns.

- **Counselling Skills.** Excellent communicator with strong interviewing and mediation skills. Proven ability to maintain composure with difficult clients and stressful situations. Trained and experienced in suicide risk assessment and crisis intervention.

- **Case Management Experience.** Work closely with 5 other case managers to case conference and share resources. Experienced with making referrals and working together with service providers. Excellent knowledge of resources for youth and families. Accurate and thorough with case recording practices. Experienced with case management software.

- **Knowledge of the Justice System.** Bachelor of Arts Degree in Criminology preceded by a Criminology Diploma. Knowledge of the Youth Justice Act and youth corrections.

- **Group Facilitation Skills.** 4 months experience facilitating life skills workshops for youth and planning curriculum. Comfortable with leading, supervising and evaluating groups of youth.

- **Additional Qualifications.** Proficient with MS Office and Internet research. Valid and clean driver's licence with a safe and reliable vehicle. Fluent in both English and French.

EMPLOYMENT HISTORY

Case Manager – Career Corner, City   20XX–Present
Provide counselling for youth in an employment services centre. Conduct needs assessments, establish collaborative action plans, and refer to appropriate community interventions. Support clients through multiple barriers. Maintain follow-up records for a caseload of 100+.

Youth Counsellor – Youth Probation Society, City   20XX
Counselled youth probation clients, most of whom faced multiple barriers to obtaining long-term attachment to the labour force. Supported clients reintegrating into an educational program. Worked closely with professionals from social services, mental health, and addiction services.

Life Skills Facilitator – Sun Valley Community Project, City   20XX
Facilitated life skills workshops to groups of 10-15 youth in a probationary program. Collaborated with employers to set-up and monitor work placements. Assisted with program planning.

ACADEMIC ACHIEVEMENTS	Bachelor of Arts Degree, Criminology Major – City University	20XX
	Criminology Diploma – Worthington College	20XX
WORKPLACE TRAINING	"Tools for Dealing with Clients in Crisis" – Youth Probation Society	20XX
	"Cultural Diversity" – Youth Probation Society	20XX

Becky Belle
DAYCARE WORKER / EARLY CHILDHOOD EDUCATOR

Home Phone • Cell Phone • Email Address
Mailing Address

CHILDCARE TRAINING

EARLY CHILDHOOD EDUCATION
Howell Career College, City
Sep 20XX – Jul 20XX

Earning a high B average in this intensive 44-week program that includes a 1-week and a 3-week practicum, and these courses:

‹ Introduction to Early Childhood Education

‹ Community/Family Support

‹ Behaviour Management

‹ Activity Planning and Implementation

‹ Indoor and Outdoor Safety

‹ Communicating with Kids

‹ Developing Programs

‹ Child Growth and Development

‹ Drama and Creative Expression

‹ Artistic and Creative Development

‹ Health, Safety, and Nutrition

‹ Psychology of Play

‹ Language Lessons

‹ Children and Music

‹ Math and Science

‹ Social Studies and English

‹ Daycare Operations

‹ Professional Development

CHILDCARE EXPERIENCE

KIDS CORNER DAYCARE, City   Sep 20XX – Present
Work with 8 other daycare staff supervising 30 children aged 4 to 10. Prepare and distribute snacks, update parents on accomplishments and concerns, plan and implement play activities, assist children with outerwear and footwear, and clean and prepare the centre for the next day.

CHERISH BEARS, City   Aug 20XX – Dec 20XX
Hosted birthday parties with up to 9 children at a time, aged 3 to 12. Managed all aspects of the parties including bear playtime, taking pictures, teaching and singing theme songs, playing games, and processing payments. Merchandised sales floor and assisted guests with questions or concerns.

TANIA'S TREEHOUSE DAYCARE, City   Mar 20XX – Jun 20XX
Volunteered 3 days a week in a centre with 20 children. Worked with 7 other staff members, supervised children, prepared and distributed snacks, and taught arts and crafts.

ART PALLADIUM, City   Jul 20XX
Volunteered to work with up to 60 children in the Summer Art Program. Helped teachers with classroom organization, assisted students with projects, escorted them to classes, and supervised them during breaks.

ADDITIONAL QUALIFICATIONS

Fluent in English and conversant in Spanish.

Graduated with honours from Barrie High School in 20XX.

Elected chairperson of high school graduation committee.

Earned Food Safe Level One certificate in Foods 11 course.

Proficient with both Windows and Mac operating systems.

Passed a Criminal Record Test in October of 20XX.

MAILING ADDRESS ◆ HOME PHONE ◆ CELL PHONE ◆ FAX NUMBER ◆ EMAIL ADDRESS

MICHAEL LENNON
Non-Profit Program Coordinator

Compassionate advocate and dedicated organizer in the animal rights movement with 2 years' experience in program development, event planning, and fundraising. Conceived, launched, and managed an awareness and fundraising program focused on the concept of how glass walls in slaughterhouses would lead to national veganism. Surpassed all targets and expectations.

PROGRAM COORDINATOR, GLASS WALLS CAMPAIGN   **20XX–Present**
Farm Animal Sanctuary, City
Local farm animal protection and advocacy organization with a 100-acre sanctuary for the care and treatment of rescued and abandoned farm animals.

Program Development

- Visualized the framework for the campaign, prepared a comprehensive business plan, and presented it to the Executive Director of Farm Animal Sanctuary as part of a directed studies course at Glendale College. Hired to implement the program immediately after graduation.

- Secured initial budget approval based on business plan. Prepared and delivered tailored presentations to various departments within the organization to develop partnerships and cross-marketing opportunities. Compiled lists of donors and supporters.

- Recruited and hired 3 volunteers. Oversaw the design and production of all marketing and promotional materials such as brochures, position statements, press releases, web pages, and social media sites. Launched the campaign through donor lists, media, and events.

Event Planning

- Planned and conducted a 2-day music festival featuring several local bands in September of 20XX. Coordinated all logistics, scheduling, production, and food services. Managed an advocacy table throughout the festival. Grossed over $60,000 from 10,000 attendees.

- Conceived and organized several peaceful demonstrations outside an animal production facility to raise awareness of the conditions inside. Coordinated all online communications and averaged more than 250 supporters and 4-5 print and TV reporters per event.

- Produced numerous food awareness and fundraising events at local vegan and raw food restaurants. Marketed and advertised through college and university groups. Attracted an average of 75 supporters and raised more than $1,000 per event.

Revenue Development

- Surpassed all revenue development targets in the first year. Generated $93,000 from events with a $75,000 goal, $32,000 from direct mail with a $25,000 goal, and $23,000 from online donations with a $20,000 goal.

- Planned and launched a marketing initiative to grow the number of direct mail recipients. Approached and partnered with several other non-profit organizations in the animal rights movement and increased the contact list by 66% in the first year.

- Designed and implemented a donor appreciation program to recognize and reward major donors. Developed a system to provide supporters with consistent updates on campaign progress. Negotiated space in the monthly newsletter to recognize major contributors.

Diploma in Non-Profit Management, Glendale College, 20XX

MISCELLANEOUS

Chapter 6

Chapters 1 to 5 cover the major industries that hire youth. However, there are many other jobs that teens and young adults enjoy that don't fit into those categories.

These may include Soccer Coach, Actor, Car Lot Attendant, Hockey Referee, Library Assistant, Hair Stylist, Lifeguard, Traffic Counter, Photographer, and many more. This final chapter begins by analyzing the resume of an aspiring Loss Prevention Officer, and continues with 27 more resume samples and four FAQ tips.

DESIGNING MY ALTERNATIVE RESUME//
THOMAS CHEUNG : LOSS PREVENTION OFFICER

Thomas Cheung has security training and customer service experience, and seeks an entry-level position as a loss prevention officer, deterring internal and external theft in such industries as retail, hospitality, or banking.

He works the graveyard shift at a gas station where he has been involved in and documented many security and loss prevention incidents common to a 24-hour service station. Thomas' resume can be viewed on the following page.

1. Objective

Rather than using a typical objective such as, "To obtain a position as a Loss Prevention Officer," Thomas projects the image of an assertive and competent candidate by stating his desired job title clearly at the top of his resume.

2. Training

Thomas understands that without direct work experience in loss prevention, his most attractive and relevant qualification is his security training. Therefore, he prioritizes education above experience by featuring it first and using bold for emphasis. Even if the reader only scans the top quarter of his resume, they will see his Advanced Security Diploma and be compelled to read the entire page.

Because he knows there are many different security training programs offered by private colleges, Thomas clearly states this was a ten-month, full-time, advanced diploma program to differentiate it from the typical four-month, part-time, certificate programs his competitors may have taken. He also lists his other certificates, even those completed in high school, because of their relevance to his job target.

3. Employment

Thomas has several areas of responsibility at the gas station including cash handling, customer service, merchandising, pricing, and store maintenance. However, he focuses his employment section on the aspects most related to security and loss prevention to appeal to his targeted reader. In addition to duties, he expands on his experience by including a relevant accomplishment as well as recognition he received for his loss prevention awareness.

4. Availability and Other Qualifications

Availability and reliability are very important in loss prevention, and Thomas provides a detailed explanation of his flexibility in these areas. He also includes his martial arts training to demonstrate his capability in physical altercations, as well as his conditioning, mental toughness, and personal discipline, all beneficial character traits in this field.

	THOMAS CHEUNG **❶ Loss Prevention Officer**
TRAINING **❷**	**Advanced Security Diploma** – On Guard Security Academy – 20XX
	Completed this 10-month, full-time, advanced program with the following courses:

Arrest & Control Techniques	Firearms Safety	Self-Defence
Emergency Services	Criminal Code	Report Writing
Property Protection	Bomb Threats	Surveillance
Private Investigation	Crowd Control	Mobile Patrol

	Basic Security Skills Certificate – On Guard Security Academy – 20XX
	Emergency First Aid Level 1 / CPR Certificate – On Guard Security Academy – 20XX
	High School Diploma – Meadow Lane High School – 20XX
	Hazardous Workplace Materials Certificate – Meadow Lane High School – 20XX
	Workplace Safety Certificate – Meadow Lane High School – 20XX
EMPLOYMENT **❸**	Dover Point Self-Serve Fuel Station – 20XX to Present
	Responsible for the security of all company assets including the building and lot during the
	graveyard shift, in addition to cashier and service duties. Experienced with resolving diverse
	customer issues, mediating disputes between customers, and enforcing store policies and
	procedures with regards to security and loss prevention. Frequently contacted the appropriate
	authorities for assistance with handling criminal, medical, or other incidents with customers.
	Involved in a store robbery and praised by officers for remaining calm in a very tense and
	stressful situation, doing exactly what the person asked, and providing a detailed description
	afterwards. Earned top marks on last performance evaluation for loss prevention awareness.
AVAILABILITY **❹**	Available to be scheduled any days or shifts needed including early mornings, afternoons,
	evenings, graveyards, weekends, and holidays. Able to start immediately. Very flexible and
	willing to accept a full-time or part-time schedule. Able to work on short notice. Easy to
	contact with 2 phone numbers, a fax number, and an email address.
OTHER **❹**	6 years' experience in karate and kickboxing. Clean driver's licence and reliable vehicle with
	3 years' driving experience. Physically fit and accustomed to standing for long periods of time.
	Excellent communication skills; fluent in verbal and written English and Cantonese.

CONTACT	Mailing Address	Home Phone	Cell Phone	Email Address	Fax Number

SANDRA BELL

BAGPIPE INSTRUCTOR

email address

home phone

cell phone

mailing address

PIPING HISTORY

- ♫ 11 years' experience playing the bagpipes.
- ♫ Member of Western Highland Pipe Band from 20XX to 20XX.
- ♫ Alternate member of Sather University Pipe Band from 20XX to 20XX; permanent member since 20XX.
- ♫ Student of William Malcolm Piping School for first 4 years.

EVENT PARTICIPATION

- ♫ Participated in several parades including the Pearl Parade, the St. Patrick's Day Parade, the CityFest Parade, and the County Thanksgiving Parade.
- ♫ Performed at various holiday events including the national birthday in 3 different cities, New Year's Eve, and Christmas.
- ♫ Played solo and with the band for such charitable events as the Kids' Club Telethon and the Spring Multicultural Celebration.
- ♫ Travelled in North America, Scotland, and England for events.
- ♫ Played at numerous funerals and weddings for family, friends, associates, and acquaintances.

AWARDS & ACCOMPLISHMENTS

- ♫ Earned 9 solo 1st place awards from competing in 28 Highland Games in North America and overseas.
- ♫ Won several 1st place awards with the band including the World Championships in Scotland in 20XX and 20XX and the National Championships in 20XX, 20XX, and 20XX.
- ♫ Awarded 5 solo 2nd place medals and 8 solo 3rd place medals from various Highland Games.

TEACHING SKILLS

- ♫ Proficient at developing mutually acceptable action plans and following up on progress. Effective communicator who lets the student advance at their own comfortable pace.
- ♫ Empathetic and patient; adept at providing both encouraging, positive feedback in addition to constructive criticism.
- ♫ Firm belief in allowing the student to define their own success.

REFERENCES

- ♫ Jack Garrison – Pipe Major, Sather University Band
- ♫ Barry Gordon – Lead Drummer, Sather University Band
- ♫ Scott Finley – Pipe Sergeant., Sather University Band
- ♫ Kent Harrison – Instructor, William Malcolm Piping School

Brian McLachlan   **Library Assistant**

HOME PHONE • CELL PHONE • FAX NUMBER • EMAIL ADDRESS • MAILING ADDRESS

CAPABILITIES

- Assisting visitors with locating and using library resources such as books, magazines, newspapers, audio and video, reference materials, government publications, and community brochures. Registering guests and providing professional service.

- Shelving, shifting, and shelf-reading aisles. Maintaining organization and cleanliness of library and all resources. Searching shelves for repair, sale, or disposal books.

- Operating and maintaining library equipment such as reader/printers, digital readers, coin-op photocopiers, overhead projectors, audio-visual equipment, scanners, printers, and Internet workstations. Conducting equipment demonstrations.

- Planning and facilitating Internet and word-processing training sessions. Coordinating and conducting class visits, tours, story times, and holiday programs. Promoting library programs and events in-house and in the community.

- Troubleshooting computer hardware and software concerns. Technical knowledge and skill includes Windows and Mac systems, MS Office, Lotus SmartSuite, the Internet, HTML and web design, and a variety of graphics software. Keyboard 50 wpm.

EMPLOYMENT

SALES ASSOCIATE / CASHIER   20XX–Present
National Home and Auto, City

Worked part-time through high school, averaging 20-30 hours a week. Assisted customers with locating items and carrying purchases. Operated computerized cash register and inventory control system. Processed sale, refund, exchange, and void transactions, as well as stock transfers and shipment receipts. Merchandised stock according to planograms from head office. Earned "Employee of the Month" award on 3 occasions.

EDUCATION

Certificate in General Business Studies • MLD Community College   20XX
High School Diploma • Battleford High School   20XX

COMMUNITY INVOLVEMENT

Volunteer Coordinator • Annual Run for Ronald, City   20XX
Volunteer Caregiver • Bridgeport Care Association, City   20XX–20XX
Volunteer Caretaker • Green Timbers Wildlife Refuge, City   20XX–20XX

Krystal Knightley

Email Address • Home Phone • Cell Phone
Mailing Address

Animal Attendant, Wildlife Rescue Society

EDUCATION

Bachelor of Science Degree – Animal Science
Pacific University College
Enrolled in 2nd year; expected completion 20XX

Working towards a Bachelor of Science Degree with a major in animal science and a minor in anthropology. Completed or currently enrolled in such courses as Principles of Animal Science, Animal Behaviour, Conservation Biology, and Wildlife Ecology.

High School Diploma
South Central Senior Secondary School – 20XX

Awarded Honours of Great Distinction with a focus on math and sciences. Earned a Certificate of Merit for Leadership. Member of basketball team and chess club.

ANIMAL CARE EXPERIENCE

Animal Protection Association – 20XX to Present

Volunteered 4 hours a week for the past 8 months providing animal care and maintenance services, including walking, feeding, bathing, and caring for animals, cleaning cages and stalls, assisting the veterinarian, and helping with pickups. Letter of recommendation available upon request.

South Central Veterinary Hospital – 20XX

Completed a 3-week work practicum in Grade 12 as a veterinary assistant in this busy animal hospital. Greeted visitors, provided information on services and fees in person and on the phone, assisted the veterinarian with holding and calming the animals, and organized the filing room. Rated as "excellent" on performance review.

EMPLOYMENT

Restaurant Server – Stone Ridge Patio – 20XX to Present

Promoted from bus person to hostess after just 1 month, and then to server after 6 months. Received 4 wage increases in 16 months. Selected by the manager to help interview job candidates for server positions. "Employee of the Month" in May 20XX.

TRENT BAILEY

Physically fit, hard-working Grade 10 student seeking a part-time job as a Car Wash Attendant

---

① What would you do to ensure all your customers have a pleasant visit to Auto Suds?

I would work fast so they aren't kept waiting too long, while at the same time trying to provide the best wash I can so they are happy with the service. I would also treat them with courtesy and respect by smiling, thanking them for coming, and wishing them a great day. This will help make sure that they're pleased with the service and more likely to return in the future.

② How would you handle a situation where a customer is angry at you or the company?

I would listen to the customer explain the problem and I would do everything I can to solve it and make sure they leave satisfied. If I didn't have the authority to help them, I would find someone who could or get their phone number so my manager could call and help them.

③ What would you do if your manager asked you to perform a task you didn't agree with?

If I thought it was unsafe, illegal, or immoral, I would respectfully tell my manager why I feel that way. I would like to have a manager who would allow employees to voice concerns like that. However, after it's explained to me how it isn't unsafe, illegal, or immoral I would happily and quickly complete the job the best way I can.

④ How would you handle a situation where you didn't get along well with a co-worker?

While I get along with most people very well, I can see how not getting along with a co-worker could affect the workplace. I would talk to the person privately and do everything I could to sort it out between ourselves, without having to bother the manager or other co-workers with it. I would also do everything I can to ensure it doesn't affect how well I do my job.

⑤ What would you do if you saw a co-worker stealing from the company?

Theft is wrong and illegal, whether a customer or an employee does it. So, if I noticed someone stealing from the company, I would notify my manager right away with all the details. If I didn't, I would feel like I'm stealing from the company because I would be an accessory to the crime.

⑥ Why do you want to be a Car Wash Attendant?

Having a job where I work outdoors would make me very happy, and I'm comfortable working in all types of weather. I also like the thought of having a job that keeps me active, since I'm in really good shape and like to keep moving; I wouldn't be able to sit at a desk all day long. I have also been described as a "people person" and I like the idea of working in customer service.

⑦ Why should we hire you over everyone else who applied for this job?

I think all the different parts of the job, such as customer service, cash handling, and equipment operation, can easily be taught and I learn very quickly. I think what's more important is attitude and that's where I know you won't be disappointed. I have been told I'm very mature for my age, I come from a stable family home, and I pride myself on going "above and beyond" the call of duty. I am very confident my energy and enthusiasm will result in satisfied customers for Auto Suds!

HOME PHONE   •   CELL PHONE   •   EMAIL ADDRESS   •   MAILING ADDRESS

UNIQUE HAIR BOUTIQUE, City   20XX–20XX
Hair Stylist

- Designed traditional and contemporary hair styles for men and women of all ages.
- Developed and maintained an exclusive client list of 75, second highest in the salon.
- Generated the highest product sales out of 11 stylists in 9 different months.
- Recommended a loyalty program that was eventually implemented by management.
- Represented salon as a stylist at the Cotton Grove Mall Fashion Show in August 20XX.
- Selected by manager as "Stylist of the Month" on 6 separate occasions.
- Oversaw the orientation and training of 2 new stylists in October 20XX.

ANNA-MARIE BOUCHARD
Certified Hair Stylist

MAILING ADDRESS • CELL PHONE • EMAIL ADDRESS

✂ Skilled in all aspects of hair styling including shampooing, trimming, cutting, straightening, curling, blowdrying, layering, texturizing, highlighting, colouring, and perming. Experienced in the creation of custom colours. Portfolio and references available upon request.

✂ Proficient in the operation and maintenance of computerized cash register systems and related equipment. Accurately process cash, credit, and debit transactions, and reconcile cash and receipts.

✂ Available for full-time or part-time scheduling. Able to work any day and shift including weekdays, evenings, weekends, and holidays.

✂ Fully fluent in both English and French.

CUMBERLAND HAIR AND ESTHETICS ACADEMY, City   20XX–20XX
Certificate in Advanced Hair Design

- Graduated with a final grade of 96%, the highest mark in a class of 8 students.
- Researched numerous hair care companies in preparation for a class presentation.
- Provided discounted haircuts to over 100 volunteers during a 3-month period.

COTTON GROVE HIGH SCHOOL, City   20XX–20XX
High School Diploma

- Maintained a B average throughout Grades 10, 11, and 12.
- Completed several arts courses including Drawing 11–12 and Dramatic Arts 11–12.
- Volunteered as a peer tutor in Grade 12, assisting other students with math classes.

FRISCO GERVAIS

2 years' photography experience with Lens Art Studio in Leduc, conducting over 100 photo shoots for local schools, churches, businesses, and individuals. Gained significant experience shooting weddings, baptisms, graduations, school yearbooks, family and school reunions, births and babies, store openings, and other assignments. Comfortable working individually and with other photographers. Letter of recommendation available from the company president. Jan 20XX – Dec 20XX

Portrait experience shooting individuals and groups at Shop World during the Christmas season. Assisted customers with selecting from among multiple backdrops and choosing appropriate poses. Presented, sold, and up-sold a variety of portrait packages. Performed minor repairs on equipment and maintained a clean, stocked, and organized studio. Letter of reference available from studio manager. Oct 20XX – Dec 20XX

Professional Photography Diploma from Jasper Art School in Leduc. Core courses in this 2-year, full-time program included Medium-Format Photography, Commercial Photography, Digital Imaging Applications, Digital Restoration, Portrait Photography, Graphic Arts, Wedding Photography, Portfolios, Copyright Law, and Photography Sales. May 20XX

Available 24/7 for full-time, part-time, permanent or temporary employment, in addition to independent contract assignments. Portfolio, clean driver's licence and reliable vehicle available.

PHOTOGRAPHER

ALTERNATIVE RESUMES FAQ//
CAN I INCLUDE SOFT SKILLS ON MY RESUME?

Soft skills are personal management skills, character traits, or skills that can't be quantified or measured.

They are often used by teens and young adults who lack experience or other relevant qualifications, like Eric Schweitzer on the next page. Unfortunately, soft skills are generally opinions, not facts, and they don't carry much weight with hiring managers unless proof is offered.

It's acceptable to include soft skills on your resume if you have little training or experience, or if the employer is seeking candidates with particular soft skills. However, don't simply list them as follows:

Summary Of Qualifications

- Leadership skills

- Reliable and punctual

- Mechanically inclined

- Outgoing personality

- Excellent physical condition

You may believe you're a great leader, and perhaps past supervisors, teachers, or coaches have told you that, but just because you say it on your resume doesn't mean hiring managers will believe it. It looks like a personal opinion and unless you offer some sort of proof, that is all it will be. Therefore, include examples that demonstrate your soft skills so that readers will have a reason to believe you:

Summary Of Qualifications

- Leadership skills. Played organized hockey for 6 seasons and elected team captain 3 times. Completed leadership courses in Grades 11 and 12.

- Reliable and punctual. Maintained perfect attendance at high school and work in the past year. Copies of report cards and performance evaluations available upon request.

- Mechanically inclined. Completed metalwork, woodwork, and auto mechanics courses in high school. Rebuilt a 1967 Mustang with 2 other people. Comfortable with hand and power tools.

- Outgoing personality. Performed in 4 plays through Aspen Community Arts Club, including 2 leading roles. Won the stand-up comedy category in a 20XX talent contest.

- Excellent physical condition. Member of Trident Dance Academy for 4 years, specializing in ballet and hip hop. Enjoy rock climbing and hiking. Exercise 5 days a week.

There are two important benefits to including proof or examples of your soft skills. First, there is a much higher chance the reader will believe and trust you, and continue to read the rest of your resume. Second, it gives you an opportunity to include additional qualifications that may not fit under employment or education. Rather than listing them in a bland Interests and Hobbies section, use them to validate your soft skills.

ERIC SCHWEITZER

"Without hesitation I can say that Eric was one of the most capable, self-motivated students that I have ever worked with in my fifteen years of teaching. He always showed the qualities of a disciplined, achievement-oriented, and successful student. He was enthusiastic about learning and it showed in his production. I recommend him as someone who would be a truly outstanding employee – someone who would be a great asset to any organization."
LARRY WATTS, BUSINESS DEPARTMENT, KRAMER BEACH HIGH SCHOOL

SKILLS & CHARACTERISTICS

HIGH ACHIEVER. Accustomed to succeeding in high-pressure situations. Earned honour roll status every semester so far in high school. Won 8 trophies and medals as part of the Kramer Beach Pipe Band, competing in several competitions locally and around the country. Awarded 3 trophies and 2 individual medals with the Kramer Beach Jaguars soccer team.

ORGANIZED. Showed strong time management and prioritization skills by simultaneously balancing the following commitments over the past few years: band practices, parades, competitions, and other events; soccer practices and games; homework, studying, and other school requirements; family and household commitments.

QUICK LEARNER. Completed two Grade 10 courses while in Grade 9, including earning an A in Business Technology 10. Awarded Top Student in Computer Applications 9; placed in the top 5% in Business Technology 10. Achieved all As and Bs so far in high school.

TEAM PLAYER. Developed teamwork skills from playing soccer with the District Youth Soccer League for 6 years, and as a member of the Kramer Beach Pipe Band for 4 years. Accustomed to working together for a common goal, but also able to work alone if needed.

COMPUTER LITERATE. Developed spreadsheet, database, word-processing, and desktop publishing skills through various high school computer courses and self-study. Advanced understanding of Windows and Mac operating systems, with moderate knowledge of Linux. Capable of troubleshooting many hardware and software problems.

WORK EXPERIENCE

Mowed lawns and pulled weeds for 15 families throughout the community.	Summer 20XX
Volunteered to serve snacks and drinks at Family Day for Lupul Plastics.	20XX
Earned childcare certificate and babysat for several families.	20XX – 20XX

EDUCATION

Currently enrolled in Grade 10 at Kramer Beach High School.	20XX – Present

CONTACT

Home Phone ▪ Cell Phone ▪ Email Address ▪ Mailing Address

carmel mendes

RESIDENTIAL INTERIOR DESIGNER

MAILING ADDRESS
EMAIL ADDRESS
HOME PHONE
CELL PHONE

Bachelor of Arts Degree – Interior Design
Atlantic Art & Design School, City   20XX – 20XX

Graduated in the top 5% of the class, having completed the following core courses:

• Modern Architecture	• Textiles and Finishes	• Fundamentals of Colour
• Design Fundamentals	• Drawing for Design	• Project Management
• History of Art	• Historical Style	• Lighting
• Design Theory	• Furniture Design	• Design Materials

Diploma of Fine Arts
Athabasca Academy of Fine Arts, City   20XX – 20XX

Showcased several art projects, particularly oil paintings, at exhibits throughout the city:

- East Coast Art Exhibit, earned honourable mention   20XX
- East Coast Art Exhibit, earned 2nd place   20XX
- Artist's Place Exhibit   20XX
- Art in the Park Exhibit, earned honourable mention   20XX
- Athabasca Academy of Fine Arts Exhibit   20XX
- Athabasca Academy of Fine Arts Exhibit, earned 2nd place 20XX

Extensive personal travel experience, including three trips to Europe totalling eleven months:

- Travelled through most of Italy including Rome, Venice, Naples, Florence, and Milan
- Visited other cities including London, Paris, Amsterdam, Berlin, Hamburg, and Vienna
- Journeyed throughout the southern US including California, Texas, Louisiana, and Florida

---

Three years' sales and customer service experience in the retail sector:

- City Art Supplies, City   20XX – 20XX
- Jeans 'n' Things, City   20XX – 20XX

...to design is to dream...and to dream is to live...

FAVOURITE FILMS

All About Eve
Apocalypse Now
Bonnie and Clyde
Cat on a Hot Tin Roof
Casablanca
Chinatown
Citizen Kane
Do the Right Thing
Doctor Zhivago
Dog Day Afternoon
Gone With The Wind
It's a Wonderful Life
Jaws
JFK
Lawrence of Arabia
Midnight Cowboy
Moulin Rouge
North By Northwest
On The Waterfront
Psycho
Pulp Fiction
Raging Bull
Rear Window
Scarface
Scent of a Woman
Schindler's List
Serpico
Singin' In The Rain
Sin City
Some Like It Hot
Star Wars
Sunset Boulevard
Taxi Driver
The Bicycle Thief
The Corporation
The Godfather
The Godfather II
The Graduate
The Wizard of Oz
Titanic
Traffic
Twelve Angry Men
Vertigo

Harjit Amira ☛ Movie Critic

HOME PHONE • CELL PHONE • EMAIL ADDRESS

Eloquent and thoughtful movie reviewer for a school newspaper seeks a youth movie critic position with your publication. Very knowledgeable with regards to modern movies, classic films, actors, directors, film history, and awards. Personal knowledge spans all genres including drama, comedy, family, thriller, horror, western, biopic, and musical. Skilled at researching movies online and in print.

WORK EXPERIENCE

My background includes experience with *Freemont Freebie* newspaper, where I have written the school's movie review for the past 10 months. I have been reliable and punctual and meet every deadline and I have received many compliments from students and faculty on my movie knowledge and creative writing skills. Copies of all columns available upon request.

In addition to writing film reviews, I also help with the design, layout, and production of the paper. Through personal research and my newspaper experience, I have developed strong computer graphics skills, including PhotoShop, Corel Draw, Illustrator, and MS Office. I am comfortable with both PC and Mac, and have a keyboard speed of 45 wpm.

Through my leadership and drama courses, I have volunteered numerous hours at my high school. Organizing Parent/Teacher Nights and Open Houses, surveying graduating students on behalf of Student Council, planning the sound/lighting requirements for theatre productions, and constructing stages in the school gym are all contributions I have made. I also earned a Certificate of Merit for volunteering.

EDUCATION

I am currently completing Grade 11 at Freemont High School. My academic focus is on a combination of business and artistic courses including Marketing, Keyboarding, Entrepreneurship, Leadership, Creative Writing, Drama, and Fine Arts. Expected high school graduation is in June 20XX.

Reference letters, contact names and phone numbers are available from my teacher and career advisor.

FAVOURITE ACTORS

Al Pacino
Bill Bob Thornton
Christopher Walken
Denzel Washington
Diane Keaton
Don Cheadle
Dustin Hoffman
Ed Harris
Ellen Burstyn
Emily Watson
Faye Dunaway
Frances McDormand
Gene Hackman
Grace Kelly
Holly Hunter
Humphrey Bogart
Ingrid Bergman
Jack Lemmon
Jack Nicholson
James Stewart
Jodie Foster
John Travolta
Julianne Moore
Kate Winslet
Kevin Spacey
Lauren Bacall
Maggie Smith
Marlon Brando
Meryl Streep
Natalie Wood
Nicolas Cage
Nicole Kidman
Peter O'Toole
Robert DeNiro
Robert Duvall
Robin Williams
Samuel L. Jackson
Sean Penn
Shirley MacLaine
Susan Sarandon
Tom Hanks
Uma Thurman
Vivien Leigh

HOME / CELL PHONE
EMAIL ADDRESS

KATIE MONTANA
Account Manager, Food Industry

MAILING ADDRESS LINE 1
MAILING ADDRESS LINE 2

COMPANY	MARSHALL FOOD CORPORATION $750M packaged food and beverage wholesaler serving US and Canada.	BENJAMIN & BRADDOCK LTD. $480M manufacturer and wholesaler of frozen food in US and Canada.	GOLDEN RIPE PRODUCTS LTD. $175M produce distributor serving the western US and Canada.
JOB TITLE	Account Manager, 20XX–20XX	Junior Account Manager, 20XX	Sales Administrator, 20XX–20XX
SCOPE	Managed all business development activities in a $7M region.	Supported a Senior Account Manager in a $3M territory.	Provided administrative support to a team of 4 Account Managers.
DUTIES	Sourcing and prospecting for new accounts. Preparing and delivering sales presentations and negotiating contracts. Providing guidance to a Junior Account Manager. Analyzing and reporting sales and profits.	Prospecting for new accounts and generating leads. Developing and contributing to sales presentations. Providing support during contract negotiations. Company and product marketing and representation.	Processing sales orders and meeting monthly deadlines. Managing account inquiries on the phone and over email. Calculating profit margins for contract negotiations. Preparing statistics and reports for sales presentations.
ACHIEVEMENTS	Increased regional sales 19% and grew customer base by 23 in 1 year. Surpassed annual sales target by 9% in 20XX and 16% in 20XX. Secured the hugely successful Bower and Sons account. Awarded Account Manager of the Year in 20XX out of 18 candidates.	Increased customer base by 11 and surpassed sales goal by 4%. Contributed to the development of a new sales training program that was implemented throughout all regions in the company. Earned special recognition from the Vice President of Sales & Marketing.	Designed a prominent section of the sales presentation that won a major account worth $3M per year. Created a new profit margin report. Met every monthly deadline for sales order entry. Promoted to Sales Administrator from Receptionist after 1 month.

Bachelor of Arts Degree · Major in Marketing, Minor in Finance · Henderson University, City · 20XX

Staff reporter for hire

By Jordan Starr

EDUCATION

Graduated from NWA College in 20XX with a **Diploma of Technology in Journalism and Investigative Reporting**, a two-year, full-time program that included such courses as:

Mass Communication · News Writing/Reporting Data Gathering and Analysis · News Editing Journalism Ethics · Feature and Critical Writing Newsroom Organization · Statistical Research Economics of the Media · Technology & Media Photography and Image Editing · Internship Public Communication Law

Graduated from Andover Technical School in 20XX, earning a **Certificate in Graphic Arts** after completing a six-month, full-time program.

INTERNSHIP

Completed a three-month, full-time internship in 20XX at *Westview Tab*, a community paper that is circulated three times a week downtown. Working closely with senior reporters, covered numerous community stories, including:

Hagen serial murder case	*primary research*
Civic election campaigns	*secondary research*
Missing teen case	*primary research/interviews*
School closures	*primary research*
Downtown drug problems	*interviews*
Local gas price hike	*interviews*
Safety issues in Grace Park	*interviews*
Power Centre opening	*secondary research*
Mall walking	*interviews/writing*
City Council	*primary research/writing*
Provincial Law Courts	*primary research*
Traffic accidents	*secondary research*
Sports and Entertainment	*interviews*

REFERENCES

"Jordan demonstrated a penchant for details and the perseverance to get the facts right. He will make a valuable reporter..."
- SUSAN STRICKLAND, NWA JOURNALISM INSTRUCTOR

"He did a great job for us and we wish we could have kept him on. If something comes up..."
- JAMES FINLEY, *WESTVIEW TAB* EDITOR-IN-CHIEF

COMPUTER SKILLS

Operating Systems – Windows and Mac; limited Linux experience.

Productivity – MS Word, Excel, PowerPoint, Publisher, Access; Lotus Word Pro, Freelance Graphics, SmartCenter, 1-2-3; Corel Draw and WordPerfect; Adobe Illustrator, PhotoShop and PageMaker; QuarkXPress.

Other – Internet research; HTML; Dreamweaver. 65 wpm keyboard speed.

OTHER

Fluent in English; conversant in French with limited German and Spanish. Clean driver's licence with a reliable, late model vehicle. Good photography skills and own equipment. Skilled in desktop publishing.

CONTACT

Jordan Starr
Mailing Address
[Home] 555.555.5555   [Cell] 555.555.5555
[Fax] 555.555.5555   [Email] Email Address

ALTERNATIVE RESUMES FAQ//
SHOULD I INCLUDE SHORT-TERM JOBS?

Hiring managers are likely to assume someone with several short-term jobs on their resume is a job-hopper, or someone who is unable to hold a job for a reasonable length of time.

Regardless of whether you quit, were fired, or got laid off, it may concern hiring managers and you won't get interviewed if they assume you won't last very long. If this describes your background, here are steps you can take.

Provide appropriate reasons for leaving short-term jobs

In most cases, omit reasons for leaving past jobs. However, if you've held several short-term jobs and you're worried about how that may look, you can provide reasons for situations like the following, which are less likely to concern a hiring manager than a history of terminations and layoffs:

1. Temporary jobs

Companies often hire people with the understanding that the job will end in the short-term through no fault of the employee, and hiring managers are accustomed to seeing these temporary jobs on resumes. However, if you fail to state that a position was meant to be temporary, the reader will believe you left prematurely and possibly assume you were fired or laid off. It's easiest and clearest to include the word temporary or contract by your job title, as Robert Murray has done on the following page. Even though Robert shows four jobs within a short span, he wouldn't be viewed as a job-hopper.

2. Promotion or transition

Sometimes job-seekers who have been promoted, made the transition to a new position, or transferred from one location to another, list these different job titles separately on their resume and repeat the company name with each position. At first glance it can appear as if they held completely distinct short-term jobs, even though

they worked for the same company the entire time. While it is important to list the different job titles you had, make it clear you were with the same employer by listing the company name once at the top.

3. Returned to school

If you quit a short-term job to return to school, and you have several unexplained short-term jobs on your resume, indicate in your cover letter or on your resume that you left to continue your education. Explaining the true reason is better than letting them assume you were fired or laid off, or quit because you couldn't handle it or didn't like it.

4. Moved out of the city

Similar to returning to school, indicating that you quit because you moved out of town is better than allowing hiring managers to jump to their own conclusions.

Leave off one or more irrelevant jobs

Resumes are designed to advertise your most compelling qualifications to potential employers. That means you don't have to list every job you've had if it's not relevant. For example, if you've held four short-term jobs and one was completely irrelevant to the position or industry you're targeting, leaving if off may lessen your risk of being considered a job-hopper and help make your overall resume appear more focused.

EDUCATION & TRAINING	**Advanced Security Service Certificate**	MAR 20XX – JUN 20XX
	Emergency First Aid Level 1 Certificate	MAY 20XX
	S.S.T. Certificate – Standard Security Training I & II	FEB 20XX

"Robert showed himself to be a diligent and motivated student while he was with us. I first met him in February during the SST courses, which he easily completed. I was impressed that he then wanted to enhance his skills by taking the Advanced Security Service Certificate. Most students want to take the quickest route to a job, but he showed that he wasn't only interested in finding employment – he wanted the skills! He continued this approach to education in the certificate program and received a B average in the 6 courses. He also overcame his shyness. When he started, he had a fear of public speaking and receiving attention. We worked on his confidence and he persevered. I was very proud to work with Robert and wish him well in his career."
MARTIN SHROEDER – INSTRUCTOR, ALERT SECURITY ACADEMY

Violence in the Workplace Certificate	JAN 20XX
High School Diploma	DEC 20XX
Customer Service Fundamentals Certificate	NOV 20XX

ROBERT MURRAY, Security Officer

MAILING ADDRESS · HOME PHONE · CELL PHONE · FAX NUMBER · EMAIL ADDRESS

WORK EXPERIENCE

WESTERN COUNTY EXHIBITION, City	JUL 20XX – SEP 20XX
Security Patrol Officer	FULL-TIME, 7-WEEK CONTRACT

"Rob worked as a Security Patrol Officer during our 20XX fair. His responsibility was to patrol the grounds on foot, provide a security presence for guests, and resolve any issues that arose. These issues included physical altercations between juveniles, verbal disputes between guests, lost children, road rage incidents in the parking lots, vandalism, pickpockets, and ill/injured guests. In all cases, Rob showed maturity in his attitude and care in his work. I was very impressed with his report writing; he was articulate, detail-oriented, thorough and factual. Overall Rob performed very well for us and we would hire him back next year should he be available. I don't hesitate to recommend Rob to any organization in need of professional security personnel."
TERRY MCALLISTER – SECURITY MANAGER, WESTERN COUNTY EXHIBITION

JEFFERSON SPEEDWAY, City	SEP 20XX
Security Gate Officer	4-DAY CONTRACT FOR RACE WEEKEND

"Robert should enjoy a great career in security services. He is a bright young man who understands the seriousness of the business and that shows in his work. It was a pleasure to have him on our team and we would welcome him back next year."
GREG DONNER – HEAD OF SECURITY, JEFFERSON SPEEDWAY

COUNTRY FALL FEST, City	SEP 20XX
Security Guard	3-DAY CONTRACT

"Rob was a great addition to our staff for what is usually a difficult event. He showed skill, maturity, and professionalism, and obviously received great training from Alert Security. I wouldn't hesitate to hire him again for similar events. Please contact me anytime at 555-555-5555 if more information is required."
ALEXANDER YOUNG – SECURITY CHIEF, COUNTRY FALL FEST

CORNER MART, City	OCT 20XX – JAN 20XX
Convenience Store Clerk	PART-TIME WHILE IN SCHOOL

DEBORAH ROBERTS
Competitive Gymnastics Coach
PHONE • EMAIL • ADDRESS

GYMNASTICS HISTORY

- 11 years' gymnastics experience, including 5 at competitive levels.
- Former member of United Gymnastics Academy and Carlton Gymnastics Club.
- Specialized in floor and beam routines; earned reputation for thriving under pressure.
- Travelled to several cities across the country to participate in national competitions.
- Trained with national team coach Clare Berkley for 3 months.

GYMNASTICS ACCOMPLISHMENTS

- Senior member of team that won silver at regional championships.   20XX
- Earned gold for all-around solo performance at regional championships.   20XX
- Received bronze for floor performance at national championships.   20XX
- Member of team that won bronze at national championships.   20XX
- Awarded bronze for beam performance at regional championships.   20XX
- Won silver for all-around solo performance at national championships.   20XX

CERTIFICATIONS & LICENCES

- National Gymnastics Federation Level 1 Coaching Certificate.   20XX
- Emergency First Aid & CPR Certificate from Care-Aid Training Society.   20XX
- Customer Service Skills Certificate from Lancaster Continuing Education.   20XX
- Transporter Class Driver's Licence.   20XX

WORK AVAILABILITY

- Mondays, Tuesdays, and Thursdays   4:00 pm to 10:00 pm
- Wednesdays and Fridays   1:00 pm to 10:00 pm
- Saturdays, Sundays, and Holidays   8:00 am to 10:00 pm

WORK EXPERIENCE

- Pleasure Palace – 20XX to 20XX. Worked part-time during school as a hostess at a busy toy store. Planned and facilitated birthday parties for up to 12 kids at a time. Worked with parents to customize events and ensure a memorable experience.

- Jubilee Sunset Daycare – 20XX. Completed a 150-hour work practicum while in high school. Assisted staff with caring and supervision of up to 60 children at a time, aged 6 months to 8 years. Letter of recommendation available upon request.

EDUCATION

- Viscount University – 20XX to Present. Currently enrolled in 3rd year with a major in kinesiology and minor in drama.

- Sumner City School District – 20XX. Earned a high school diploma through home schooling. Challenged government exams and earned an 89% average grade.

GORDON JONES · Car Lot Attendant

Mature, honest teenager seeking an entry-level position with an auto dealer. One year experience working in a fast-paced environment as part of a team. Physically fit; willing and able to work outdoors in all weather conditions. Excellent attitude and very safety conscious.

DRIVING EXPERIENCE

Valid class 5 driver's licence since November of 20XX; zero demerits on driver's test. Clean driving record; no tickets or accidents. Driver's abstract available upon request. Capable of operating both manual and automatic transmissions.

EDUCATION

One course shy of high school diploma; currently completing through night school. Elective courses included Automotive 11 and 12, Metalwork 11, and Drama 11 and 12.

EMPLOYMENT EXPERIENCE

Bus Person – Stew's Bar & Grill, August 20XX to January 20XX. Worked on a team of 10 to 15 servers, bussers and hostesses to ensure efficient and profitable table turnover.

Grill Cook – Cosmic Café, February 20XX to July 20XX. Worked on a team of 4 to 5 kitchen staff to ensure quality food was prepared quickly and in the manner requested.

VOLUNTEER EXPERIENCE

Fashion Model – Meadowbrook Mall Spring Fashion Show   May 20XX
Fashion Model – Centaur Centre Fashion Show   May 20XX and Sep 20XX

PERSONAL ACCOMPLISHMENTS

Assisted with the rebuilding of a 1967 Ford Mustang, including installing a brand new engine and performing extensive bodywork.

Helped design and build a 10' x 6' x 8' wood shed on a concrete foundation. Installed the insulation and assisted with the electrical wiring.

AVAILABILITY

Able to work any day or shift needed, except Wednesday evening due to night school. Able to start immediately and comfortable working either a full-time or part-time schedule.

CONTACT

Home Phone   Cell Phone   Email Address   Mailing Address

LINDSAY BEAUMONT • REAL ESTATE APPRAISER
Mailing Address • Home Phone • Cell Phone • Email Address

ECONOMICS OF REAL ESTATE DIPLOMA   20XX–20XX
Carrington Business and Technical College, City
Graduated from this 2-year, full-time diploma program with credit for the first year.

Core Courses:

- Residential Appraisal
- Real Estate Investment Analysis
- Mortgage Analysis
- Industrial, Commercial & Investment
- Real Estate Pre-Licensing Course
- Residential Management
- Real Estate Marketing
- Governments in Real Estate

Major Projects:

- Conducted a market appraisal of a local shopping mall using 3 different techniques. Analyzed and compared the results and presented the final report to the owners. Awarded a grade of 92%, second highest in the class of 22.

- Compared the difference between listing prices and selling prices on the sale of over 500 homes in the region between 20XX and 20XX. Prepared a thorough analysis and received a grade of 96%, highest in the class of 22.

- Analyzed all government-issued quarterly housing reports for the region from 20XX to present, and prepared a comprehensive report on market discrepancies. Earned a grade of 93%, second highest in the class of 21.

BACHELOR OF COMMERCE DEGREE   20XX–20XX
East Coast University, City
Graduated with a major in Economics and a minor in Finance.

University Involvement:

- Volunteered in multiple capacities with the International Student Union in the first 3 years. Coordinated "Student Orientation Week" in partnership with other groups and assisted with all aspects of club operations and office administration.

- Member of the Bridge Builders Club each year, dedicated to building bridges between different cultural and ethnic communities and increasing respect for diversity on campus. Elected President in the final year.

- Member of the University Math Club in the second year. Met weekly to discuss and debate mathematical theories and problems.

Employment:

- Worked as a Resident Advisor in years 3 and 4, assisting new students with locating and securing residences on and off-campus.

- Employed in an off-campus sportswear and sporting goods store in the first 2 years.

MAILING ADDRESS
TELEPHONE
EMAIL

CARLOS MONTOYA
Self-Defence / Karate Instructor

athletic history

4th Degree Black Belt in Karate, awarded in 20XX
8 years' karate training and competitive experience

National Amateur Wrestling Champion in 20XX
Earned an additional 4 individual and 6 team awards
as a member of university wrestling team from 20XX to 20XX

Member of wrestling and track & field teams in university

teaching experience

Instructor – Self-Defence / Karate
Hercules Athletic Club, City – 20XX to 20XX

Taught self-defence and karate classes to adults and children, age 8 and over.
Delivered self-defence workshops to a variety of community organizations
including Trail Guides, Youth International, and Teen Clubs.
Taught classes ranging in size from 6 to 15 students.

education

Bachelor of Science Degree – Physical Education
St. Stephens University, City – 20XX

Certificate – Violence in the Workplace
The Care Institute, City – 20XX

Certificate – Occupational First Aid with CPR
First Responders Association, City – 20XX

Certificate – Health & Fitness Instruction
Hercules Athletic Club, City – 20XX

Bilingual – English and Spanish

~ Available for Group Classes, Individual Instruction and Demonstrations ~

179

ALTERNATIVE RESUMES FAQ//
WHAT IS WRONG WITH USING A RESUME TEMPLATE?

Templates make resume writing as simple as possible. If you need a resume quickly and you can't or won't put much effort into it, use a template.

You will probably finish it in less than an hour, and can start your job search immediately. Just realize, however, that your finished resume will look very similar to most of your competitors'. It will not work nearly as well as a custom-designed one. Here are the most important reasons for NOT using a resume template:

1. Standard Sections

Resume templates use standard layouts that include all the traditional sections, such as Objective, Summary of Qualifications, Work Experience, Education, and Interests and Hobbies. Some even add References Available upon Request at the bottom. Since you often have limited flexibility with these sections, adding new ones or changing the headings may be out of the question. In the end, you will have a resume that will not promote your qualifications as effectively as a custom-designed one.

2. Limited Flexibility

No two people are exactly the same, and therefore no two resumes should be exactly the same. Even if two job-seekers have a similar work history, they may have different job targets, different skills and achievements to highlight, and different flaws to hide, such as lack of training, gaps in employment, terminated jobs, or unfinished education. A resume template will not help with any of these. Only a custom-designed resume can maximize your positives and minimize your negatives.

3. Generic Appearance

Job searching is a competition and your success depends on how you compare with other people who apply for the same jobs you do. It's not about whether you meet the requirements of the position; it's how well you meet or exceed them compared to other applicants. Therefore, your resume needs to stand out and differentiate you from your competitors. A template will have a difficult time achieving that because the appearance will be almost identical to so many others the hiring manager receives.

4. Lazy Impression

Most hiring managers, who have seen hundreds or even thousands of resumes in their time, will immediately recognize a template and know the candidate put minimal effort into applying for that job. Hiring managers want to feel special. They understand you may be applying for many different jobs, but they want to feel like you really want the job they have available. By submitting a resume made with a template, you're telling them their opportunity doesn't excite you enough to warrant a better effort, meaning a more personalized and targeted resume.

Resume templates are quick and easy. However, your resume is your primary tool for getting job interviews and you need it to be the best it can be. Quick and easy doesn't cut it. Writing an original, targeted resume takes more time and energy, and the results are worth it.

TIFFANI SARANDON

ICE RINK ATTENDANT

CAPABILITIES

Ensuring all skaters observe the rules and policies of the ice rink.

Using music and on-ice activities to entertain guests during public skating sessions.

Operating sound systems; using appropriate music and volume levels for each event.

Issuing rental skates and other equipment as needed.

Collecting payment for skate rentals, skate sharpening, and other rentals and services.

Using computer systems to process cash, credit card, and bank card payments.

Assisting with maintaining the ice surface to ensure customer fun and safety.

Staying aware of ice conditions; monitoring ice surface for holes, ruts, or other dangers.

Shovelling snow and relocating nets during ice re-surfacing.

Sharpening and maintaining guest skates and rental skates.

Keeping centre organized and cleaned by performing custodial duties when needed.

Distributing information to the public on all programs, in person and on the phone.

EMPLOYMENT EXPERIENCE

ICE RINK ATTENDANT   Oct 20XX – May 20XX
Baskerville Place Ice Centre   City

CASHIER   Nov 20XX – Jan 20XX
Baskerville Superstore   City

ADDITIONAL QUALIFICATIONS

Over 12 years' skating experience; competitive figure skater from the ages of 10 to 16.

Certified in Emergency First Aid Level One with CPR from Safety First Training Society; January 20XX.

Certificate in Customer Service Fundamentals from the Service Excellence Organization; July 20XX.

Excellent physical conditioning; accustomed to work environments that demand a lot of activity.

Available to work weekday afternoons, from 4:00 pm to close, in addition to weekends and holidays.

Own skates, gloves, safety vest, and helmet.

Proficient in Word and Excel on both Windows and Mac systems; 45 wpm keyboard speed.

Letters of recommendation available upon request from both previous employers.

EDUCATION

Mainland College   Jan 20XX – Present
Enrolled in first year of sales and marketing program.

Fairmont College   Sep 20XX – Dec 20XX
Completed first semester of general business courses.

CONTACT

Mailing Address
Home Phone   ·   Cell Phone   ·   Email Address

Diana Stratten   Lifeguard

National Lifeguard Certificate, Waterfront Option – Brentwood Lifeguard Academy – 20XX
Training focused on natural environments such as lakes and beaches, with topics including waterfront scanning and rescue procedures, emergency preparedness and response, rescue equipment, and crowd control.

Silver Swimmer Certificate – Brentwood Lifeguard Academy – 20XX
Earned nationally recognized intermediate level swimming certification on first test.

Bronze Swimmer Certificate – Brentwood Swim Club – 20XX
Passed the beginner level swimming certification with top marks.

First Aid Level 2 Certificate – Hudson Health Care – 20XX

CPR Level C Certificate – Hudson Health Care – 20XX

Top Physical Condition
Exercise 5 days per week; excellent cardiovascular fitness level.

Accomplished Swimmer
Competitive swimmer for 2 years and diver for 3 years with Brentwood Swim Club.

Optimum Senses
20/20 vision as of May 20XX. Normal hearing efficiency as tested in September 20XX.

Open Availability
Able to work any days or shifts needed including evenings, weekends, and holidays.

Clean Criminal Record Check

High School Diploma – 20XX

Camp Counsellor – Mount Baron Campgrounds – Summers 20XX/20XX
Worked full-time for the summer at a camp for children aged 8 to 12. Supervised games and activities including swimming, canoeing, badminton, soccer, tennis, and hiking. Worked closely with kids in groups, generally up to 7 at a time, and individually.

Travelled in Europe from October 20XX to February 20XX. Backpacked across 8 countries with a friend while visiting family members and sightseeing. Performed odd jobs when needed. Planned trip for 6 months prior to departure. Learned basic French and German.

KIERAN O'REILLY
Home Phone • Cell Phone • Email
Mailing Address

HOCKEY REFEREE
Bow Valley Hockey Association
Minor Youth Division

Played minor youth and major youth ice hockey in the Bow Valley Hockey Association for 8 seasons from 20XX to 20XX. Maintained knowledge of policies, teams, and personnel by attending brothers' practices and games. Full understanding of league rules and regulations. Excellent skater in top physical condition. Available every evening and weekend for games.

EMPLOYMENT

EDUCATION

Construction and Renovation Assistant
Hunter and Sons Contracting, City
Summer 20XX

History/Philosophy Degree Program
Pennington University, City
20XX–Present

Cashier and Sales Representative
Bountiful Hardware, City
20XX–20XX

Communication Diploma
Danville College, City
20XX–20XX

Grocery Stock Associate
Food Plus More, City
20XX

Mediation Certificate
Danville College, City
20XX

Car Wash Attendant
Soap 'n' Suds, City
20XX

First Aid / CPR Certificate
PLR Training, City
20XX

Kimberly Efron

Home Phone • Email Address • Mailing Address

Grade 7 student at Kelly Elementary School. Actively involved in many extracurricular activities, while maintaining good grades at the same time. Lots of volunteer experience at the school and in the community, especially in raising funds for causes and special projects.

SCHOOL ACTIVITIES

ENVIRONMENTAL PROGRAM

Student member of the school's environmental team in Grade 7. Attended meetings at our school and the district head office with the rest of the team, including the principal, the maintenance staff, and science teachers. Discussed ways to lower the school's impact on the environment. Created new programs and presented them to the students in a school assembly.

PEER TUTORING PROGRAM

Tutored Grade 5 students in math while enrolled in Grade 6. Tutored Grade 6 students in science while enrolled in Grade 7. Dedicated one afternoon per week to the peer tutoring program.

BIG BUDDY PROGRAM

Helped new students during the first month of school each of the past two years. Gave tours to groups of students, helped them find their classrooms and other areas of the building, and helped them to feel welcome at their new school.

LIBRARY MONITOR

Volunteered as a library monitor for one week in Grade 6. Helped the librarian with checking student's library cards, scanning books in and out, and putting books on the shelves.

SPORTS INVOLVEMENT

Member of the school track & field team in Grades 5, 6, and 7. Won 1st in the regional long jump competition in May 20XX out of 34 students. Won 2nd in the short sprint and 3rd in long distance in June 20XX at the regional championships.

COMMUNITY ACTIVITIES

FUNDRAISING

Collected over $600 from family and friends to donate to the SPCA for construction of a new animal shelter in 20XX.

Participated in the annual Run for Equality in 20XX, 20XX, and 20XX. Helped family members raise over $1,000 each year.

Created "Christmas Shoe Boxes" to donate to needy children in less developed countries in 20XX, 20XX, and 20XX.

Helped raise over $2,000 to send a local youth activist on a mission to Kenya to help build a school for a community in need.

GYMNASTICS

Participated in competitive girl's gymnastics from ages 8 to 12 at Westcoast Gym. Won numerous medals and ribbons.

COMPUTER SKILLS

Use Mac computers at school and Windows systems at home. Experienced with AppleWorks and Word software. Know how to compose, send, and receive emails. Familiar with many online social networking and chat sites such as WebTalk and IM-Chat.

TREVOR YOAKAM
Theatre Actor

5'10" ▪ 165 lbs. ▪ Black Hair ▪ Brown Eyes ▪ D.O.B. 05/26/XX

DATE	PRODUCTION	ROLE	THEATRE
Aug 20XX	*Hamlet*	Horatio	Gastown Actor's Studio
Aug 20XX	*Annie Get Your Gun*	Frank Butler	Gastown Actor's Studio
May 20XX	*The Elephant Man*	John Merrick	Shepherd Senior Secondary
Dec 20XX	*Miracle on 34th Street*	Bryan Bedford	Shepherd Senior Secondary
Aug 20XX	*Oliver!*	The Artful Dodger	Gastown Actor's Studio
May 20XX	*Othello*	Iago	Shepherd Senior Secondary
Dec 20XX	*A Christmas Carol*	Bob Cratchit	Shepherd Senior Secondary
May 20XX	*Romeo and Juliet*	Mercutio	Barnston Junior Secondary
Dec 20XX	*A Christmas Story*	Randy Parker	Barnston Junior Secondary
Jun 20XX	*Grease*	Doody	Barnston Junior Secondary
Dec 20XX	*Oliver!*	Noah Claypole	Barnston Junior Secondary

THEATRICAL TRAINING

Gastown Actor's Studio, City   20XX – 20XX
Attended three consecutive summers and completed the following acting classes:

Acting Levels I, II and III • Behind the Scenes • Scene Study
Introduction to Auditioning • Commercial Acting • Cold Reading

Shepherd Senior Secondary, City   20XX – 20XX
Completed drama and advanced theatre courses in Grades 11 and 12.

Barnston Junior Secondary, City   20XX – 20XX
Completed drama classes in Grades 9 and 10.

ACADEMIC EDUCATION

Central City University, City   20XX – 20XX
Enrolled in the first year of a general studies program with courses in psychology, history, western art, religion, and international relations.

Shepherd Senior Secondary, City   20XX – 20XX
Graduated with a High School Diploma. Member of Senior Social Committee in Grade 12 and elected as Junior Government Rep in Grade 11.

ALTERNATIVE RESUMES FAQ//

WHAT IS A PLAIN TEXT RESUME?

The purpose of this book is to provide readers with options for the appearance of their resumes as well as the content.

Every resume sample in this book, except the one on the following page, is considered to be a formatted resume because they contain elements such as page borders, bold, justification, and graphics that cannot be used in a plain text resume. Simply put, formatted resumes use bells and whistles to enhance the appearance, while plain text resumes cannot.

What can and cannot be used in a plain text resume?

Plain text resumes can use any keyboard key including letters, numbers, lowercase characters such as / and =, and uppercase characters such as # and *. UPPERCASE can be used as a text enhancement. Everything is aligned to the left. The following elements cannot be used:

- Bold
- Underlining
- Italics
- Lines
- Bullets
- Graphics
- Shading
- Page borders

- Tables
- Columns
- Text boxes
- Fancy fonts
- Special characters
- Centre justification
- Right justification
- Tabbed indents

When should a plain text resume be used?

Whenever you copy and paste your resume into forms on company websites, forms on Internet job boards, or into the body of an email.

Anytime you copy and paste your resume into something that isn't your word processor, you lose control over formatting. Online job boards and the career sections on company websites will often ask you to copy and paste your resume into an e-form, or electronic form. If you're using an e-form paste the plain text version of you resume because the e-form application likely won't recognize the formatting elements of your word processor.

Although you may retain some control over formatting when you copy and paste your resume into the body of an email, you can't control how the recipient will view it. If they receive their emails in plain text, or use mobile options such as smartphones or other hand-held devices, your advanced formatting will be altered or lost, if your resume can be viewed at all.

When should a formatted resume be used?

Whenever you email your resume as an attachment, upload your resume online as an attachment, or print your resume for mailing, faxing, or delivering in person.

Formatted resumes are eye-catching and easy to read, and should be used whenever possible. You can make the page appear balanced and symmetrical, demonstrate your creativity with different layouts, project a professional image with a suitable graphic, and attract the reader's attention using bold or italics. You can't do any of this with a text resume.

If you email your resume to an employer, add it as an attachment unless instructed otherwise and use the body of the email for your cover letter. Attach it as a PDF file rather than a Word document, because a PDF file can be viewed the same by everyone.

SAMANTHA COOMBS
Youth Soccer Coach
Mailing Address - Home Phone - Cell Phone - Email Address

SOCCER EXPERIENCE

- Played organized soccer for 9 years in the Central Region Youth Soccer Association.
- Won championships in 20XX and 20XX as a member of the Greenville Jaguars.
- Awarded "Player of the Year" in 20XX, while placing 2nd in 20XX and 4th in 20XX.
- Elected team captain each year from 20XX to 20XX.

COACHING EXPERIENCE

Youth Recreational Coach
Greenville Community Services, City, 20XX-20XX

- Volunteered to develop and facilitate recreational sports activities for disadvantaged youth aged 6 to 12 throughout the region.
- Created and led programs in soccer, basketball, floor hockey, volleyball, and tennis for groups of up to 20 at a time.
- Developed the framework for a soccer program that was adopted by the Teen Program Manager for use with his 13 to 18 age group.
- Received a letter of recommendation from the Youth Program Manager and letters of appreciation from 5 parents; copies of all available upon request.

EMPLOYMENT

Staff Trainer and Cashier
Burrito Emporium, City, 20XX-20XX

- Worked part-time through high school as part of the customer service team in a busy fast food restaurant. Assisted with prep cook duties when short-staffed.
- Operated a touch-screen register and a banking terminal for bank card payments.
- Rewarded with a wage increase and additional responsibility for training several new employees after just 4 months. Created a new orientation and training program.
- Selected by management to assist with the after-hours installation and setup of a local area network with 8 brand new cash register systems and a back office server.
- Recognized as "Employee of the Month" on 3 separate occasions.

EDUCATION

High School Graduate
Elizabeth Palliser Senior Secondary School, City, 20XX

- Completed business and technology courses such as Communications 11, Business Systems 11, Information Technology 12, Entrepreneurship 11/12, and Leadership 11/12.
- Maintained a B average throughout junior and senior high.
- Earned a Certificate in Emergency First Aid and CPR; expires June 20XX.
- Awarded a Certificate of Merit for Excellence in Community Leadership in Grade 12.
- Served as a peer tutor in the first semester of Grade 12 as part of the leadership class.
- Volunteered 3 hours per week as a computer lab monitor throughout Grade 11.

Perry Cannon

MAILING ADDRESS • HOME PHONE • CELL PHONE • FAX NUMBER • EMAIL ADDRESS

PHOTO LAB TECHNICIAN

Photo Lab Technician Certificate
Altrans Technical College, City, May 20XX

Completed this 6-month, part-time program with such courses as Colour Film Processing, B&W Film Processing, Photography Basics, Tinting and Toning, The Business of Photography, and Digital Imaging. Achieved an average grade of 88%, finishing in the top 5% of the class.

High School Diploma
Charles Campbell Senior Secondary School, City, June 20XX

Worked on the school yearbook in Grade 12 as a key member of the Graphic Arts Program. Photographed sports events, student council meetings, and student rallies. Assisted with page layout and design, as well as scanning and photo imaging. Administered a poll among graduating students to get their input on the project.

Certificate in Hazardous Materials Management
District Continuing Education, City, February 20XX

Completed a 4-hour workshop that explained how to use chemicals properly and safely, how to read chemical labels and warning signs, and how to dispose of dangerous materials.

Workplace Safety Certificate
District Continuing Education, City, January 20XX

Completed an 8-hour workshop that demonstrated proper communication among customers and co-workers and showed how to deal with violence in the workplace.

AVAILABILITY

Available to work any days or shifts needed, including early mornings, afternoons, evenings, weekends, and holidays. Have no other commitments that will interfere. Flexible with either a full-time or part-time schedule. Able to start immediately.

EMPLOYMENT EXPERIENCE

Bus Person / Host	The Waffle House, City	August 20XX – May 20XX
Cashier	Strawberry Hill Café, City	June 20XX – August 20XX

PAIGE ANDERSON
Instructor & Demonstrator – Piano Emporium

mailing address ♫ telephone ♫ email address

PIANO SKILLS

12 years' current piano playing experience. Won several awards for recitals and competitions, including 1st place finishes at the 20XX and 20XX National Conservatory Competition. 3 years' current experience teaching piano to children.

WORK EXPERIENCE

SELF-EMPLOYED PIANO INSTRUCTOR   20XX–PRESENT
Taught over 20 different students on a weekly basis, aged 8 to 13, for durations ranging from 4 months to 2 years. Provided children with constructive, encouraging feedback in addition to written evaluations for parents every month. 3 letters of recommendation available upon request.

SERVER, DANIELLE'S DELICIOUS DESSERTS   20XX–20XX
Prepared and served food/beverages in this downtown bistro-style dessert bar. Often covered for the Assistant Manager, accepting responsibility for the premises and company assets including cash management and closing duties. Authorized to hold store keys and retain safe combination and alarm codes.

CASHIER, CENTRON SERVICE STATION   20XX–20XX
Worked part-time through high school and university, averaging 20 hours per week. Often worked alone at this self-serve station, operating a cash register and banking terminal, and providing customer service through a security window.

EDUCATION

BACHELOR OF ARTS DEGREE, CHARLOTTE UNIVERSITY   20XX
Music Major, Philosophy Minor

FLEXIBILITY

Available for any shifts needed, including evenings, and weekends. No other commitments that would interfere with work availability.

Priyanka Shivani • Mailing Address • Phone Number • Email Address

TRAFFIC COUNTER for TRANSPORT DATA SERVICES INC.
as advertised in the September 16, 20XX edition of *The Citizen Gazette*

 Qualifications Desired
Candidate Qualifications

Employment experience performing work of a technical nature, ideally outdoors and preferably involving vehicular traffic.

2½ years' experience as a Flag Person for Mark Cafferty Construction from 20XX to 20XX. Controlled traffic patterns and speeds at over 30 construction sites in the region.

Comfortable working in inclement weather conditions including heavy rain, wind, and snow with exposure to traffic, vehicular emissions, and noise.

Significant experience working in all types of weather including sun, heat, rain, snow, cold, and ice, with exposure to traffic, vehicle emissions, and related noise.

Ability to draw accurate, detailed maps of basic and complex traffic intersections, incorporating lanes, traffic flows, lights, stop signs, and pedestrian crosswalks.

Created and contributed to basic maps portraying vehicle traffic flows, intersections, and pedestrians affecting construction areas. Extremely detail-oriented with knowledge of all elements affecting traffic flows.

Excellent hand-eye coordination with the ability to quickly and accurately operate hand-held computerized equipment during periods of high pressure.

Developed strong hand-eye coordination through several years' experience playing hand-held video games. Sound technical skills with the ability to learn new electronic equipment quickly and easily.

Available to work during all high-volume traffic periods including 6–9 am, 11–1 pm, and 3–7 pm. Able to work any day of the week.

Able to start immediately and work any days or shifts needed including weekdays and weekends. No other commitments that will affect availability.

Current Certificate in Work Zone Safety.

Earned first Certificate in Work Zone Safety in November 20XX. Renewed in July 20XX after completing refresher training. Also hold current Emergency First Aid Level 1 certificate.

Valid driver's licence with no restrictions.

Maintained a valid driver's licence with no restrictions since December 20XX.

High school graduate.

Graduated with a diploma from Kendall Patterson Senior High School in May 20XX.

MARTIN BAUR
Whitewater Rafting Guide

7 Years' Rafting Experience

Kenmore River – Location
Alahonuk River – Location
Constantine River – Location
Athabasca River – Location
Serpentine River – Location

Accomplished Swimmer

Trained and Licensed Lifeguard
County Parks & Recreation, City
May 20XX – September 20XX

Skilled Scuba Diver, Snorkeller, and Diver

Wilderness Guiding Experience

Hiking Guide, Casual
Mount Bastion, City
May 20XX – August 20XX

Other Outdoors Experience

Trail Builder and Landscaper, Casual
Mount Bastion, City
June 20XX – July 20XX

Physically Fit

Maintain proper diet and regular exercise
6 years' organized soccer experience
2 years' high school wrestling experience

Own Equipment

Drysuit, wetsuit, booties, gloves, whistle, knife

Primitive Camping Experience

Jenkins State Park – Location
Garrison Provincial Park – Location
Valdez State Park – Location
Glacier National Park – Location
Yasmat National Park – Location
Sunwood Valley – Location

Whitewater Rafting Guide
Level 1 Licence

Adventure Academy, City, May 20XX

Wilderness Adventure Guide
Level 1 Certificate

Adventure Academy, City, Dec 20XX

Lifeguard Level II Certificate

County Parks & Recreation, City, Apr 20XX

First Aid Certification

Emergency First Aid with Level "C" CPR

High School Graduate

Completed high school in June of 20XX

PHONE NUMBER
EMAIL ADDRESS

Scarlett Jolie
TATTOO ARTIST APPRENTICE

Email Address
Mailing Address
Home Phone • Cell Phone

Portfolio Available Upon Request

ARTISTIC TRAINING

POWELLVILLE CONTINUING EDUCATION. Completed several drawing classes at night school including Level 2 Drawing, Level 3 Drawing, Charcoal Drawing, The Human Figure, and Colour Theory. 20XX–20XX

HENRY STRONG HIGH SCHOOL. Completed all available arts courses up to and including Grade 11, such as Drawing & Painting, Studio Arts, Sculpting, and Photography. 20XX–20XX

ARTISTIC ACHIEVEMENTS

REGIONAL YOUNG ARTISTS FESTIVAL. Earned 2nd place award for a Greek Goddess Series of 7 charcoal drawings. 20XX

CHEMAINUS VISUAL ARTS FESTIVAL. Earned an "Honourable Mention" for a charcoal drawing of Aphrodite, Goddess of Love. 20XX

SPECIALTIES

Portraits, Goddesses, Celtic Designs, Animals, Landscapes, Figures

PERSONAL TATTOO COLLECTION

Aphrodite, Goddess Of Love	Small of Back, Self-Drawn, Age 20
Athena, Goddess Of Wisdom	Left Shoulder, Self-Drawn, Age 19
Diana, Goddess Of The Hunt	Right Shoulder, Self-Drawn, Age 19
Celtic Knot	Left Ankle, Artist-Drawn, Age 18

INTERESTS

Greek and Roman Mythology, Celtic Art, Ancient History, Guitar, Piano

EMPLOYMENT EXPERIENCE

MARVIN'S CLUBHOUSE. Hired as a hostess; promoted to server position after 3 months. Earned "Employee of the Month" 4 times. 20XX–20XX

JUICE JOINT. Employed as a part-time cashier during high school. Processed cash and bank card payments on a computerized register system. 20XX

"The tattoo attracts and also repels...precisely because it is different."

RESUME WORKSHEETS

Appendix

A comprehensive, step-by-step guide to help you identify job qualifications from your education, interests, employment history, and volunteer experience.

An easy way to create your own alternative resume and impress employers!

ALTERNATIVE RESUMES WORKSHEETS//

The following resume worksheets are available for job-seekers, career educators, resume writers, and employment counsellors to copy, distribute, and use as needed. You can download the worksheets at www.alternativeresumes.com.

It is designed to help job-seekers fully examine their education, work history, volunteer experience, training, skills, and personal life to uncover all potential qualifications for employment. Some sections, such as employment experience and volunteer experience, can be copied multiple times depending on the number of positions the job-seeker has held.

HIGH SCHOOL EDUCATION //

1. What is the name and location of your school?

2. What level or diploma did you achieve and when?

3. What elective courses did you complete?

4. If you took computer courses, what specific skills or hardware/software knowledge did you gain?

5. Describe any major projects you completed individually or in a group.

6. List high grades, scores, or marks in any specific courses or projects.

7. List high grades, scores, or marks averaged over a semester or school year.

8. List any certificates you earned, such as first aid, food safe, customer service, or workplace safety.

9. Describe any work experience placements, practicums, or internships you completed.

10. Describe any volunteer work you completed for the school.

11. Describe any extra-curricular activities in which you participated.

12. Were you involved in school sports, either on a team or as an individual?

13. Were you involved with any other teams, clubs, committees, or organizations?

14. Did you participate in peer tutoring or other leadership initiatives?

15. Were you involved with student government?

16. Did you earn Honour Roll or other special academic standing at any time?

17. Did you receive any other awards or recognition such as certificates of merit or achievement, academic awards, athletic awards, or scholarships?

18. Describe any other high school experiences that don't fit into the above categories.

19. Do you have copies of report cards or attendance records to help market yourself?

20. Do you have any letters of recommendation from teachers, principals, or counsellors?

21. Can you use any teachers, principals, or counsellors as references?

POST-SECONDARY EDUCATION //

1. What is the name and location of your college, institute, or university?

2. What level, citation, certificate, diploma, or degree did you achieve and when?

3. Did you attend full-time or part-time? What were the most courses you took at the same time?

4. What was the name of your program? What courses did you complete?

5. If you took computer courses, what specific skills or hardware/software knowledge did you gain?

6. Describe any major projects you completed individually or in a group.

7. List high grades, scores, or marks in any specific courses or projects.

8. List high grades, scores, or marks averaged over a semester or school year.

9. List any certificates you earned, such as first aid, food safe, customer service, or workplace safety.

10. Describe any work experience placements, practicums, or internships you completed.

11. Describe any volunteer work you completed for the school.

12. Describe any extra-curricular activities in which you participated.

13. Were you involved in school sports, either on a team or as an individual?

14. Were you involved with any other teams, clubs, committees, or organizations?

15. Did you participate in peer tutoring or other leadership initiatives?

16. Were you involved with student government?

17. Did you earn placement on the Dean's List, Honour Roll, or other special academic standing?

18. Did you receive any other awards or recognition such as certificates of merit or achievement, academic awards, athletic awards, or scholarships?

19. Describe any other post-secondary experiences that don't fit into the above categories.

20. Do you have copies of report cards or attendance records to help market yourself?

21. Do you have any letters of recommendation from professors or instructors?

22. Can you use any professors or instructors as references?

EMPLOYMENT EXPERIENCE//

1. What is the name and location of the company?

2. Describe this company. What are their products and services? Are they local, regional, national, or international? How many staff/locations? Annual sales? Are they a division of another company?

3. What was your job title?

4. What was the start and end date of your employment?

5. Were you full-time or part-time? How many hours did you work per week?

6. What position did you report directly to?

7. What position(s) reported directly to you, if any, and how many people were in those positions?

8. What was the scope of your position? What were you accountable for? Use numbers if possible.

9. Describe your duties and responsibilities. Include regular duties as well as responsibilities that were more random or infrequent. Place particular emphasis on tasks that are relevant to your job target.

10. List tools/equipment you used such as hand tools, computers, cash registers, and office equipment.

11. Describe the skills you used, such as math skills, following detailed written directions, mechanical skills, professional telephone etiquette, hardware troubleshooting, or organizational skills.

12. Describe your work habits or character traits. Did you stay late when needed? Did you work on short notice? Did you go above and beyond? Did you cover for your supervisor when needed?

13. Did you belong to any committees, such as Health & Safety or Social? What was your role?

14. Fully describe your accomplishments. Think about achievements that go beyond "what you did" and demonstrate "how well you did it." Recall ways in which you increased revenues, lowered costs, or improved productivity. Try to quantify in numbers, dollars, or percentages. For example: "achieved sales of $6,000 in one 4-hour shift," or "processed an average of 2 skids of new stock every hour."

15. Describe how your performance was recognized. Think of winning awards such as Employee of the Month, winning contests, or being selected for a project. Be specific about the scope of any awards or recognition. For example, instead of "won employee of the month," put "awarded Employee of the Month 3 times out of 20 eligible employees."

16. Did you earn a raise? How much? Can you explain why you received it?

17. Did you earn a bonus? How much? Can you explain why you received it?

18. Did you earn a promotion? From what to what? When? Can you explain why you received it?

19. Do you have any letters of recommendation from supervisors or managers?

20. Can you use any supervisors or managers as references?

21. Do you have any positive performance evaluations?

22. Do you have any complimentary letters from customers or management?

23. Do you have any secret shopping reports that highlight your job performance?

VOLUNTEER EXPERIENCE //

1. What is the name and location of the company or organization?

2. Describe this company. What are their products and services? Are they local, regional, national, or international? How many staff/locations? Annual sales? Are they a division of another company?

3. What was your job title?

4. What was the start and end date of your volunteering?

5. How often did you volunteer? How many hours per week or month?

6. What position did you report directly to?

7. What was the scope of your position? What were you accountable for? Use numbers if possible.

8. Describe your duties and responsibilities. Include regular duties as well as responsibilities that were more random or infrequent. Place particular emphasis on tasks that are relevant to your job target.

9. Did your responsibilities increase while you were there? In what way? After being there how long?

10. List tools/equipment you used such as hand tools, computers, cash registers, and office equipment.

11. Describe the skills you used, such as math skills, following detailed written directions, mechanical skills, professional telephone etiquette, hardware troubleshooting, or organizational skills.

12. Describe your work habits or character traits. Did you stay late when needed? Did you work on short notice? Did you go above and beyond? Did you cover for your supervisor when needed?

13. Did you belong to any committees or boards? What was your role?

14. Fully describe your accomplishments. Think about achievements that go beyond "what you did" and demonstrate "how well you did it." Recall ways in which you increased revenues, lowered costs, or improved productivity. Try to quantify in numbers, dollars, or percentages. For example: "unloaded 5 pallets of donated food per day," or "solicited donations from 100 homes every 4-hour shift."

15. Describe how your performance was recognized. Think of winning awards such as Volunteer of the Month, winning contests, or being selected for a project. Be specific about the scope of any awards or recognition. For example, instead of "won volunteer of the month," put "awarded Volunteer of the Month 3 times out of 20 eligible candidates."

16. Did you receive any perks or gifts of appreciation? Can you explain why you received them?

17. Do you have any letters of recommendation from supervisors or managers?

18. Can you use any supervisors or managers as references?

19. Do you have any positive performance evaluations?

20. Do you have any complimentary letters from customers or management?

21. Do you have any secret shopping reports that highlight your job performance?

MISCELLANEOUS//

1. When are you available to be scheduled for work?

Monday: Friday:
Tuesday: Saturday:
Wednesday: Sunday:
Thursday: Holidays:

2. Do you have any certificates not included elsewhere? Have you completed any workplace training?

Food Safe:
Customer Service:
WHMIS – Workplace Hazardous Materials Information Systems:
First Aid:
CPR:
Workplace Safety:
Conflict Resolution:
Violence in the Workplace:
Other:

3. List any night school, weekend, correspondence, or other courses/workshops you have taken.

4. Describe your computer skills. Indicate whether you are beginner, intermediate, or advanced.

Operating Systems:
Office Productivity Software:
Other Software:
Internet Skills and Knowledge:
Hardware Troubleshooting:
Keyboard Speed:
Other:

5. Have you participated in any individual or team sports not listed elsewhere? How many years?

6. Did you achieve any leadership positions, such as team captain or coach?

7. Did you win any championships, tournaments, events, trophies, or medals?

8. Have you belonged to any clubs, associations, or groups? How long? What was your role? What were your accomplishments?

9. Do you have other hobbies or interests not listed elsewhere? Indicate your level of involvement, knowledge, and skill.

10. In what languages are you fluent? In what other languages can you manage a simple conversation?

11. Do you have a valid driver's licence? How long? Do you have a clean driving record? Do you own, or have access to, a reliable vehicle?

12. If necessary, are you comfortable with frequent heavy lifting?

13. If necessary, are you comfortable working at heights?

14. If necessary, do you own any safety equipment or clothing?

15. If necessary, do you own your own tools?

16. If necessary, do you own anything else you would need for this job? Apparel, footwear, equipment?

PERSONAL ACHIEVEMENTS//

**Describe any personal accomplishments or projects
that are not related to work or school that may interest an employer.**

Many of these could be considered important qualifications, depending on the type of
job you are applying for. Some examples include:

- Invented a metal bracket system to hold plastic grocery bags upright in the trunk of a vehicle.

- Had the lead role in a theatre production of Grease; performed 10 shows over 4 weeks in front of 300+ guests.

- Completely restored a 1977 Corvette with my father.

- Own over 500 DVDs from all genres in my personal movie collection.

- Journeyed through 8 Eastern European countries over 6 weeks in the summer of 20XX.

- Designed and constructed a 120-foot long gated fence in my backyard.

- Played the drum in a bagpipe band for 4 years.

- Created an online message board and chatroom for science fiction fans.

- Travelled to Montreal to watch 4 World Cup of Hockey games in 20XX.

ABOUT THE AUTHOR//

Michael Howard is a freelance writer in British Columbia, where he designs resumes for clients all over Canada and the United States.

His background includes extensive experience on all sides of the youth employment issue. As a hiring manager in sales and service industries that primarily hire youth, Michael was involved in recruiting, screening, interviewing, and hiring hundreds of teens and young adults. As a youth employment counsellor and job search facilitator, he used his employer's perspective to assist hundreds of clients with developing job search plans, writing resumes and cover letters, and preparing for interviews.

Visit Michael's website at www.alternativeresumes.com.

LaVergne, TN USA
20 September 2010
197730LV00001B/15/P